ERIC
BLOODAXE
THE VIKING

O, 'tis a good song the sea makes when
Blood is on the wave,
And a good song the wave makes when its
Crest of foam is red!
For the rovers out of Lochlin the sea is a
Good grave,
And the bards will sing tonight to the sea –
Moan of the dead!

Fiona Macleod: *Washer of the Ford*

ERIC BLOODAXE THE VIKING
'I SHALL DIE LAUGHING'

JOHN SADLER

AMBERLEY

For Sebastian

First published 2025

Amberley Publishing
The Hill, Stroud
Gloucestershire, GL5 4EP

www.amberley-books.com

Copyright © John Sadler, 2025

The right of John Sadler to be identified as the Author of this work has been asserted in accordance with the Copyright, Designs and Patents Act 1988.

ISBN 978 1 3981 2233 8 (hardback)
ISBN 978 1 3981 2234 5 (ebook)

All rights reserved. No part of this book may be reprinted or reproduced or utilised in any form or by any electronic, mechanical or other means, now known or hereafter invented, including photocopying and recording, or in any information storage or retrieval system, without the permission in writing from the Publishers.

British Library Cataloguing in Publication Data.
A catalogue record for this book is available from the British Library.

1 2 3 4 5 6 7 8 9 10

Typesetting by SJmagic DESIGN SERVICES, India.
Printed in Great Britain.

Appointed GPSR EU Representative: Easy Access System Europe Oü, 16879218
Address: Mustamäe tee 50, 10621, Tallinn, Estonia
Contact Details: gpsr.requests@easproject.com, +358 40 500 3575

CONTENTS

Acknowledgements		7
Maps		10
Timeline		15
A note on sources		17
Abbreviations		20
Introduction		22
One	Streamers of Fire	31
Two	Tangle-Hair	44
Three	Sword Song	62
Four	Wood-wreathed Ships	85
Five	*Northanhymbre*	100
Six	'Never Greater Slaughter'	123
Seven	A Bad Country for old Gods	149
Eight	'Valhalla, I am coming…'	168
Nine	The Good Name Never Dies	186
Ten	Will the Real Eirik Bloodaxe…	197
Eleven	Mother of Kings	212

Notes	222
Glossary	236
Appendix 1: Egil's Drapa, The *Eiriksmal* and *Hrafnsmal*	242
Appendix 2: Genealogy of the Kings of Bernicia and Deira (after Nennius)	249
Appendix 3: Kings of Northumbria 685–867	251
Appendix 4: *Eric Bloodaxe – Axed? The Mystery of the Last Scandinavian King of York* by Professor Clare Downham	253
Bibliography	273
Index	281

ACKNOWLEDGEMENTS

> Eirik's court kept the Viking Age gossipmongers busy for a decade and his life could fill a biography of his own!
> Neil Price: *The Children of Ash & Elm*
> (London, Penguin 2020), p. 411.

I owe a debt of gratitude to all the following: to Neil Astley and Dr Suzanne Fairless-Aitken at Bloodaxe Books; to staff at the Literary and Philosophical Library, Newcastle upon Tyne, at the National Archives, Kew, at the British Library and British Museum, Viking World Reykjavik, The Viking Ship Museum, Roskilde, the Viking Museum Ladby, Goteborg City Museum, Slottsfjellmuseum, Tonsberg, Wikinger Museum Haithabu, and Archaologisches Landesmuseum Schloss Gottorf, Schleswig Germany, Royal Museums of Art & History, Brussels; the National Museum of Ireland, to library staff at the Society of Antiquaries London, to Emily North, Amy Cope and colleagues at the Yorkshire Museum Trust, To Professor Claire Downham of Liverpool University, to Professor Michael Woods of Manchester University, to Hakon Glorstad and Svein Harald Gullbekk at the Viking Age Museum Oslo, to Rebecca Ramsay and Dr Tim Pestell at Norfolk Museums; to Charles Fumunjere and Wouter Paelinck of the Fine Arts Museum of Belgium; to Sarah Marlene Moesgaard Jagd at the National Museum of Denmark; to Stephen Lines and other members of the Vikings Living History Group, to Kev Cockayne and colleagues at Jorvik and York Archaeology Trust; Bamburgh

Castle; Berwick Museum & Art Gallery; Durham County Record Office; East Lothian County Archives; English Heritage; the Explore Programme, Newcastle; Historic Environment Scotland; Literary and Philosophical Society, Newcastle; National Museum of Scotland, National Records of Scotland, Edinburgh; National Trust for Scotland; Newcastle Central Library; Glendale LHS; Coldstream & District LHS; Northumberland Archives, Woodhorn; Royal Armouries, Leeds; Society of Antiquaries, Newcastle upon Tyne; the UK Battlefields Trust; Tullie House Museum, Carlisle; Tyne and Wear Museums & Archives, Newcastle upon Tyne.

I have a great many people to thank, many who have knowingly and many others unknowingly contributed to this book, which has been a long time in the making. These include: Max Adams, Dr Lyndsay Allason-Jones, Fiona Armstrong, the late Alec Bankier, Adam Barr, Margaret Baxter, Stan Beckensall, Alix Bell, Barbara Birley, Peter Blenkinsopp, Chris Berendt, Steven Bogle, Liz Bregazzi, Robert Brooks, Colin Burgess, Chris and Barry Butterworth, Dr David Caldwell, Dr Tobias Capwell, Geoffrey Carter, Doug Chapman, the late Beryl Charlton, the late Ian Colquhoun, April Common, the late Tom Corfe, John Dale, John Day, Terry Deary, Ruth Dickinson, the late Wilf Dodds, Keith Douglas, Ulfric Douglas, Pat Dunscombe, Colin and Lindsay Durward, Margaret Eliott, Flora Fairbairn, Janet Fenwick-Clennell, Ann and John Ferguson, Tony Fox, Alistair Fraser, Jane Gibson, Bobbi Goldwater, David Goldwater, Dave Grey, Alan and Julia Grint, Anna Groundwater, Jane Hall, Tony Hall, Clive Hallam-Baker, the late Robert Hardy CBE FSA, Jim Herbert, Rob Horne, Philip Howard, Andy Jepson, the late George Jobey MC FSA, Chris Jones, Terry Kowal of the Scottish Assembly, Jennifer Laidler, Sue Lloyd, Stephen Lowdon, Paul Macdonald, May McKerrell, John Malden, Kath Marshall-Ivens, Paul Martin, Dr Xerxes Mazda, Margaret Mitchinson, Brian Moffat, Glenda Mortimer, Peter Nicholson, John Nolan, Colm O'Brien, Geoff Parkhouse, Harry Pearson, Phil Philo, Aiden Pratt, Baroness J. Quinn, Peter Ryder, Pearl Saddington, John Scott, Barbara Spearman of English Heritage, Alex Speirs, Lord Steel of Aikwood, Derek Stewart, the late Jock Tate, Anne Telfer, Paul Thompson, Neil Tranter, Graham Trueman, Anne-Marie Trevelyan MP, The Honourable Christopher Vane Chester Herald,

Acknowledgements

Jenny Vaughn, Philip Walling, Sir Humphrey Wakefield, Charles Wesencraft, Peter Woods and Dr Paul Younger.

Especial thanks are due to professor Downham for permission to include her brilliant paper on Eirik and his possible identity as appendix four. This has been reproduced, for the sake of brevity without original footnotes. The full text can be viewed online at: Eric_Bloodaxe_axed_The_mystery_of_the_la (1).pdf.

The fragment of gnomic verse included at the beginning of the introduction is reproduced by kind courtesy of the British Museum. Quotes from *Beowulf* are from the seminal translation by Seamus Heaney (London, Faber & Faber 1999). Those from *Egil's Saga* are translated by Bernard Scudder (London, Penguin 2004). For excerpts from *Orkneyinga Saga*, I have relied on the translation by Herman Palsson and Paul Edwards (London, Penguin 1981). Verses from Longfellow's 'The Saga of King Olaf' are taken from the 1902 *Complete Poetical Works*.

As for the *Anglo-Saxon Chronicle*, I've relied on my long-trusted edition, translated by G. N. Garmonsway (London, J. M. Dent & Sons 1953). Excerpts from Basil Bunting's *Briggflatts* are included by kind permission of Bloodaxe Books, *Basil Bunting, Complete Poems* ed. Richard Caddel (Bloodaxe Books, 2000) with audio CD (Bloodaxe Books, 2009; www.bloodaxebooks.com. Extracts from the *Gododdin* are primarily from Gillian Clarke's *Gododdin – Lament for the Fallen* (London, Faber & Faber 2022). The final quote of the last chapter is taken from Gordon Honeycombe's novel *Dragon under the Hill*, reproduced by kind permission of Simon & Schuster.

Yet again, I owe much to Chloe Rodham for drawing the maps, another successful collaboration, to Shaun Barrington my editor at Amberley, as ever to my agent Tom Cull and yet again to my muse and indexer, Bev Palin. As ever, I remain solely responsible for any errors or omissions and if anyone discovers they have been incorrectly quoted or necessary permissions have not been obtained please contact me through the publishers or via my website (www.johnsadler.net), and I will ensure all errors are corrected in any future editions.

John Sadler, Northumberland,
2025

MAPS

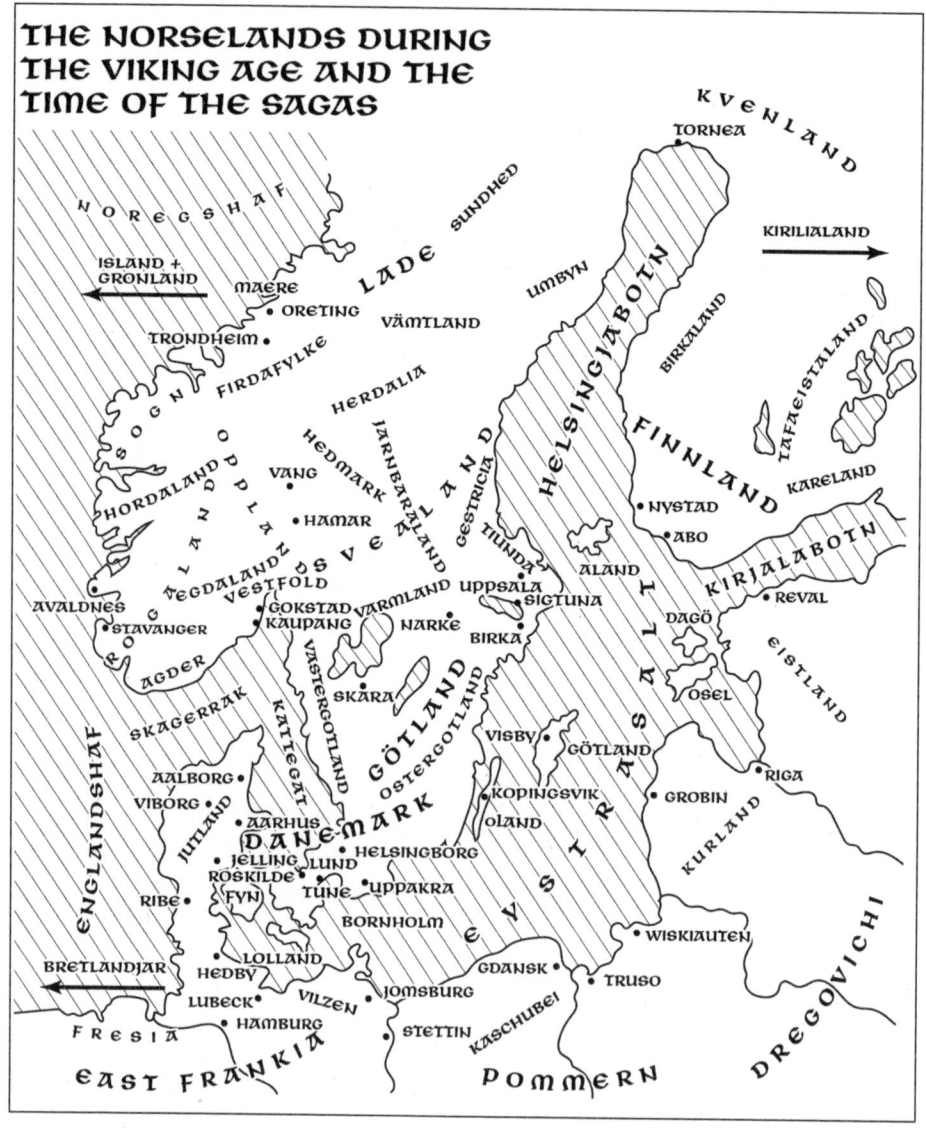

Viking Age Norway.

Maps

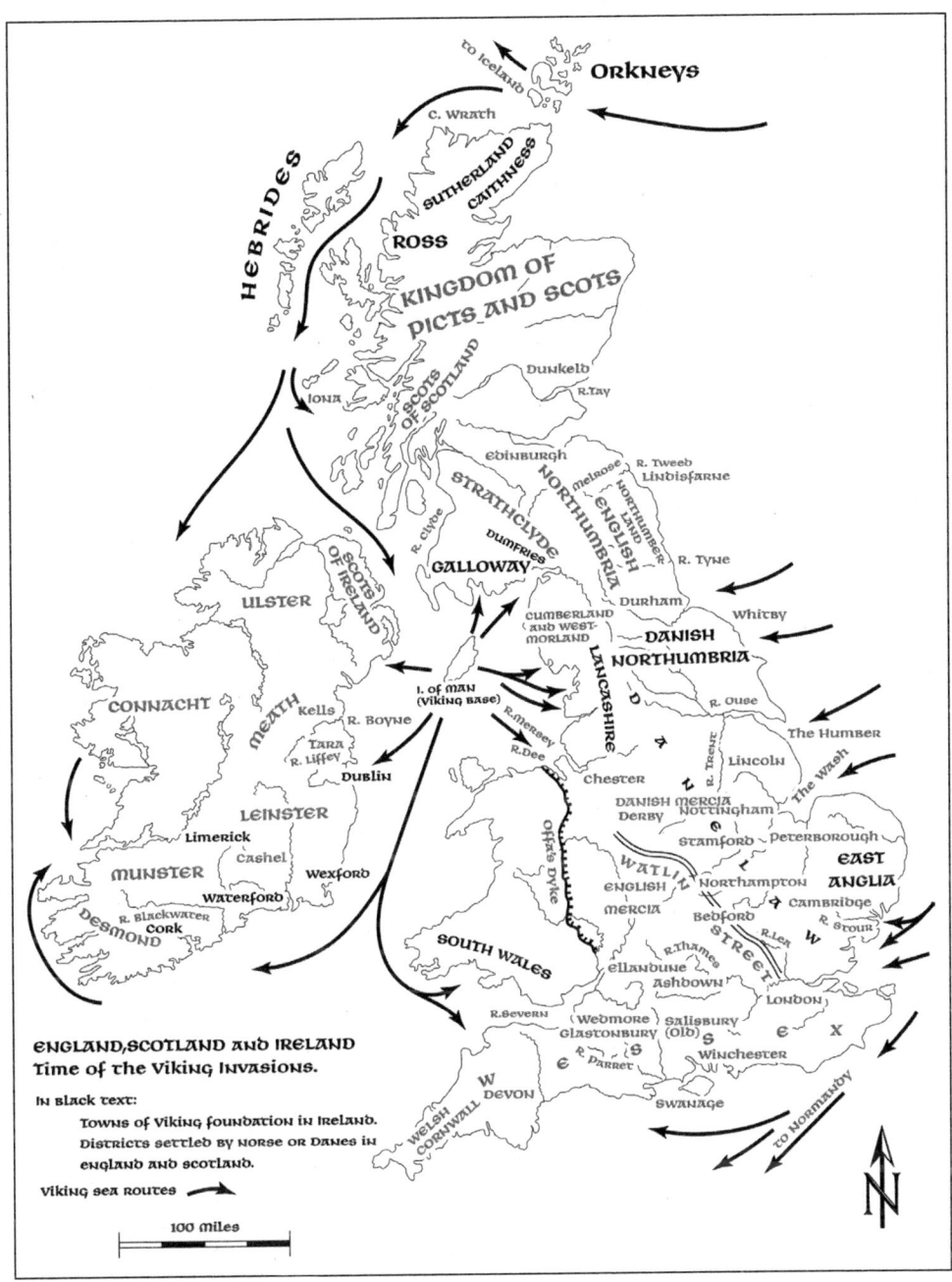

Viking Age England.

Viking Age Northumbria.

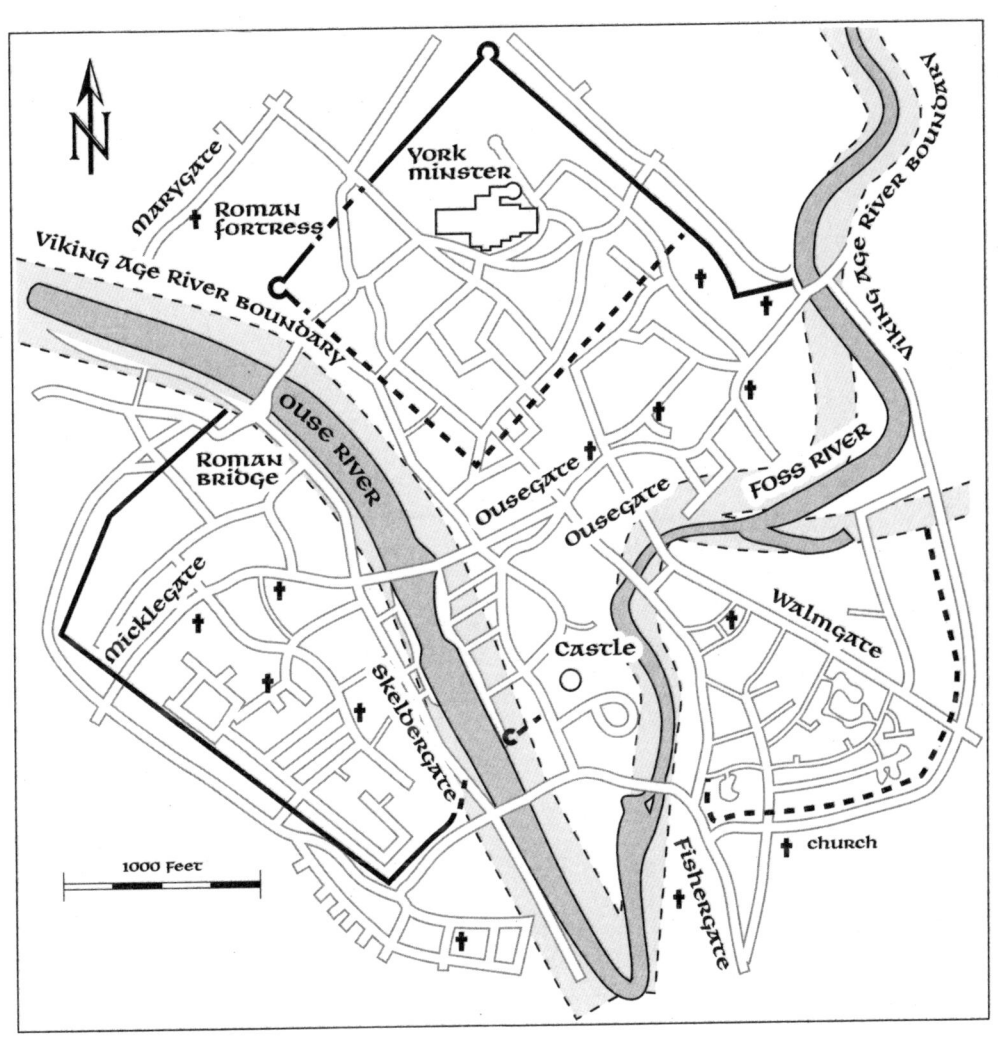

Viking Age Jorvik.

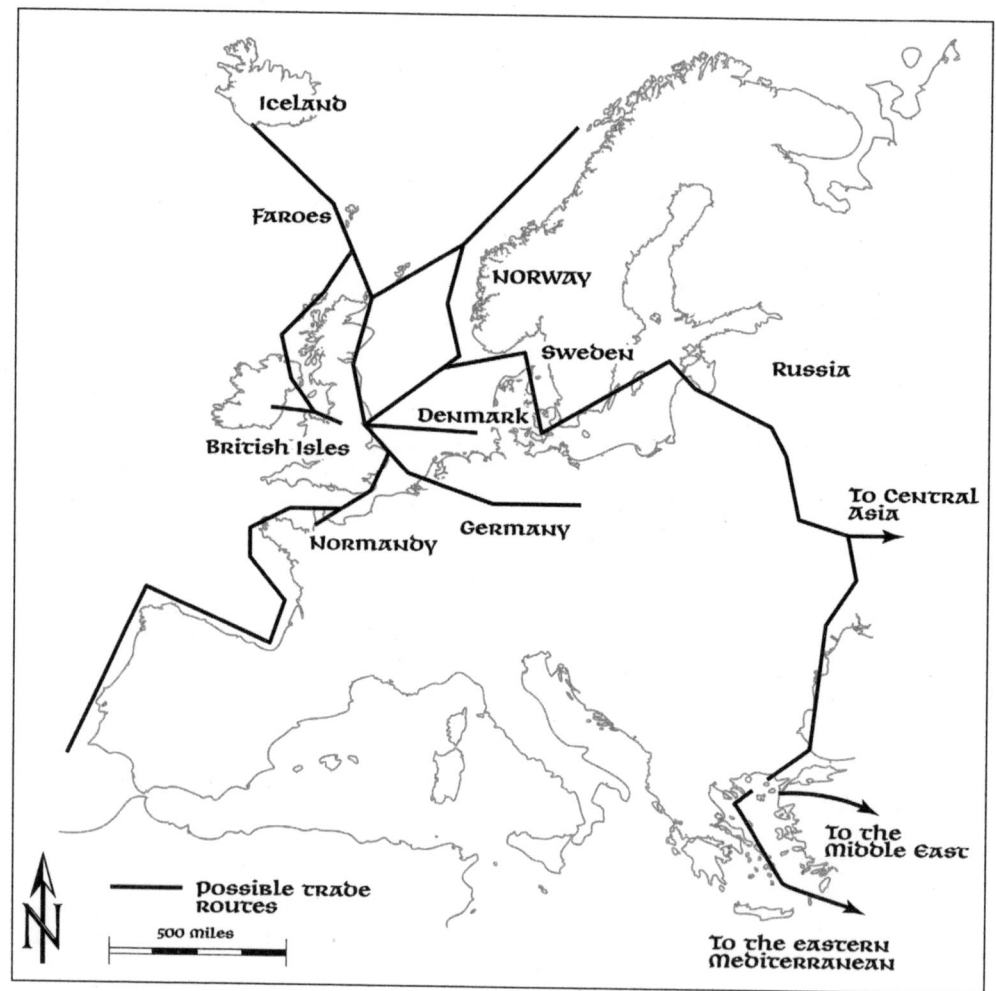

Jorvik trading networks.

TIMELINE

789	King Beorhtric of Wessex's reeve is killed by Norse raiders
793	Viking attack on Lindisfarne
795	Raid on Iona
799	Norse raids on Frankia begin
c. 800	Osberg ship constructed
835	Major attack on Wessex, Vikings defeated by King Egbert
c. 850	Birth of Harald Fairhair
851	Viking forces over winter in England for the first time
865	The Viking Great Army arrives in England, led by Ivar the Boneless
867	Ivar defeats rival kings of Northumbria at York, establishes Norse rule
c. 870	King Harald consolidates his rule over Norway
c. 870	Vikings begin to colonise Iceland
c. 872	Battle of Hafrsfjord
c. 875/6	Halfdan Ragnarsson retakes York and establishes a Scandinavian kingdom
877	Halfdan killed in Ireland
877	Great Viking Army takes Mercia
878	King Alfred defeats Guthrum at Edington

879	Northmen occupy East Anglia
883	Guthred becomes King in York
c. 884/5	Birth of Eirik
895	Death of Guthred
895–900	Rule of Siefredus (Sichfrith?)
900	Death of Alfred, accession of Edward the Elder
901	Aethelwold of Wessex becomes ruler in York
903	Death of Aethelwold
903–26	Norse rule restored in York
918	Battle of Corbridge, Ragnall rules in York
921	Sihtric replaces Ragnall
924	Death of Edward the Elder, accession of Athelstan
926	Sihtric submits to Athelstan at Tamworth
927	Death of Sihtric and West Saxon rule in York established
931–3	Eirik rules in Norway, expelled by Hakon the Good, foster-son of Athelstan
934	Athelstan campaigns in Scotland
937	Battle of Brunanburh
939	Death of King Athelstan, accession of King Edmund
939	Olaf Guthfrithson re-asserts independent Scandinavian rule in York
942	Death of Olaf, succeeded by Olaf Cuaran
944	Norse expelled from York and West Saxon rule re-imposed
946	Death of King Edmund, accession of King Eadred
947	Northumbria submits to Eadred
948	Eirik's first rule in York
948	Eirik expelled and replaced by Olaf Guaran
952	Eirik returns for second rule
954	Death of Eirik Bloodaxe at Stainmore and end of the independent Scandinavian kingdom. Northumbria is reduced to an earldom.

A NOTE ON SOURCES

Eirik Bloodaxe is, in terms of reliable sources, very elusive and any biography such as this must, to a degree, rely rather heavily on heroic assumptions. There are contemporary chronicle sources for Eirik's time in Northumbria, different versions of *The Anglo-Saxon Chronicle*, numismatic evidence from coinage, *The Life of St. Cathroe*.[1]

Skaldic, or poetic sources from Norway, which has no early chronicles, are contentious. These do indeed contain much that is historical in nature but at the same time are riddled with inaccuracies and inconsistencies and cannot ever be relied upon fully. A shame but there it is. The Eirik who was briefly King in Norway was only really identified as the same Eirik who was equally briefly twice King of York in 1901 by W. G. Collingwood.[2] At the start of this century Clare Downham has cast doubt on this, suggesting these are in fact two different individuals.[3] I have chosen to follow Collingwood and find the synergies compelling but cannot argue this is definitive.

It is most notable that there is a very marked dissonance between the chronicle sources and the kings sagas. These include a number of synoptic or compilation sources including *Historia Norwegiæ* (from *c.* 1170), Theodoricus Monachus' *Historia de antiquitate regum Norwagiensium* (*c.* 1180), and *Ágrip af Nóregskonungasögum* (*c.* 1190) together with the later Icelandic kings sagas *Orkneyinga Saga* (*c.* 1200), *Fagrskinna* (*c.* 1225), the *Heimskringla* (ascribed to Snorri Sturluson and perhaps from 1230),

Egil's Saga (1220–1240), and *Óláf's Saga Tryggvasonar en mesta* (c. 1300).

As entrancing as these are, they cannot be read as histories. Where Eirik is concerned there are no gospels, just this tantalisingly incomplete tapestry, so any biographer must tread with extreme care and be mindful when raising their head above the parapet. Contemporary historical research suggests taking a robust and critical view of the sagas as reflections of historical record and clearly this is wise, but without them, we are left with mere fragments. Throughout this narrative I have attempted to interrogate the sources – skaldic, synoptic and chronicle – as thoroughly as possible. That entails a lot of 'maybes'.

'Bloodaxe' has a real ring to it, a biographer's dream, but we can't even be sure this handle was ever applied during his lifetime. Egil leads us to think so, as does *Historia Norwegiae*. Theodoricus brands him as 'brother-killer' after the fratricidal bloodletting of the dynastic scrimmage in Norway. *Fagrskinna* tells us it derives from his equally savage reputation as a Viking raider. Whatever the exact origin, my guess is Eirik would have rather liked his soubriquet – proper Norsemen don't do Woke*.

The *Anglo Saxon Chronicle* (D version) clearly identifies Eirik as a son of Harold and this is echoed by John of Worcester writing in the early twelfth century. John contends that Eirik was of royal Norwegian stock and cites precedents from earlier kings of York, suggesting clear synergies between both crowns. Both sagas and synoptics are unanimous that Eirik was a son of Harald Fairhair. Egil is our leading advocate, but questions have been raised over both the content and dating of certain passages. As ever then, the sagas are far from cast iron. But they remain persuasive. Sticking

---

* Bloodaxe or *Bloody Axe,* as mentioned above, has an uncertain provenance. It is debatable whether its presence in two *lausavísur* by Egil and another contemporary skald means it is from the 10th century or has been coined at some stage when Eirik was becoming the focus of legend. There is no absolute guarantee that it predates the 12th-century narrative tradition, where it is first attached to him in *Ágrip* and in Latin translation as *sanguinea secures* in the *Historia Norwegie..*The sagas usually state it refers to Eric's slaying of his half-brothers. Theodoricus gives the similar nickname, *fratrum interfector* (brother-killer). *Fagrskinna* ascribes it simply to the violent reputation Eirik earns as a prolific raider.

A note on sources

with Egil, his *Arinbjarnarkviða*[4] clearly identifies a ruler in York who is a descendant of Halfdan, (Eirik's paternal grandfather), and a member of the *Yngling* Dynasty[5].

There is peripheral doubt as to who the 'Harold' in question may be, not necessarily Fairhair himself. We have Aralt mac Sitric (d. 940) who was a king of Limerick and father of both Maccus and Gofraid – the former is one of the anomalies of Eirik's final fight at Stainmore, so may be relevant. Both of these and an Eric have been described as rulers of the Isles[6]. Edward I, when penning correspondence to Pope Boniface VIII remembers an 'Eric' who he thinks may have been a very much earlier King of Scots who owed allegiance to England[7] (see chapter ten).

Another contender as Eirik's putative father is Danish King Harald Bluetooth (ruled 958–986/986). In the nineteenth century J. M. Lappenburg[8] saw Bluetooth as Eirik's parent, identifying with the Danish ruler's son Hring. In this he relied on Adam of Bremen[9] who himself relied on a lost earlier source when compiling his history of the Bishops of Hamburg, asserted that Harald had dispatched an army under his son Hring to conquer England. The invasion was successful, but Hring was undone by the treachery of Northumbria; a rather odd theory and one which doesn't really hold water.

As biographer, the writer must hedge a life of Eirik around with stiff caveats and the final view will inevitably be to some degree subjective. I will be as rigorous as I'm able in my interrogation and provenance of sources, but there will be much the reader will have to decide, if indeed any decision is possible. None of this demeans Eirik Bloodaxe or devalues his story, what we do know makes it compelling.

ABBREVIATIONS

'ASC' – *Anglo-Saxon Chronicle* (transl. G. N. Garmonsway, London, J. M. Dent & Sons 1953)

'Bede' – Bede's *Ecclesiastical History of England* (ed. J. A. Giles (London, George Bell & Sons 1880)

'*Egil's Saga*' – *Egil's Saga* transl. Leifur Eiriksson (London, Penguin 2002)

'*Fagrskinna* – *Fagrskinna – A Catalogue of the Kings of Norway* (transl.) A. Finlay (Leiden, Brill 2004)

'*Goddodin*' – *Gododdin* by Aneurin, transl. Reverend J. Williams (London, Longmans 1852)

'*Beowulf*' – Heaney, S., *Beowulf* (London, Faber & Faber 1999)

'Henry of Huntingdon' – Henry of Huntingdon, *Historia Anglorum* (Cambridge, Cambridge University Press 2012)

'*Historia Norwegie*' – *Historia Norwegie*, eds. I. Ekrem & L. B. Mortensen, transl. P. Fisher (Copenhagen, Museum Tusculanum Press University of Copenhagen 2006)

'*Jomsviking Saga*' – *Jomsviking Saga* translated N. F. Blake in *Icelandic Texts*, editors S. Nordal & G. Turville-Petrie (London, Thomas Nelson & Sons 1962)

Abbreviations

'**Nennius**' – Nennius, *Historia Brittonum* (England, independently published 2022)

'**Njal's Saga**' – *The Saga of Burnt Njal* translated R. Cook (London, Penguin 1997)

'**Orkneyinga Saga**' – *Orkneyinga Saga* (transl. Hermann Palsson and Paul Edwards, London, Penguin 1981)

'**Roger of Wendover**' – Roger of Wendover, *Flowers of History* (New York, AMS Press 1968)

'**Simeon of Durham**' – Simeon of Durham, *Historical Works*, (editor J. Stevenson, Franklin Classics 2018)

'**Heimskringla**' – Snorri Sturluson, *Heimskringla* (Kent, Dover Publications 2009)

'**The Poetic Edda**' – *The Poetic Edda* by Snorri Sturluson, transl. C. Larrington (Oxford, Oxford University Press 1996)

'**The Prose Edda**' – *The Prose Edda* by Snorri Sturluson, transl. J. L. Byock (London, Penguin 2003)

'**William of Malmesbury**' – William of Malmesbury, *The Deeds of the Bishops of England*, transl. D.G. Preest (London, Boydell Press 2002)

INTRODUCTION

A king shall have a kingdom. Cities are to be seen from far-off times, the cunning work of giants which are on this earth, a skilful shaping of wall stones. Wind is the swiftest thing under heaven. Thunder is at times the loudest. The might of Christ is great. Fate is strongest. The clouds go by. Good companions shall cheer the young prince in battle and the giving of rings. Courage shall be in the hero. The sword against the helmet shall make war. The hawk upon the glove shall remain a wild thing. The wolf in the forest shall be wretched, a recluse. The boar in the wood shall be strong in the might of his tusks. The good man in his country shall do glorious deeds. The spear in the hand shall be a weapon wrought with gold. The jewel on the ring shall sit high and broad. The tide with its waves shall stir up the ocean. The mast, the sail yard, shall stand in the boat. The sword on the breast shall be lordly, of iron. The dragon under the hill shall be ancient, proud of his treasures.

      11th-century Anglo-Saxon gnomic verse.

Then one stern in war waded forth, heaving up his weapon,
sheltered by his shield, stepped up against Byrhtnoth.
The earl went just as resolutely to the churl,
either of them intending evil to the other.
Then the sea-warrior sent a southern spear,
that wounded the lord of warriors.
Byrhtnoth shoved it with his shield, so that the shaft burst,

and that spear-head broke so that it sprang out again.
The fighting-warrior became infuriated; he stabbed with his spear
the proud Viking, who had given him that wound.
Aged was the army-warrior; he let his spear go forth
through the neck of the younger warrior, guided by his hand
so that he reached the life of that sudden attacker. (130-42)
Then he swiftly pierced another Viking,
so that the mail-shirt burst – that one was wounded in the breast
through the ring-locks, the poisonous point
stood at his heart. The earl was the happier,
then he laughed, the mindful man, said thanks to the Measurer
for the day's work which the Lord had given him. (143-8)

'Battle of Maldon'

To a Viking, how you might have lived is far less important than how you die; Valhalla sets demanding standards. Eirik Bloodaxe* (or *Brother-Slayer*) might well claim to be the last of the Vikings, his career a documentary episode of *Game of Thrones*; his life a true Norse saga, slender facts being teased out from sparse sources. But the whole picture encapsulates the very tenor and essence of the Viking Age, an age which had exploded onto the shores of Northumbria 160 years earlier: 'A furore Nordmannorum, libera nos, domine ("From the fury of the north men O Lord, deliver us") was a litany without need of vellum. It was graven on the hearts of men whenever and for as long as that fury fell.'[1]

In June 793, a year of troubling portents, three swift, square-sailed ships, their fearsome dragon heads rearing, appeared on a summer's dawn, they skimmed the bright, jewelled waters of the North Sea to make landfall in the harbour of Lindisfarne, the Holy Island, sacred seat of Aidan and Cuthbert, a dune-fringed archipelago of golden sand beneath vast skies; home to the astonishing art of the sacred gospels and God's holy church. Slaughter, pillage and a harvesting of slaves followed, sacred precints left bloodied and smouldering[2]. The Norsemen had arrived. For any interested in fictional takes on these events Robert

---

* Born *c.* 885, ruled Norway 932–934, Northumbria 947–948 and 952–954 (killed 954, age approximately 69/70). I believe.

Westall's *The Wind Eye*[3] together with Gordon Honeycombe's *Dragon Under the Hill*[4] offer an interesting perspective

For me they arrived not via *The Anglo-Saxon Chronicle* or even the sagas but via Hollywood and Richard Fleischer's 1958 movie *The Vikings* with Kirk Douglas, Tony Curtis and Janet Leigh, the latter fully aerodynamic in a rocket bra which would have raised a few eyebrows in Jorvik, I'm sure. Fort La Latte in Brittany doubled commendably for Bamburgh and I was, decades later, thrown out of the place for trying to recreate the rooftop final duel. I think I saw the film in the autumn of 1964, aged eleven and a half – an obsession was born. Odin was in the driving seat:

> Odin is the greatest and most profound of the Nordic gods ... he is many faced and terrible with a ferocious passion for knowledge and wisdom, for which he stops at nothing and sacrifices anything – anyone – even himself. Odin governs in mystic ecstasy, he fathoms the soul. He is a sorcereor and master of the runes. He inspires a frenzy in his worshippers and his warriors, so that they face the worst that fate can bring fearlessly and with a kind of rapture... He is the god of death and war, and his hall, Valhalla, is at once a symbol of the grave and the field of battle, where his warriors rest, feast and greet their ancestors. Mead is his drink and theirs. The wolf, the eagle and raven are his creatures For nine days and nine nights he hung on the world tree, in the manner of his sacrifices, and endured with a spear impaling him. Thus he won the secrets of the runes!*

A few years later while visitng family in Norway I got the chance to visit the Museum of The Viking Age near Oslo.** After a rickety train ride up the length of the fjord from Tonsberg, my first glimpse of the real thing, the Gokstad Ship, blew me clear out of the gallery. Here was the whole essence of the Norsemen built in timber, unbelievably sleek and slender, yet imbued with grace and

---

* Honeycombe, G., *Dragon under the Hill* (New York, Simon & Schuster 1972), pp. 276–277.
** https://www.vikingtidsmuseet.no/english/

Introduction

a true pagan exuberance, spirit, style and elegance. That rather settled things.

Within a century of the raid on Lindisfarne, Ivar the Boneless had led a great heathen army to conquer Northumbria and establish his kingdom at Jorvik (York). In Scandinavia, would-be kings struggled to achieve hegemony and make themselves supreme, a dangerous and violent process that would take a couple of centuries and fuel the outward urge as independent-minded Vikings sought new lands, free of centralised control.

During the late ninth and early tenth centuries Harald Fairhair managed to carve out a fragile supremacy over Norway, certainly in the west and south, but his rule would ever be resented. Against all odds, he managed to live to a ripe old age and die in his bed, leaving, it is said, a score or so of sons by various wives. Of these, Eirik was probably the youngest yet seems to have shared power with his father during Harald's declining years. The old king may have nominated Eirik to be his sucessor. Saga sources tell us that by the age of 12, Eirik was already a warrior and a fearsome one, leading terrible raids against Balts and Scots, building his reputation and harvesting resources to pay his *hird*. He'd be needing both if he was to rule. Norse kingship was a bit like modern electioneering, it took cash, lots of it, to grease all the outstretched palms waiting to be motivated.

Promogeniture was as yet an unknown concept in Norway and on his father's death Eirik chose or was forced into a bloody civil war with several of his half-brothers. He defeated and killed them, and his personal rule became increasingly oppressive and despotic. One of his siblings, Hakon, had been sent to the English court as a foster son to King Athelstan. Powerful allies amongst the Norwegian magnates encouraged Hakon to return and Eirik was soon driven into exile.

At this point the record goes dark, but it seems he headed for Orkney where he possibly intimidated the local jarls into accepting him as a kind of overlord, thought this cannot be substantiated. From there he resumed his earlier vocation as a pirate – a means both of subsistence, keeping his war band together and of amassing resources for a return bout with Hakon who, though no mean fighter himself, was known as 'The Good', possibly in contrast to his brother.

Meanwhile, the situation in England and especially in the north was complex. In 927, Athlstan had taken York under central authority. His crushing victory a decade later when he thrashed

Olaf Guthfrithson, Constantine of Scotland and their allies so soundly at Brunanburh, served, pointedly and brutally, to underline West Saxon supremacy. Yet barely two years after and Athlstan was dead, succeeded by his 18-year-old half brother Edmund. At the outset of his reign Edmund proved incapable of exerting this same level of influence, alowing Olaf Sihtricsson (cousin of and co-ruler with the other Olaf, now dead), to slip back in. Within a couple of years, Edmund reasserted West Saxon dominance but was himself dead by 946, murdered at the age of 25.

Relations between north and south were never easy. The old rump of Northumbrian grandees resented the power of Wessex and were wont to find Norse rulers more acceptable than southern English ones. The shifting sands of politics at this time are unmappable and invariably involved both Scots and Dublin Norse. Edmund's brother Eadred succeeded after the former's assassination and soon showed himself highly effective, ruthlessly so. His reponses to Northumbrian secessionist tendencies were simple, burn them out; stamp on the embers of home rule with an iron fist. It wasn't nice but it was a pretty powerful incentive for toeing the West Saxon line.

Barely had the ashes cooled than the Northumbrians broke out in fresh tumult, abetted by Scottish raids, which may have been opportunistic or collaborative. Eirik had clearly been waiting in the wings, his claim was credible, his credentials as a strong ruler impeccable. Eadred responded and torched the north once more, but Eirik, biding his time, inflicted heavy losses on the southerners' rearguard in a battle at Castleford.

Eadred might have had his nose bloodied but the terror he could unleash, even the promise of it, was sufficient to undermine Eirik. In 948, it was Olaf's turn for another try but he didn't last long, being expelled in 952, which gave Eirik his own second season. He lasted two years before his final *Ragnarok* in the obscure ('dim weird') battle at Stainmore. He would be nearly 70 years of age by that time. Eirik was always a trier. Most of this is clouded by a paucity and confusion of sources. There is doubt, as examined in the final chapter, whether Eirik Bloodaxe and Eirik of York were even the same person.

During the early Victorian era, Thomas Carlyle was keen to promulgate the notion that the British are of Norse descent. His first standard lecture (1840) – 'The Hero as Divinity' – fosters the idea that Odin the God was in fact once a mortal man: '[He]

Introduction

was not only a wild captain and Fighter; discerning with his dark flashing eyes what to do, with his wild lion heart daring and doing it; but a Poet too, all that we mean by a Poet, Prophet, great devout Thinker and Inventor – as the truly Great Man ever is'[5]. Total tosh but the appeal resonated.

We consider Eirik's legacy in chapter nine and how he somehow exemplifies the ideal of the Viking, not a nice man to be sure but one to be respected. I know many people who have researched their own DNA and a common desire is to find they have Norse blood pulsing in their 21st-century veins. Why? What's so wonderful about the Vikings we're so keen to claim their bloodlines? Much ink has been expended in recent years revisiting our traditional image of bloodthirsty warriors, slavers, oppressors and hooligans.

Revisionists cite the Northmen's achievements as farmers, builders, craftsmen, navigators and explorers. Yes, they were all of those, but they were vain, hungry for honour, irredeemably violent and upgraded slavery, the terrible trade in human suffering, from a cottage industry to a global one. When not attacking others, they revelled in incessant blood feuds and the ritualised killing of the *holmgang*, or formal duel. They glorified war and fetishised weapons. To be fair, we still tend to do so today. One only has to read *Orkneyinga Saga* or *Njal's Saga* to wonder why Tarantino hasn't filmed it – and you can see what inspired George R. R. Martin, it's a rollercoaster of non-stop gratuitous sex and violence.

Recently, I attended a wargames fest in my locale. Games varied across the centuries, some reprising wars I'd never heard of, but the idealised view of the warrior elite pervades all. At such events the actual participants almost universally fail to live up to the ideal, most are middle-aged or look it, often overweight, moving at best at a slow shuffle. Eirik wouldn't have been impressed. Sadly, Vikings became poster boys for the Nazis, who hijacked or imposed their image as symbols of Aryan supremacy. But we still like them.

We like them so much that one of the most popular TV series in recent years has been *Vikings*.* Many of we Viking enactors

---

* Created by Michael Hirst for The History Channel, its first season premiered in Canada during February 2013 and the series ran until December 2020. A sequel, *Vikings: Valhalla* first reached our screens in February 2022 and a third season is about to begin at the time of writing.

in England wanted to be extras but this was reserved for Irish nationals only. In the north of England, we had to be content with swinging swords in ITV's dire fantasy adaptation of *Beowulf* – least said about that the better! Based, very loosely, on the Saga of Ragnar Lothbrok (who may or may not have existed), *Vikings* is a rollicking carousel of endless mayhem, high adventure with sharp swords, yet close enough to history (and with sumptuous production values) to be compelling.

Back in 1973, I took part in one of the first large-scale Viking Age battle reenactments in the north, located in Trow Quarry South Tyneside and with the then Norse Film and Pageant Society (now made over as 'The Vikings' and still going strong). It was great fun, even if there was an awful lot of dodgy faux-fur and some seriously weird outfits. There were some there whose sympathies lay more with fantasy Third Reich and what would now be called 'far right' tendencies (see chapter nine).

Eleven years earlier in Jarrow, just up the coast, a new sixties shopping mall, the Viking Precinct, was embellished, not necessarily to its advantage, with a modernist, or what masqueraded as modernist at the time, statue of two Vikings; and yes, they do have horned helmets. This was period installation art at its most unfortunate. Since then, the years have not been kind and the whole place looks horribly like East Germany just before the Berlin Wall came down. Recent reviews have been unkinder still – in the wake of the Black Lives Matter protests, South Tyneside Council, working with the police, carried out a survey of monuments to see which gave most offence to zealots. These Vikings (along with Queen Victoria) were labelled with an 'amber' sticker, indicating they could be linked to oppression and a beacon for Neo-Nazi types (as reported in *The Telegraph*, 11 February 2023).

Fifty years on and we're still donning mail and hefting linden shields for the crowd's delight. The Norsemen really are in our blood, whatever the DNA results suggest, and Eirik Bloodaxe embodies all that makes them unendingly exciting to us; courage, indomitable spirit, warrior ethos and skills and perhaps, above all – a fierce independence. Norsemen don't bend the knee. Eirik spent his long career trying to ensure they did – to him!

Dr Thomas Williams curated a major Viking Exhibition at the British Museum through 2013–2014. One reviewer lamented:

Introduction

'There's no stage setting. No gory recreation of the Lindisfarne Raid, say, to get us in the mood... I felt like crying. Where were the swords?'[6] Dr Williams ably countered in his subsequent book, querying whether glorification of horror – 'sensationalizing violence for the entertainment of children – is ever appropriate'. He's quite right of course but yes, I would have liked more swords. He then goes on to ask if we'd relish an exhibition gloating over the carnage of Srebrenica. We'd be appalled and rightly so. Eirik Bloodaxe wouldn't even blink. Welcome to his world. Horror was a tool, terror a policy. Different times of course, infinitely harder in every respect to our lives in western Europe today. Ask the residents of Lindisfarne in June 793, they could have told you exactly what October 7, 2023, was like.

Our modern perceptions are irrelevant. My main task is to try and get under the skin, into the mindset of the subject, near impossible, as we've really no idea how these far-off Northmen really thought. Their world is more distant than the passage of a single millennium might suggest. They are not like us, and yet very like us in being prone to anger, fear, jealousy, ambition – all our petty vanities. Eirik is a difficult case, the chronicle and synoptic sources are both vague and at times contradictory, and while the skaldic accounts are far fuller, their authenticity needs to be robustly interrogated.

What I do hope to do is to open as many windows as I'm able into the world of those Norse Kings of Dublin and York. Eirik was the last Viking King of York, scion of a line of Norwegian kings whose long and tempestuous career spans the Norsemen's world. Context, as Uhtred of Bebbanburh might say, (alongside fate, *wyrd*), is all.

Byrhtnoth looked to heaven:

> 'I thank you, Wielder of peoples,
> for all these joys that I have experienced in the world.
> Now I have, mild Measurer, the greatest need
> that you should grant my spirit the good
> that my soul may be allowed to venture unto you
> into your keeping, Prince of Angels
> ferrying with peace. I am a suppliant to you

that these hell-harmers shall not be allowed to injure it.'
(172-80)
Then the heathen warriors cut him down
and both of the men who stood beside him,
Ælfnoth and Wulfmær, both lay there,
when they gave up their lives beside their lord. (181-4)

'Battle of Maldon'

The 'northern heroic spirit' is an expression coined by J. R. R. Tolkien. Byrhtnoth with his final defiance in the face of violent death and a willingness for self-sacrifice exemplifies this. At the same time 'this northern heroic spirit' is never quite pure; it is of gold and an alloy. Unalloyed it would direct a man to endure even death unflinching, where necessary; that is when death may help the achievement of some object of will, 'or when life can only be purchased by denial of what one stands for'.[7]

Yet this obsessive honour can drive a fellow beyond 'bleak heroic necessity' to 'excess', which Tolkien classes as 'chivalry'. Byrhtnoth is heroic but he's also vain, egotistical and downright stupid in allowing the Norsemen to cross the fatal causeway unhindered and form up for battle on even ground. A sensible general would have forgotten about honour and focused on expediency – on winning the fight. Byrhtnoth's misplaced chivalric notions get himself and so many of his followers killed and he ultimately fails in his obligation to keep his march safe, ushering in a new age of Viking aggression and untold woe for England.

Where does Eirik fit in all this? As ever, we don't really know. It would be neat to see his final march to Stainmore in a similar light, a doomed heroic crusade propelled by personal honour. Another 'dim weird battle in the west' or perhaps rank folly, treachery or plain bad luck, we can't say. I'm sure Eirik would have liked his last stand to be another Maldon, but history hasn't been able to give his memory that consolation.

One

STREAMERS OF FIRE

> See the grisly texture grow,
> ('Tis of human entrails made,)
> And the weights that play below,
> Each a gasping warrior's head.
> Shafts for shuttles dipt in gore,
> Shoot the trembling cords along.
> Sword, that once a monarch bore,
> Keep the tissue close and strong.
>
> Thomas Gray: 'The Fatal Sisters' (1768)

At the centre of the Norse world sprouts the great life-giving tree Yggdrasill ('steed of the terrible one'),[1] an ash whose leafy canopy forms the roof of the world. Worlds lie beneath its vast spread of roots. Deer graze on its overhanging branches and a quick-footed squirrel scampers up and down its Olympian trunk, carrying tidings good and bad. Deep beneath the root structure in a subterranean chamber lives Nidhoggr, a fearful dragon.

We're not sure if the tree was planted by the gods, whether they strained its seed from the oceans or recycled body parts from Ymir, a dismembered giant. We don't know if it can survive the apocalypse of Ragnarök. But there the great ash stands, life giving, life itself, almost human in its ability to experience all the senses. We know that Valhalla lies directly beneath and that Heidrun the goat, squatting on its roof, nibbles at its leaves. There's plenty of livestock and fauna about, the Norse cosmos has lots of natural touches. A great eagle perches at its very pinnacle. Yggdrasill's roots are just as important as what stands above. One plunges downwards into the dark reaches of the underworld, ruled by the goddess Hel, a second to the frozen realm of the frost giants and the third connects directly to the world of men. Despite its seeming omnipotence, irritating snakes, a myriad of them, chew its branches, the dragon's constant gnawing at the roots, these promote decay, signs of which are visible. Decay isn't just a human affliction.

Back to Valhalla's roof and Heidrun has the deer Eikpyrnir for company. Moisture flicks from his proud spread of antlers into the pool Hverglemir ('Roaring Kettle') [Larr. 28]. Another water source, Mimir's Well, also stands at the tree's base. Somewhere at

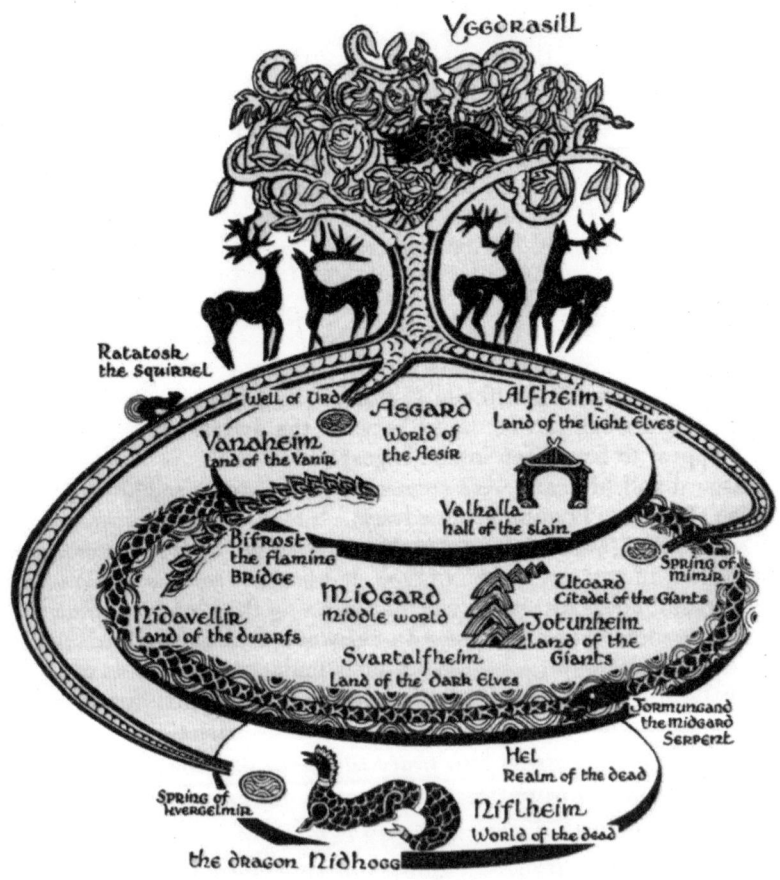

One of the many and varied representations of Yggdrasill.

the bottom lies Odin's missing eye. This wasn't left by accident or carelessness; the father of the gods traded an eye for wisdom. Mimir is an oracle, a northern Delphi but at the same time, an active player, a mysterious chess-master, except nobody quite knows what his game actually is.

This is the world Eirik Bloodaxe believes in, his inheritance and burden.

Eirik was the man who would be king and was, for a while at least, King of Norway then (possibly) twice King of York. There's a long context in both cases and he straddles no small part of the Viking World. Kings in Norway had a long and tricky pedigree: 'Norway is said to have taken its name from a king called Nor. Its territory is immense but for the most part uninhabitable, due to the huge numbers of its mountains, forests and cold temperatures'[2]. *Historia Norwegie* cites the Swede Yngve (from whom his line the Ynglings derive their name) as the first of a long and colourful list of rulers, most of whom meet unusual and violent ends: one is drowned in a tun of mead, another suffocated by a goblin, one is immolated in a hall by descendants anxious to accelerate the inheritance process, another hanged by the Swedes, one dies in battle against the Danes, and so on.

I first saw Norway sailing up the Oslo Fjord on a bright late summer's day in 1967. This was the old Vestfold region and my family lived in Tonsburg. Dating from the ninth century, the city, lying on the west flank of the Oslofjord around 60 miles (100 kilometres) south of the capital, can claim to be one of the oldest urban centres in the country. Once a royal residence, its great economic boom came in the nineteenth century when, together with neighbouring Sandefjord, it developed into a major whaling station. Now, the wharves and old timber framed warehouses are thoroughly made over, mostly as bars. Many people from Oslo have their weekend retreats there and they come down the fjord in small boats.

Netflix's *Lillehammer* series[3], which was rather good and very tongue in cheek, showed contemporary Norwegians as being deadly serious, right on and fully 'woke'. Eirik might have struggled with that, he'd have probably had less difficulty in identifying with fictional Frank Tagliano, the re-located mafioso.

Attitudes may have shifted, but Norway is still rugged. Some 32 per cent of the ground lies above tree level and a hunched spine of mountains forms its backbone running north to south. It's one of Europe's most northerly realms. These interlocking knuckles link to their continuations across Scotland, into Ireland, over the Atlantic to form the Appalachians, part of a vast prehistoric range.

During the last ice age, a frozen straitjacket covered the whole mass, gouging out steep-sided and plunging valleys. Sognefjord is the world's deepest. When the ice at last released its grip, it left a jagged coastline, scattered like the Hydra's teeth with over 50,000 offshore islands, studded with narrow fjords and hemmed in by high hills. Millennia afterwards, the land is imperceptibly but surely returning, clawing back a couple of millimetres every year. The mountains are a bit like Scotland's western highlands, but very much bigger brother and they split up the relatively fertile areas into distinct regions. A fair part of the country stretches inside the cold grip of the Arctic Circle.

It's no surprise that Norse mythology tends toward the dark and monumental, a natural home for giants, trolls and elves: 'Beneath the sky ranged a vast assortment of wild turrets, gnarled spires and pinnacles which prodded at it... High in the flickering darkness, silent figures stood guard behind long shields, dragons crouched gaping at the foul sky as Odin, father of the Gods of Asgard, approached the great iron portals which led to his domain and on into the vaulted halls of Valhalla.'

> The table he was crouched behind was one of countless slabs of oak on trestles that stretched away in every direction, laden with steaming hunks of dead animals, huge breads, great iron beakers slopping with wine and candles like wax anthills. Massive sweaty figures seethed around them, on them, eating, drinking, fighting over the food, fighting in the food, fighting with the food[4].

Snorri Sturluson[5] tells us that Odin was a Trojan, a son of Troy who came north to absorb new lands: 'Odin had the gift of prophecy, as his wife also did, and through this learning he became aware that his name would become renowned in the northern part of the world and honoured more than other kings. For this reason, he was eager to set off from Turkey, and he took with him on his journey a large following of people, young and old, men and women'[6]. One would think this must be entirely fanciful, but archaeology has shown that there were large-scale battles, or at least a battle, fought in Northern Europe. Diggers have been investigating a site along the banks of the Tollense River, 14 kilometres north of the town of Schwerin, municipality for the Mecklenburg-Vopommern region in Germany[7].

What, if anything, this may have to do with Troy and Odin we cannot possibly say or even speculate, but the great clans of Norse mythology, the Aesir and Vanir, may well represent some form of real ancestors. They squabble, fight, connive and deceive much like any real dysfunctional family or tribal group. Their propensity for constant warfare has a distinctly Homeric feel:

> The Northern Gods have an exultant extravagance in their warfare which makes them more like Titans than Olympians, only they are on the right side, though it is not the side that wins. The winning side is Chaos and Unreason – mythologically, the monsters – but the gods, who are defeated, think that defeat no refutation. And in their war men are their chosen allies, able when heroic to share in this absolute resistance, perfect because without hope. At least this vision of the final defeat of the humane (and of the divine made in its image), and in the essential hostility of the gods and heroes on the one hand and the monsters on the other, we may suppose that pagan English and Norse imagination agreed[8].

Norse mythology has the first two human types fashioned by the gods as Ash (male) and Elm (female), crafted from two pieces of driftwood the promenading Aesir chanced to discover on the shore. The human race is descended from them. Archaeology suggests that first incomers followed the retreating ice sheet after 10,000 BC, hunter gatherers who clung to the coasts now being warmed by a benign gulf stream. Several millennia later and early Neolithic settlements were forming, primarily along the Oslo Fjord. By 1500 BC these had proliferated across southern Norway and an emerging aristocracy were throwing up hillforts.

During the Nordic Bronze Age (*c.* 1800–500 BC), a pattern of larger and more permanent communities emerges around Oslo, then further north by what is now Trondheim and in other fertile enclaves. Prosperity creates plenty and then generates surplus, stimulating trade. Grain, skins and furs are moved on through Jutland. In the far north after, say, 1000 BC an influx of Uralic (Finno-Ugric) speakers, merging with older indigenous folk, creates the Sami people.

Iron begins to dominate after 500 BC when the climate also goes colder, older woodlands of elm, lime, ash and oak begin to be supplanted by forests of birch, pine and spruce. Iron-working technology transforms land clearance and facilitates the spread of settled farming communities. This trend in turns fosters the genesis of extended family and affinity-based structures, the emergence of clans, so local strongmen gain status and achieve prominence. Free men meet at assemblies, the *Thing*, to debate and settle disputes. Some Norwegians may latterly serve as mercenaries in Rome's armies while local magnates become petty kings. Things hot up during the Migration period (*c.* 400–550 AD), levels and sophistication of fortifications increases, and trade in iron, furs, and soapstone stretches across the North Sea.

So much of Norway is mountainous, so settled, farmed areas are dotted between massifs and inevitably assumed strong regional characteristics and an independence of spirit which would severely inhibit any transition towards centralized authority. This would become a protracted and often bloody contest between those who sought to assert a 'national' identity and the rest who preferred to remain free of control. Eirik would be a part of this long saga. There was no fixed border with what would be Sweden, states *per se* did not exist. In Norway, the area south of and around Oslo Fjord became the Vestfold. Moving west around the coast were Jaeder, Rogaland, Hordaland and Sogn, filling the knuckle of south-west coastal districts. Northwards up the coast towards Trondheim lay the Trondelag, then further north still, towards and into the Arctic Circle, was the Halogaland region.

As mentioned, two contrasting visions of Norse society emerge, one chooses to see the Vikings as essentially predatory: raiders, slavers, brawlers, iconoclasts and pillagers with overtones of racial supremacy thrown in. Another school prefers to view them as pastoralists, craftsmen, traders and explorers. In fact, they were all these things. *Orkneyinga Saga* gives us the wonderfully buccaneering Svein Asleifsson, a colourful rogue you can relate to but only from a distance, who stays on his island farm over winter, sows his fields then sets out in spring for his first piratical cruise of the year. He's back in time for harvest, then rounds off the season with an autumn cruise. His preferred targets are the Hebrides or Ireland, where he finally comes to grief (see next chapter).

At one level, Svein's relationship with crewmates and freemen would have been broadly egalitarian, but at the same time the society he came from was rigidly hierarchical and much of the hard labour on farms was the lot of slaves, no equality for them. By the late eighth century, when Viking raids first struck Britain, Norse society was headed up by regional magnates who acted as and were recognised as, petty kings. Below them, on the next layer of the pyramid, stood the nobility or *jarls* (from which we derive our term 'earl'). These men were local lords. Specific communities recognised the *hersir*, a knightly class, as local gentry, the kind of individual who, certainly in the early days, would be likely to command an expedition of one or two ships.

Now we come to freemen or *bonders*. These made up the bulk of the free classes, farmers or fishermen, craftsmen and traders. They also formed warrior elites clustered beneath their lord's banner. They were the backbone and cutting edge of Norse society. Our later, imposed differentiation between farmers and raiders would have meant nothing, all formed parts of the job description. At home, the *bonder* was a basic peasant farmer who worked the land with his family, kin and a handful of thralls (slaves).

He would work his own smithy, produce his own tools and iron gear, husband his own stock, trading for whatever else he needed. He had power of life and death over his slaves. These were his property, mere chattels. If he felt he needed to kill one, he could do so without sanction or redress (provided only that he declare the fact at a following *Thing*). This was his acknowledged prerogative – even if it was considered rather bad form. Being a thrall had nothing to recommend it, for them life truly was nasty, brutish and usually short.

A *bonder* could take time out from beating thralls to play a highly competitive ball game, *knattleikr*, almost a training for war in itself. During the long, cold and very dark nights of winter, when sunlight gave only a fitful glance before retreating again, he could play *hnefatafl* (a kind of proto chess) or listen to the violent lays of sagas with their cycle of conflict and killing. Life, even for the free, was grindingly hard and laborious. Slaves didn't get R & R. There was no concept of retirement. Once you were past working then it was likely a quick bash to the head and dumped in a ditch. Meanwhile, any children you might bear became your master's property, a bonus for him. Not all *bonders* were so harsh, a decent owner might allow his slave scope to work towards manumission and even a rented plot of his own. All round though, it was a most unenviable fate.

Slaves, if they enjoyed no rights, did have value as a cash crop. Vikings were perennial slavers, and they would elevate their pernicious trade into a global enterprise. Captives were sold through busy slave markets from Dublin to Constantinople and beyond. When he set off on his bi-annual cruise the Viking might sail as a slaver, a pirate or as a trader, hawking his wares around market centres such as Hedeby or Birka. He wouldn't have perceived any marked distinctions between these roles.

Norway during the early decades of the Viking Age, say from the late eighth century onwards, had few if any major urban settlements. The nature of the topography meant that farms were scattered along the coasts and throughout those narrow fertile regions. During the summer months, stock was moved to higher ground for warm weather grazing, a form of transhumance which endured until the 20th century. This practice preserved the lower meadows which would then (hopefully) yield sufficient forage to see men and beasts through the long ordeal of winter. In the autumn, some livestock, the weakest of the herd, would be slaughtered and the flesh salted or smoked. Nothing was wasted; hides were tanned for leather wear, bones ground as fertiliser.

Jarls might boast of fine timbered halls and lavish boards groaning with abundance, *Heorot* (Hrothgar's great hall in *Beowulf*) might be a marvel of the age, but the average *bonder* seldom ran to such magnificence. His home was more likely to be a timber-framed, turf-roofed longhouse, narrow, long and low, seeming almost a part of the landscape it sprang from. Living space was separated off into three or four sections, not quite rooms perhaps, divided by screens or curtains, timber platforms served for daytime seating and beds at night. The central hearth provided both warmth and heat for cooking. Smoke would be dreadful, but it could help to cure meats hung in the rafters and thin out the omnipresent legions of vermin. In towns, craftsmen would incorporate their workshops into their domestic structures. Thralls did not live well, crammed into squalid huts.

This was the everyday world of Eirik Bloodaxe. It must have appeared largely immutable in an age long before industrialisation and notions of continuous progress that came with it. Things changed very slowly and by far the majority of folk were tied to their land and to the seasons. Raiding, as we've seen, wasn't anything out of the norm, it was an annual activity. It was just what you did. It was always brutal and it could be very risky, but life in general inclined that way. An average male would be lucky to make it past forty, women perhaps a little longer, though childbirth was a major killer[9]. What would be changing was the nature of governance. Eirik's father had successfully begun a process which, falteringly perhaps, would grow over the next two centuries to transform Norway into a centralised and legitimised monarchy – in the teeth of persistent and determined resistance from local entrenched interests.

Eirik's queen Gunnhild generally gets a bad press from her contemporaries (see chapter eleven), Egil and she appear to have cordially detested each other. She is accused of being a conniving witch, sorceress and shapeshifter. It's clear she was a strong-minded and forthright woman, yet this would not of itself be out of kilter with women's perceived roles. When the *bonder* went a-Viking, he entrusted his property and affairs to his wife. She would already hold the keys to the family strongbox or strongboxes. Whilst marriages, by way of dynastic or affinity connection, were often arranged, women did enjoy considerable freedom of choice and could both inherit and hold property. A wife could instigate divorce proceedings against her husband and petition to recover her dowry. If widowed, she wasn't obliged to seek a new husband, she could choose a life of independence.

TV viewers, fans of Netflix' *Vikings*, clearly embraced those feisty, sword-wielding heroines, especially the shield-maiden Lagertha (allegedly wife, or a wife, to Ragnar Lodbrok). Whether women warriors either existed, or existed in the sort of numbers the series would have us imagine, is very much open to question. But very strong-minded women – the rather awe-inspiring Aud the Deep-Minded[10] springs to mind – certainly existed and Gunnhild is very evidently one of these. The sagas abound with vengeful females, every bit as steeped in the blood feud as their men. Aud's great-grand-daughter Freydis[11], portly Leif's sister, would have a huge appeal for Webster or Tarantino.

Faith was important to the Norse, their Gods were every day and all-powerful, as well as being deeply flawed by the worst of human weakness. It would become an element in the fight to establish centralised royal authority. Would-be rulers such as Olaf Tryggvason[12] used the sword of Christianity as a tool to enforce both his will and general conformity to a new order. Christ, the 'nailed' god was now the only god in Norway. Olaf's proselytizing came at the point of a spear and was wholly motivated by political aims. New religion – new era – new king. A strong centralised authoritarian power on the throne, validated by the Pope. Christianity was a major policy statement. The old faith sustained the old ways, and those ways were now gone.

What about Eirik, was he Christian or pagan? Like many, he probably accommodated both, wore the hammer and the cross. Christianity had barely begun to filter into Scandinavia during his father's time, but in Viking York, the church, mainly in the person of Archbishop Wulfstan, was a major player and Eirik would desperately need that validation to shore up his shaky tenure on the throne.

Viking paganism was a subject which excited attention from distinguished Victorian historians and philosophers, none more erudite, or more romantic, than Carlyle:

> Of the chief god, Odin, we shall speak by and by. Mark at present so much; what the essence of Scandinavian and indeed of all Paganism is: a recognition of the forces of Nature as godlike, stupendous, personal Agencies – as Gods and Demons. Not inconceivable to us. It is the infant Thought of man opening itself, with awe and wonder, on this ever-stupendous Universe.
>
> To me there is in the Norse system something very genuine, very great and manlike. A broad simplicity, rusticity, so very

different from the light gracefulness of the old Greek Paganism, distinguishes this Scandinavian System. It is Thought; the genuine Thought of deep, rude, earnest minds, fairly opened to the things about them; a face-to-face and heart-to-heart inspection of the things – the first characteristic of all good Thought in all times. Not graceful lightness, half-sport, as in the Greek Paganism; a certain homely truthfulness and rustic strength, a great rude sincerity, discloses itself here.

For the Norse people, the Man now named Odin, and Chief Norse God, we fancy, was such a man. A Teacher, and Captain of soul and of body; a Hero, of worth immeasurable; admiration for whom, transcending the known bounds, became adoration. Has he not the power of articulate Thinking; and many other powers, as yet miraculous? So, with boundless gratitude, would the rude Norse heart feel. Has he not solved for them the sphinx-enigma of this Universe; given assurance to them of their own destiny there?[13]

It's all stirring stuff; but did Eirik and his contemporaries ponder such philosophy? Most unlikely. Their lives were dictated by established patterns, regulated by instinct. Even for those standing at the apex of the social pyramid, life was neither easy nor certain. Kingship was hard-won and succession uncertain. Failure was apt to have fatal consequences. Religion was just part of the package at the end of the day. *Ragnarök*: 'The sun turns black, land sinks into the sea, / The bright stars vanish from the sky, / Steam rises up in the conflagration, / hot flame plays high against heaven itself.'[14]

'There's a wicked wind tonight, wild upheaval in the sea. No fear now that the Viking hordes will terrify me.' To their victims the Vikings appeared like devils out of hell. We only hear about them, never from them. That said, a visit from the predatory Norsemen would have been a truly horrible experience. No glory, no honour, just violence and savagery, small populations terribly and quickly thinned by murder and abduction.

A sense of that shock echoes from the outraged pen of Alcuin as he rebukes Northumbrians for their ungodliness, leading to such severe divine retribution: 'Never before has such terror appeared in Britain, as we have now suffered from a pagan race. Nor was it thought possible that such an inroad from the sea could be made.

Behold the Church of St. Cuthbert, spattered with the blood of the priests of God, despoiled of all its ornaments. A place more venerable than any other in Britain has fallen prey to pagans.'[15]

How and why did this horror strike as it did and when it did? Several factors have been suggested and none of these can wholly and satisfactorily account for the phenomenon on their own. As described above, Norse society had been developing a knightly and magnatial class, a warrior elite, and very likely growth in population overall encouraged 'freelances' to look abroad, as land became harder to acquire. Quite obviously, the major incremental expansion of ship-building technologies must be a major factor (see chapter three). Ships became the means, perfectly developed and adapted for raiding.

Warrior elites need regular employment, or they became dangerous at home, factionalism and disaffection follow boredom. Having trained war bands means a lord has to find employment for them. Young men full of testosterone seek glory, riches and expect lands in reward. All this needs to be added to opportunity. Increasing trade widens horizons and identifies likely targets. Raids were never wholly opportunistic. The medium of commerce provides ample intelligence. Means, motive and opportunity. The British Isles and Europe were to discover what a lethal concoction this heady brew was.

'Far and wide through the world, I have heard, / orders for work to adorn that wall-stead, / were sent to many peoples. And soon it stood there, / finished and ready, in full view, / the hall of halls. Heorot was the name, / he had settled on, whose utterance was law. / Nor did he renege, but doled out rings, / And torques at the table.'[16]

From 793 and after, a chorus of lamentation is heard around the coasts of Britain and the hornets continue to sting, as the anonymous Irish chronicler records:

> Even if there were a hundred loud, unceasing voices from each tongue, they could not recount or narrate ... what all the Irish suffered in common, both men and women, laity and clergy, old and young, noble and ignoble, of hardships and of injuring and of oppression, in every house, from those valiant, wrathful, purely pagan people [the Vikings] because

of the greatness of their achievements and of their deeds, their bravery, and their strength, and their venom, and their ferocity.[17]

Eirik is an inheritor of this. He, like several of his successors, Olaf Trygvasson, St Olaf and Harald Hardradi, would harvest the means to follow political ambitions at home by raiding abroad. Successful warlords are ring givers, they load their followers with silver to buy loyalty, they distribute largesse to buy 'votes'. Politics in that respect is generally unchanging. Wealth buys support and support leads to power. For Eirik as well, his father would be a very hard act to follow.

Two

TANGLE-HAIR

> Then an old harrower of the dark
> Happened to find the hoard open,
> The burning one who hunts out barrows,
> The slick-skinned dragon, threatening the night sky,
> With streamers of fire. People on the farms
> Are in dread of him. He is driven to hunt out,
> Hoards underground, to guard heathen gold
> Through age-long vigils, though to little avail.
>
> *Beowulf*, lines 2271–2278, p. 72.

Odin, father of the gods, is all-powerful yet oddly human, giving rise to the suggestion his cult and that of the other gods originally stems from some form of ancestor worship. The sagas insist that the god, together with his rather obscure siblings Vili and Ve, were the spawn of giants. Their mother was Bestla, herself the progeny of the giant Bolborn. Odin's father was called Borr, a kind of Adam who was fashioned from ice by the powerful tongue of the earth mother cow Audhumla, whose milk was the staple of the very first sentient being, another giant named Ymir.

Now, Odin with his brothers pretty much makes everything. He might have dragged the earth up from out of the crashing waves, organised and regulated the cosmos, using (possibly) handy components body parts from Ymir, who they'd done away with. Once this basic creative chore is complete Odin's two brothers disappear from the record. He is now headman of the godly tribe, the Aesir.

> *Despite all this grand divinity and making of things, Odin is a part of the world of men for whom he has a special affinity. He encourages heroes, even influences kingship, but he has his cultural side as well. He liberates the gift, the balm of poetry, so important to the Norsemen, hitherto guarded in a mountain lair by yet another giant, Suttungr. Odin walks among men and women.*

Eirik came from a long line of kings, or so his lineage would suggest. As precedents these were not entirely encouraging, as most died in an impressive variety of unpleasant ways. One of those many kings (as listed in *Historia Norwegie*), Egil Vendelkrake, was ousted by a mere bonder, one Tunne who bested his master in eight out of nine duels but lost the ninth, when Egil finally killed him. Not that it did the king any good, as shortly afterwards he himself was gored to death by a bull[1].

Most of his successors continued this unfortunate family trait, meeting violent ends. One king who achieves special mention is the one who lives to old age and dies in his bed. Harald Fairhair's grandfather, Gudrod the Hunter, was killed by one of his squires at the instigation of his wife. His son Halfdan the Black sired Harald. It's only with the arrival of Harald and his stellar career that we begin to sweep aside the fustian and depart mythos for history. Given the ultra-violent nature of Fair/Finehair's rise and dominance, it is astounding he lasted so long and ended his days peacefully.

> Hálfdan Svarti (the Black), son of Guäröär veiäikonungr (Hunting king) had a larger kingdom than his ancestors; he had numerous followers and was popular. His wife was Ragnhildr, daughter of King Haraldr gullskegg (Gold-beard) of Sogn. They had one son called Haraldr.* His maternal

---

* There is some confusion over dates. An early source is Ari's *Islendingabok*, a history of early Iceland settlement written by the monk Ari Þorgilsson in the 12th century, which survives in two manuscript versions from five hundred years later. Snorri and subsequent scholars up to the nineteenth century follow Ari, who dated Harald's birth to 850, the victory at Hafrsfjord occurring when he was 22, and 932 as the year of his death. Subsequent scholarship pulls these dates forward, 865-870 for his birth, *c.* 900 for the sea battle and 945 for the accession of his son Hakon the Good, which also encompasses Eirik's brief tenure as sole ruler. A revision of the revisionists pushes the date for Hafrsfjord back another 15 years to 885[27].

grandfather, who had given him his own name, took him to live with him and made him his foster-son, and left him all his kingdom after his death. When the young Haraldr was ten years old his grandfather died, and because he died without sons, his estate was inherited, as had been promised earlier, by his daughter's son.

He was accepted as king over the district of Sogn, and in the same year he died. And then his father Hálfdan succeeded his son, and he appointed over the realm the jarl who was called Atli inn mjóvi ('The Lean'). In the same year that these two kings had died, Ragnhildr, the wife of King Hálfdan, fell sick and died, and the king took a second wife. She was also called Ragnhildr; her father was Sigurär ormr í auga (Snake-in-eye), son of Ragnarr Lodbrok (Hairy-breeches). Hálfdan and his wife had a son who was named after his brother and called Haraldr.[2]

Halfdan ruled over the Vestfold region and died by accidental drowning aged 40, when he and several companions went through the ice when attempting to cross, unaware it had been weakened by shepherds punching through to provide water for their flocks. Previously, it had been revealed to Harald's mother that her son would flourish like a great tree with blood-red roots, green trunk and snow-white branches, which would cover the whole of Norway together with lands yet further afield. With his father dying relatively young, Harald inherited as a minor with his mother's brother Guthorm as regent, repelling attacks by former enemies seeking to reassert their independence. Halfdan had been both aggressive and acquisitive.

When young Harald came of age, more battles were fought as he extended his sway over Ringerike, Hedemark, Gudbrandsal, Hadaland, Toten, Raumarike and northern Vingulmark. Denmark set a precedent for an ambitious young man. Viking princes winning kingdoms overseas like Olaf of Dublin added further encouragement:

After the battle King Harald and Guthorm turned back and went with all the men they could gather through the forests towards the Uplands. They found out where the Upland kings had appointed their meeting-place, and came there about the time of midnight, without the watchmen observing them until their army was before the door of the house in which Hogne Karuson was, as well as that in which Gudbrand slept.

They set fire to both houses; but King Eystein's two sons slipped out with their men, and fought for a while, until both Hogne and Frode fell. After the fall of these four chiefs, King Harald, by his relation Guthorm's success and powers, subdued Hedemark, Ringerike, Gudbrandsdal, Hadeland, Thoten, Raumarike, and the whole northern part of Vingulmark. King Harald and Guthorm had thereafter war with King Gandalf and fought several battles with him; and in the last of them King Gandalf was slain, and King Harald took the whole of his kingdom as far south as the river Raum.[3]

This was an era for power-hungry princes to soar in England, after Alfred had stemmed the seemingly inexorable progress of the Viking Great Army. He had turned back Guthrum its general and then begun the irresistible rise of the House of Wessex. His successors had energetically carried on this work. It was his grandson Athelstan who would finally, if only for a while, establish himself as *primus inter pares* across the whole of mainland Britain.

Across the water, Denmark, too, was emerging as a recognisable kingdom. Strong rulers in the mid-eighth century had begun construction of the massive Dannevirke, a huge defensive rampart sealing off the Jutland Peninsula. Early in the following century, King Godfred treated (unsuccessfully) with mighty Charlemagne but refused to be intimidated by imperial bullying. By Eirik's day, Gorm the Old, (ruled *c.* 936–958), was on the throne of Denmark (he was very probably Gunnhild's father). Emperor Charlemagne had, of course, established his strong centralised rule over much of western Europe and his legacy, if fractured, would endure.

Now kings need wives of equal mettle and aspiration, and Harald found one:

> King Harald sent his men to a girl called Gyda, daughter of King Eirik of Hordaland, who was brought up as foster-child in the house of a great bonder in Valdres. The king wanted her for his concubine; for she was a remarkably handsome

girl, but of high spirit withal. Now when the messengers came there, and delivered their errand to the girl, she answered, that she would not throw herself away even to take a king for her husband, who had no greater kingdom to rule over than a few districts. 'And methinks,' said she, 'it is wonderful that no king here in Norway will make the whole country subject to him, in the same way as Gorm the Old did in Denmark, or Eirik at Upsala.'

The messengers thought her answer was dreadfully haughty, and asked what she thought would come of such an answer; for Harald was so mighty a man, that his invitation was good enough for her. But although she had replied to their errand differently from what they wished, they saw no chance, on this occasion, of taking her with them against her will; so, they prepared to return. When they were ready, and the people followed them out, Gyda said to the messengers, 'Now tell King Harald these my words. I will only agree to be his lawful wife upon the condition that he shall first, for my sake, subject to himself the whole of Norway, so that he may rule over that kingdom as freely and fully as King Eirik over the Swedish dominions, or King Gorm over Denmark; for only then, methinks, can he be called the king of a people.'[4]

Behind every strong man, so the cliché runs, stands a strong woman. This would surely be true for Harald, as it would be for his eldest son. As befits a Norse Titan, he had the looks and style to match his ambition:

He had a luxuriant growth of hair of wonderful colour, most like beautiful silk in appearance. He was the handsomest and strongest of all men, and how big he was can be seen from his tombstone, which is in Haugesund...

He was a man of great wisdom, far-sighted and ambitious; in addition, he was supported by his good fortune and the providence that he should be the overlord of the realm of Norway, so that the land has been made glorious by his family up till this time, and so it always will be. Old men attached themselves to him with wise counsels and support for his plans. Young warriors and men of prowess loved him for the sake of his splendid gifts of money and royal pomp, as says the poet Hornklofi, an old friend of kings who had been in courts constantly since his childhood.[5]

The stage at last was set for an expansionist, almost golden rule, if by no means a peaceful one.

'King Harald inherited the titles of his father Halfdan the Black and swore an oath not to cut or comb his hair until he had become sole king of Norway.'[6] *Fagrskinna* echoes this: 'Then Haraldr made a vow that his hair should never be cut until he received tribute from every inland valley and outlying headland, as far as Norway extends east to the borderlands and north to the sea. After this, many battles took place over a long period.'[7]

Harald 'Tangle-Hair' as he was dubbed gradually extended his sway by the sword: '... he took over Oppland and proceeded northwards to Trondheim where he fought many battles before gaining full control.'[8] His methods were vigorous:

> After this the two relations gather a great force, and prepare for an expedition to the Uplands, and northwards up the valley (Gudbrandsdal), and north over Dovrefjeld; and when the king came down to the inhabited land, he ordered all the men to be killed, and everything wide around to be delivered to the flames. And when the people came to know this, they fled everyone where he could; some down the country to Orkadal, some to Gaulardal, some to the forests. But some begged for peace, and obtained it, on condition of joining the king and becoming his men. He met no opposition until he came to Orkadal. There a crowd of people had assembled, and he had his first battle with a king called Gryting. Harald won the victory, and King Gryting was made prisoner, and most of his people killed. He took service himself under the king and swore fidelity to him. Thereafter all the people in Orkadal district went under King Harald and became his men.[9]

Harald established a reputation for utter ruthlessness, even by the more elastic standards of his day. His reputation was growing as his attention turned northward and toward cold dark realms lying beyond.

This was the Trondelag. These Trondheim Jarls, like trolls, guarded their narrow remote realms – originally an enclave far to the north by the Malangenfjord – from where they traded furs, hides, cables, sea-ivory and down. To ensure continuity of commerce they needed a safe passage to markets further south such as the entrepot of Hedeby. So, to control the sea routes, these northerners from Tromso had pushed down south of the Arctic Circle to Trondheim. Locals there were like minded if not kin, and the two soon fused. If they could absorb the whole Trondelag, they would have the natural resources of the north bolstered by good agricultural land further south.

Harald Grjotgardsson could have been a threat to Harald Fairhair's rising dominance, but he was prepared to bend the knee whilst still retaining significant autonomy as Jarl of Hladir. Harald sealed the bargain by marrying his daughter (marriage arrangements could be flexible). An expedient move, but those independent Tronds would remain a thorn in the flesh of his successors and constitute a constant barrier to full unification of Norway. At Stiklestad in 1030, they outfought and killed St Olaf, torpedoing his final attempt to regain hegemony.

For Harald, his hair still tangled, Vestland would prove a more challenging proposition. A spirit of fractious independence was just as strong here in the west as further north, terrain guarded by a rampart of mountains and a jagged coastline cleft with narrow fjords and a dense scattering of islands. Much hard fighting lay ahead as Harald waged a steady, unrelenting war of attrition. Egil tells us that Harald defeated King Hunthjof of More, killing him in the fight, thus winning control of North More. The dead king's son Solvi Klofe begged help from his southerly neighbour King Arnvid, wailing that Harald had brought 'slavery and suffering' to all he had subjugated.

Arnvid, moved by a mix these entreaties and a spirit of self-preservation, resolved to resist this encroaching tyrant. The pair then solicited aid from King Audbjorn controlling Fjordane Province, who circulated a war arrow around his domain to summon all able-bodied warriors. An ensuing battle was long and hard-fought. Harald lost a brace of jarls, together with two of Jarl Hakon of Lade's sons. The Vestlanders lost far more, including both kings. Solvi Klofe made good his escape and resorted to piracy, 'and often raided in King Harald's kingdom'. Harald had scotched this snake, not killed it. It could and would still bite.

The following spring [868 AD?] King Harald raised a great force in Trondheim and gave out that he would proceed to South More. Solve Klofe had passed the winter in his ships of war, plundering in North More, and had killed many of King Harald's men; pillaging some places, burning others, and making great ravage; but sometimes he had been, during the winter, with his friend King Arnvid in South More.

Now when he heard that King Harald was coming with ships and a great army, he gathered people, and was strong in men-at-arms; for many thought they had to take vengeance of King Harald. Solve Klofe went southwards to Firdafylke (the Fjord district), which King Audbjorn ruled over, to ask him to help, and join his force to King Arnvid's and his own. 'For,' said he, 'it is now clear that we all have but one course to take; and that is to rise, all as one man, against King Harald, for we have strength enough, and fate must decide the victory; for as to the other condition of becoming his servants, that is no condition for us, who are not less noble than Harald. My father thought it better to fall in battle for his kingdom, than to go willingly into King Harald's service, or not to abide the chance of weapons like the Naumudal kings.' King Kolve's speech was such that King Audbjorn promised his help, and gathered a great force together and went with it to King Arnvid, and they had a great army. Now, they got news that King Harald had come from the north, and they met within Solskel. And it was the custom to lash the ships together, stem to stem; so, it was done now.

King Harald laid his ship against King Arnvid's, and there was the sharpest fight, and many men fell on both sides. At last King Harald was raging with anger, and went forward to the foredeck, and slew so dreadfully that all the forecastle men of Arnvid's ship were driven aft of the mast, and some fell. Thereupon Harald boarded the ship, and King Arnvid's men tried to save themselves by flight, and he himself was slain in his ship. King Audbjorn also fell; but Solve fled. Of King Harald's men, fell his earls Asgaut and Asbjorn, together with his brothers-in-law, Grjotgard and Herlaug, the sons of Earl Hakon of Lade. Kolve became afterwards a great sea-king, and often did great damage in King Harald's dominions.[10]

Neil Price, in his superlative history of the Vikings, asserts that early 'kingships' had depended, as Snorri stipulates, less upon lineage than on the number of ships a ruler could command, and the names of some of these, as Professor Price points out, sound like early versions of Edward Teach or Henry Morgan, pirates. He goes on to argue that each of these local swashbucklers created his own kingdom by the sea, a petty maritorium or thalassocracy, and that status relied less upon control of territory and more on control of maritime resources, mini-Tortugas. He suggests that Harald was, at the outset, just another one of these but with greater drive and ambition, possibly his nickname of 'Tangle-Hair' or 'Mophead' was another buccaneering sobriquet like 'Blackbeard' or 'Calico Jack'.[11]

Earl Rognvald, soon to be Jarl of Orkney[12] was given custody of the whole of More and Romsdal, surprising and burning out King Audbjorn's surviving brother Vemund who had been trying to cling on to Fjordane district, seizing ships and materiel for war. Next spring, Harald set out from his winter quarters at Trondheim to set his seal firmly on Fjordane. The king's terms were uncompromising, the defeated could bend their knees, or leave, or suffer the consequences of further resistance: 'Some had their arms and legs maimed.'[13] Everywhere he went, Harald consolidated his grip, appointing his own followers in charge and keeping a strict eye on potential defectors. Generally, few enjoyed a second chance. Harald was proving utterly determined. Kings, especially those setting out to stamp their will on a militarised and truculent nobility, can't afford too much diplomacy.

Of determined dissenters, there was no shortage. Another rebel confederation massed their fleet gathered from Agder, Rogaland and Hordaland; the final and decisive round, in the words of Gwyn Jones among the most decisive in medieval Scandinavian history (for details of fighting at sea, see chapter four). The clash occurred at Hafrsfjord, an inlet just west of Stavanger, where Harald was awaiting this new confederation of western jarls determined to keep their freedom. This would prove 'The greatest battle King

Harald ever fought, and there were heavy losses on both sides.' With his shock troops, berserkers, in the gunwales of his vessel, Harald led from the front: 'The King kept his ship to the fore in the thick of the battle.'[14]

Rebel casualties were catastrophic: 'Thorir Long Chin, king of Agder, was killed there,' as were many others, the remnants fled. Harald, too, had lost heavily but the day and the kingdoms were his. Harald showered his own survivors with honour and praise, together with cascades of silver. 'This was the last battle King Harald fought in Norway, for he met no resistance afterwards and gained control of the whole country.'[15]

Momentous as this series of victories proved, it wasn't yet time for Harald to sheath his bloodied sword but, if we believe the story, it was now time to get a haircut:

> After this the land was brought under control, and taxes were paid by both inland and coastal regions. Now he had become a man fully developed in strength, stature and counsels. His hair was long and tangled; for that reason, he was called Lúfa (Shock-head). Then Ragnvald, Jarl of More, cut his hair and gave him a nickname, calling him Haraldr inn *hárfagri* (Fine Hair). He was more than twenty years old then. He had many children, and all the kings of Norway are descended from him. It was for ten years that he fought to gain the country before he became the sole king of Norway. He brought good peace and reformation to the country.[16]

It has been suggested, and indeed this is plausible, that those defeated and oppressed weren't ready just to succumb. Many preferred to seek fresh territories or kingdoms around the coasts of Britain, build their halls there and still call themselves free men. From these new bases in Orkney, Shetland and the Hebrides, they simply changed tack, now they raided in Norway rather than from it, a form of profitable guerrilla warfare which robbed Harald of any sense of closure. Such prolonged defiance was more than an aggravation, it was a rallying point for the disaffected. Harald knew his grip was tenuous. What had been won could very easily be lost. Men might call him king and smile to his face, but he hadn't won their hearts and minds – and never would.

Harald responded by setting up standing offshore patrols. These drained his treasury but did little good. His enemies were after profit and propaganda, not direct confrontation, and Norway's long and ragged western seaboard could never be effectively sealed off, especially against men who knew its most secret and complex passages. Sterner measures would be needed, and these rebellious ruffians soon re-discovered why Harald was a very bad man to cross.

He harnessed his maritime resources to expeditionary warfare, just as Ivar the Boneless had done, and brought retribution to his enemies' doors, burning their halls, seizing their ships. Knees were bent and oaths extracted. Jarl Rognvald of More was appointed satrap[17]. Harald also appears to have exerted sway over the Faroes, that rearing cluster of 18 volcanic stumps, known as 'The Islands of sheep ... for the peasants there have a rich abundant flock ...'[18] His tentacles also reached out to the new colonies established on distant Iceland. He needed, and he was forging, an outer pale of suzerainty, shoring up his homeland rampart. Relaxation wasn't an option.

Egil's Saga, whilst its historical accuracy might be and indeed is questionable, does cast light on the dichotomy many freemen farmers now found themselves in. Should they submit, make an outright show of loyalty to the king, or just keep their heads down and hope for better times? Equally, service under so powerful a magnate as King Harald provided opportunities for young men fuelled with fire and ambition:

> When they were talking together, Thorolf asked about the business of Harald's messengers. Kvedulf told him that the king had sent word ordering him or one of his sons to join him. 'What did you tell them?' asked Thorolf. 'I said what I was thinking that I would never join King Harald, nor would you or your brother, if I had any say in the matter, I think we will end up losing our lives because of that King.'[19]

Thorolf demurs, he sees what great advantages he may win from joining with King Harald and what fame and fortune he may win. In the end it proves a poor decision. Yet for younger men of ambition, the glitter of King Harald's court was a beacon.

It offered adventure and reward. A successful ruler can afford to be, indeed needs to be, magnanimous. Silver was the cement which bound sovereignty.

Harald was now master of his domain, even if the north was still semi-independent and the west seething, but no one man had ever set his stamp so firmly on what would one day be Norway than Harald Fairhair. He also enjoyed the inestimable boon of longevity. Even if he didn't rule for 70 years as his saga suggests, he certainly kept his throne for half a century and more, a remarkable feat. It is one of the ironies of the age that he, the most bloody and contentious, lived far longer than most of his predecessors and enjoyed so much more success.

Snorri tells us that the king attempted to impose centralised control through land rights and taxation, *scatt*. Nobody has ever liked paying tax, but Harald used his fiscal administration as a tool of statecraft. Hereditary obligations were scrapped in favour of direct payment to the crown. Harald appointed local jarls, his placemen, to each shire (*fykli*) and these men owed their allegiance directly to him, ideally unfettered by the ties and drag of local affinity. Gwyn Jones points out that his may be too tidy and his description better fits Norway some centuries later, during Snorri's own time.

> King Harald made this law over all the lands he conquered, that all the udal property should belong to him; and that the bonders, both great and small, should pay him land dues for their possessions. Over every district he set an earl to judge according to the law of the land and to justice, and also to collect the land dues and the fines; and for this each earl received a third part of the dues, and services, and fines, for the support of his table and other expenses. Each earl had under him four or more *herses*, each of whom had an estate of twenty marks yearly income bestowed on him and was bound to support twenty men-at-arms, and the earl sixty men, at their own expenses. The king had increased the land dues and burdens so much, that each of his earls had greater power and income than the kings had before; and when that became known at Trondheim, many great men joined the king and took his service.[20]

Next it would be the turn of the Swedes. Harald's expansion had not gone unnoticed:

> King Harald came with his fleet eastward to Viken and landed at Tonsberg, which was then a trading town. He had then been four years in Trondheim, and in all that time had not been in Viken. Here he heard the news that Eirik Edmundson, king of Sweden, had laid under him Vermaland, and was taking scat or land-tax from all the forest settlers; and also, that he called the whole country north to Svinasund, and west along the sea, West Gautland; and which altogether he reckoned to his kingdom, and took land-tax from it. Over this country he had set an earl, by name Hrane Gauzke, who had the earldom between Svinasund and the Gaut river and was a mighty earl.
>
> And it was told to King Harald that the Swedish king said he would not rest until he had as great a kingdom in Viken as Sigurd Hring, or his son Ragnar Lodbrok, had possessed; and that was Raumarike and Vestfold, all the way to the isle Grenmar, and also Vingulmark, and all that lay south of it. In all these districts many chiefs, and many other people, had given obedience to the Swedish king. King Harald was very angry at this, and summoned the bonders to a Thing at Fold, where he laid an accusation against them for treason towards him.
>
> Some bonders defended themselves from the accusation, some paid fines, some were punished. He went thus through the whole district during the summer, and in harvest he did the same in Raumarike, and laid the two districts under his power. Towards winter he heard that Eirik king of Sweden was, with his court, going about in Vermaland in guest-quarters.[21]

Harald had moved from a regional to national league and was now a player on the international stage. His prestige was such he could arrange for Hakon, his younger son after Eirik, to become a fosterling at King Athelstan of England's court. For Eirik, this arrangement would have very far-reaching consequences. He may have thought this neatly removed his younger sibling from court and thus from influence. If so, he was very wrong.

Whatever land reforms/redistribution Harald put in place he would still need cash. Campaigns are expensive, ships are expensive, men crave rewards, and nothing guarantees continued loyalty and service better than silver. Obviously, his enemies could suffer forfeitures, now handed out to allies, but enemies are better bought off than left embittered. Blood feuds are always dangerous and kings are very far from being immune, as the violent ends of so many of his forbears could attest. Harald's rise was impressive, but he rose on a spring tide of blood. Moreover, any legacy demanded affinity. Playing the tyrant, a robber-baron would only breed fresh insurrection. Harald was too canny for that. The fact he lived and ruled for so long and died in his bed are ample proofs. His son would be less fortunate and almost certainly less astute.

As King, Harald was, to a significant degree, able to live off his own properties. He held extensive royal estates, the revenues of which came directly into his exchequer. His in-laws and their affinities in the north paid dues on their thriving export trade. He had appropriated additional property from his defeated enemies in Vestfold. Raiding expeditions might be expensive to finance, but they were expected and generally did yield attractive returns. He taxed goods coming in and goods going out. Those expecting favour could be relied on to provide sweeteners. Whether he was able to levy tax from Rognvald and further afield is unclear. He could very likely compel at least some form of annual tribute.

Like his successors, Harald would be largely peripatetic, though his main base was at Avaldsnes in Karmoy District of Rogaland Province. This was no random choice, a rich town grown fat on control of passing maritime traffic, one of those foci for the kind of sea-kingdoms Professor Price writes of. The place already had a reputation as a royal residence, said to be home to the semi-mythical king Augvald who held sway there a century or so before Harald. Again, here was policy: legitimising his rule by association with past rulers.

Kings couldn't afford to sit still, though, Harald's grip, for all his success, was always flimsy, never more than skin deep, and he knew it. His court would progress around regional centres, gathering taxes, pressing flesh, breaking heads or accepting backhanders as expediency dictated. The very notion of any form of national kingship was new and nowhere welcome. Harald would be feared, in some places respected – but never universally loved. He wasn't a King Arthur with a gleaming gilded court. His world might be lauded by skalds and his deeds immortalised in verse, but his reign was tightly rooted in realpolitik, expressed all too often in terror.

These royal progresses would be a logistical challenge, moving the entire court in one sprawling caravanserai, a long winding trail of pack animals and light carts. The roads were abysmal, little better than rutted, sunken tracks, washed out by spring thaw after winter's gouging. The king wouldn't travel light, pomp and circumstance part of policy. Circuses can be statecraft, Harald wasn't some successful brawler, he knew what kingship was about, he knew how to play the game.

With mail-clad household men, Harald would never be short of muscle. Servants, slaves, skalds and scribes, livestock on the move, a heaving train that would stretch back several miles, a riot of rich colours and cacophony of noise traversing a silent, sometimes sullen landscape, potential fear of ambush around every corner. Royal wives with their attendant women were mounted as befitted their status, Even if his hosts secretly loathed and dreaded their monarch, they would be very careful not to let it show.

Affinity was key. Marriage had secured the loyalty of Hakon Grjotgardsson, so the north was quiescent. He had put family and allies into key positions throughout the former rebel lands. He had blitzed his far-flung Atlantic provinces and secured Orkney by appointing Rognvald (once a former enemy). Even remote Iceland paid him dues. Many other foes would be forgiven and bound in by fresh ties (that doesn't mean he wasn't watching them). The King would have a well-funded intelligence network, a layer cake of spies and informants who, as well as being eyes and ears, would serve to sow doubt and fears in the bosoms of any aspiring dissenters. Keeping your enemies guessing was as vital as keeping them close.

Harald could harness the whole business of district governance by controlling local decision making through the *Thing*. These mini parliaments were scattered across his realm. But the three big regional meetings were (1) to the east in Uppland (2) within the Trondelag which had its own session, held every June, set up near the outflow of the River Nid and (3) the *Gulathing* (model for the Icelandic assembly), staged south of the mouth of the Sognfjord.

Harald did not institute any of these hallowed proceedings, all were well established by his time, but he could use the *Gulathing* especially to keep a hold on the troublesome Vestland.

Law or the perversion of it, has always been a powerful tool for despots. It can be manipulated and modified to afford legitimacy and to harness revered tradition to the chariot of an otherwise authoritarian regime. Harald was happy to use these mechanisms of proto-democracy without feeling the need to practise any enfranchisement. His dynasty, the Ynglings, despite their long pedigree, needed all the legitimacy they could steal – and what better platform than a sacred assembly of free men, cheering for their king?

Distributing some silver beforehand probably helped reap the dividend of general approbation. And it would be a brave or foolhardy man who dared to speak out. Harald would ensure plenty of his brawny *hird*-men were on hand to deal with hecklers. Today, Vladimir Putin has appropriated the shell of democracy to justify his own autocracy. Ask Alexei Navalny and other dissidents, many of whom seem prone to fatal falls. King Harald's opponents probably got the same message.

The warp and weft of local affinities yielded another and significant bonus. Local chieftains had traditionally managed ship musters to defend their stretches of coastline. Harald needed this and more. Here, from the seas, he was most vulnerable, as the Orcadians had so annoyingly and pointedly demonstrated. What he needed was a system of national conscription, a seaborne militia. In one aspect this wouldn't be that difficult to set up. Regional networks were in place and any man could see the need to defend his own coastal beat.

Having said that, transforming communal convention into a national muster was no easy task, levy rosters would have to be worked out in considerable detail. How many able-bodied men from each community, what standard of vessel with how many oars, who paid for the ships, who funded maintenance and repairs? Evidence from Harald's time is very scanty, but the rule seems to have been that each neighbourhood of three free families must be able and willing to supply one recruit. He would need two months provisions for campaigning and with enough left inside his pack to get him back home afterwards[22].

Egil paints a picture of the despotic Harald, susceptible to paranoia, as whisperers poison his suspicious mind against his loyal adherent Thorolf who had bled for him at Hafrsfjord, proving that Thorolf's old father had been right all along to doubt the 'gratitude of princes'. Harek, the main whisperer, knew how to play on the king's fears: 'I cannot imagine that you would be pleased to hear everybody when they are free to speak their minds at home, accusing you of imposing tyranny on them ... but to tell the truth, the only thing that prevents the common people from rising up against you is the lack of courage and leadership. And it is not surprising that people like Thorolf regard themselves as superior'[23]. The poisonous Harek proceeds to careful character assassination, portraying Thorolf as the jealous underling greedy for his master's share. The king is suspicious enough to swallow the bait and it's bad news all round for Thorolf. He loses land and eventually life.

All things considered; Harald's career is utterly remarkable. He largely succeeded in the Homeric task of bringing together a united Norway. He vanquished all his foes, extended his reach forcibly across the Atlantic and helped found a lasting dynasty on Orkney. He rewarded his friends, killed, drove out, bribed, or won over his enemies and lived to a ripe old age, almost certainly into his eighties. Yet his rule was personal, his kingdom only lasted as long as he did. Sustained by a complex weave of alliances and allegiances, unchallenged centralised control did not become an established system of kingship, that was still a century away. What he could not achieve was to ensure a peaceful succession for his nominated heir. His funeral pyre soon fanned a wider conflagration. Happily, his saga survives, a paean in his honour, 'The Lay of Harald' (*Hrafnsmal*) – reproduced in appendix one, (largely culled together from fragments and the *Fagrskinna*).

Not only did he live a very long life, but Harald also produced an impressive crop of sons, arguably as many as a score, born of various mothers[24]. The two who would prove most significant were Eirik himself and his younger sibling Hakon, to be known to history as 'The Good'. Eirik, too, would achieve lasting fame, but nobody ever accused him of goodness: 'When King Harald Fairhair began to age he appointed his sons as rulers of Norway and made Eirik king of them all... Harald handed the kingdom over to Eirik. At this time, Gunnhild bore Eirik a son, whom Harald sprinkled with water and named after himself, adding that he should become king after his father if he lived long enough. King Harald then withdrew to live a quieter life, mainly staying at Rogaland or Hordaland. Three years later King Harald died at Rogaland and was buried in a mound at Haugesund'[25].

Eirik thus seemed to have it all, the keys to his father's unified realm, a fertile queen and sons to come after him. All he had to do now was hang on to it all:

> King Eirik ruled Norway for one year after the death of his father, before another of King Harald's sons, Hakon, arrived in Norway from England where ... he had been fostered by King Athelstan... Hakon went north to Trondheim and was accepted as king there. That winter, he and Eirik were joint kings of Norway. The following spring, they both gathered armies, and Hakon's was by far the more numerous. Eirik saw that he had no option but to flee the country, and left with his wife Gunnhild, and their children.[26]

Eirik's own rich saga was just beginning. He'd never be as successful as his father, who must have haunted him like the spectre at the feast, but he would be even more famous. And fame is surely what heroes crave.

Three

SWORD SONG

> We come from the land of the ice and snow
> From the midnight sun where the hot springs flow
> The hammer of the gods
> Will drive our ships to new lands
> To fight the horde, sing and cry
> Valhalla, I am coming...
>
> Henry Wadsworth Longfellow:
The Challenge of Thor (1863)

Ragnar Lodbrok may never have existed though his many fans from TV's Vikings *would be sorry to hear that, and though the series is a drama, not documentary, and plays fast and loose with history at best, Ragnar emerges credibly as a larger-tha- life figure who comes to typify the Viking Age and whose career, real or imagined, forms a template for his very real successors. If he did in fact live, then the Icelandic sagas tell us he was of royal blood, a son of Sigurd Ring, King of Sweden, himself sired by Randver, the ruler of Denmark. His ancestry was illustrious.*

Though he might have been big and strong, Ragnar became as celebrated for his marriages as for deeds of valour. He began his career in the public eye by disposing of a huge serpent which was bothering the eligible Thora Borgarhjort, daughter of Swedish Jarl Herraud, the girl's hand in matrimony being his prize. To tackle this formidable snake, Ragnar kitted himself put with 'hairy breeches', thus earning his soubriquet.

Quite what these handy trousers were made of we don't know, perhaps some early form of fireproofing or venom defence. Anyway, the gear worked, and he fathered two sons by Thora, Erik and Agnar. She died and he took another wife, a Norwegian beauty named Kraka, something of a prophetess even if her social circumstances were (apparently) somewhat reduced.

With her he sired his famous brood of warrior offspring, Ivar the Boneless,* Bjorn Ironside, Hvitserk, Ragnvald and not forgetting Sigurd-Snake-in-the-Eye.** After she had borne this formidable quartet, Kraka was revealed as in fact being Aslaug, daughter of the hero Sigurd Fafnesbane. As his brood grew up and became famous warriors, Ragnar decided he needed a major victory to keep up, so he attacked Northumbria – but with only two ships. This time the ageing champion's luck finally ran out. He was bested and captured by King Aelle – one of the claimants to the disputed crown of Northumbria.

In PR terms this was a big win for the Saxon and the dreaded Ragnar was thrown into a pit of snakes. If he still had on his shaggy breeches, they were clearly out of guarantee and so Ragnar perished. Aelle would live long enough to rue the day. Eirik would be raised on such tales and taught that this was his birthright. Real or not, Ragnar was a hard act to follow.

Eirik fights battles, you don't earn a soubriquet like 'Bloodaxe' by staying at home and herding sheep. We know the later King (latterly Saint) Olaf was always rather contemptuous of his stepfather Sigurd Syr, who preferred peaceful farming to swordplay. Vikings need renown and that comes in the shield wall. We know very little about these battles. Egil tells us of a sea fight in the White Sea region where his brother Thorolf stood at Bloodaxe's side,

---

* Opinions differ over Ivar. Some say the name refers to the fact he was a slippery as a snake but other cite references in the sagas that point to a physical disability, speculatively identified as osteogenesis imperfecta, or brittle bone disease. The Vikings had a robust policy for dealing with children born with physical handicap – they were exposed and left outside to die. But Ivar was of noble blood so might have been spared. Alternatively, 'Boneless' may have been a reference to impotence.

** Sigurd, if he existed, and this can't be verified, is said to have been born with a cast in one eye in the shape of a snake biting its own tail.

(see following chapter). We know Eirik wins but we don't know who he is fighting, or why or how the action unfolded[1]. Later, after his father's death, Eirik takes on his two brothers Olaf and Sigurd, killing both in a battle at Tonsberg[2]. Again, he doesn't offer any further detail – Eirik's own saga is now long lost[3]. A Viking without a saga is a bit like a cowboy without a horse, no riding off into the sunset (and no movie rights).

The Viking Age in England alone features some three-score battles, with countless minor affairs that barely made it into the chronicles. Scandinavia witnessed a near endless cycle of civil wars: so many more major fights, big enough to count as a battle, must have occurred there. How many warriors need to be involved to justify the term 'battle' can't really be defined – generally described as a lengthy encounter between hostile military forces. That doesn't really mean much in the early medieval context, but we can say that armies weren't large, no juggernauts such as Rome's legions.

We also know that as king of Northumbria Eirik attacks the rearguard of King Eadred's Army, after the southerners had rudely chastised their northern contemporaries for electing Bloodaxe as king. The men of Wessex burnt down Wilfrid's famous minster at Ripon, but Eirik bided his time and hit back, ambushing Eadred's rearguard at Castleford and cutting them up quite badly[4]. Even his famous last battle at Stainmore, if indeed it was ever such, is shrouded in skeins of mystery. That doesn't harm your legend but seriously frustrates subsequent biographers.

Regarding these battles, we know Eirik commands in every case and emerges as winner (aside from the last one), but that's really it. We've no idea of exact ground, numbers involved, casualties or specific tactics. To reconstruct a clash such as Eirik might have fought, we need to look at what we do know of conflict in this period. Egil, as ever, comes in handy, even if we must be very careful about just how much credence we allow. He does give us a stirring description of the fight at Vin Heath/Brunanburh[5], unconstrained by any degree of personal modesty. The English victory, if he is to be believed, rests on his personal valour and that of his brother Thorolf:

> A tough battle ensued, Egil attacked Adils, and they fought hard. Despite the considerable difference in numbers, more of Adils'

men were killed… Then Thorolf began fighting so furiously that he threw his shield over his back, grabbed his spear with both hands and charged forward hacking and thrusting to either side. Men leapt out of the way all around, but he killed many of them. He cleared a path to Earl Hring's standard and there was no holding him back. He killed Earl Hring's standard-bearer and chopped down the pole. Then he drove his spear through the earl's coat of mail, into his chest and through his body so that it came out between his shoulder blades, lifted him up on it above his own head and thrust the end into the ground. Everyone saw how the earl died on the spear.[6]

This is wonderfully graphic and even allowing for skaldic bombast, may well represent a real description of battle's fury.

We think of the Vikings as ever hungry for battle, for the sword song and reputation it brings. The plain fact is early medieval commanders generally avoided battle, other than when unavoidable. It was messy, bound to be costly and very, very uncertain. Once forces were committed, then leaders could exercise little control over events. Tactics, while some flexibility was possible, relied primarily on the shield wall formation. Vikings were mainly concerned for loot and if this could be gained without fighting, so much the better. If the victims or those who might become victims were ready to buy the raiders off, better still.

Their ships (see next chapter) afforded Northmen great agility and superior navigation allowed them to choose targets at will. Good intelligence revealed tempting settlements, perhaps filled with pilgrims on holy days, which offered a richer haul. But if it came to fighting, both sides would deploy in a linear shield wall formation.

Author Bernard Cornwell describes this shield wall; this is fiction of course but nonetheless resonates:

Men do not relish the shield wall. They do not rush to death's embrace. You look ahead and see the overlapping shields, the helmets, the glint of axes and spears and swords, and you know you must go into the reach of those blades, into the place of death, and it takes time to summon the courage, to heat the blood, to let the madness overtake caution.[7]

A commander could seek to break the stalemate of locked shields by deploying the 'Boar's Snout'. This was a wedge of chosen men in an arrowhead formation and backed by weight of numbers, whose function on the field was to smash a hole in the enemy's front and roll up their line which, once fractured, became easy meat. To be successful, such a tactic needed to be finely judged. Timing, momentum and cohesion would determine success or failure. Done right, the snout could be a battle winner, but if it misfired, the consequences could be disastrous.

Saint Olaf, on course for martyrdom, deployed a boar snout in his last, apocalyptic battle at Stiklestad in July 1030. Outnumbered, his *hird*-men facing a far more numerous army of *bonder* led by dissenting jarls, tired of the king's heavy-handed tyranny and his steel-edged proselytizing. Leading from the front, Olaf punched a salient into the enemy line but failed to break through. His blitzkrieg ran out of momentum and he out of luck. The king was cut down and the fight lost (though he did get a sainthood out of it). Happily, or otherwise, his younger half-brother Harald, who came to be known as Hardradi or 'Hard Ruler', survived. His Little Bighorn came decades later at Stamford Bridge in 1066.

However tough and experienced you may be, battle is utterly terrifying. We look at images of formations in books where troops are marked by neatly denoted squares and, as with computer games, they move around the field with precision. But battle would be a bowel-loosening horror of near total confusion, a tsunami of sound confusing all the senses. In the shield wall, you can't see much, just a metre or so around you. And there's the smell, this is what we can't properly envisage. Old sweats felt a chill remembrance of the smell of the trenches from the first World War. On the medieval field, you would be assailed by the combined odours of sweat, piss and shit, a portion of which would be your own.

Your attention tends to be focused on the man who's trying to kill you. and should you succeed in killing him, there are plenty more behind. Your chances of getting out wound-free are generally minimal. Even victors would still bear the scars. It's a simple enough game, whichever side breaks, they lose, and they will die. It would have been nothing like the movies, where generally both sides run gleefully into a furious melee. Discipline, cohesion, stamina and experience were what mattered.

By Eirik's day, the shield wall had a long provenance, favoured by classical armies and much relied upon by late Roman and Byzantine forces. The idea is blessedly simple. The troops deploy in aligning linear formations, fronting shields which can overlap to solidify the defence. The phalanx can be up to s six or even eight ranks deep, with the first three lines formed from the 'best' men. These would be the trained and armoured retainers of the officer elite formed by the jarls, accompanied by their crack household fighters. Such men trained and messed together, they were primarily professional warriors, a superior caste. Freemen, bonders, made up the rest, generally without mail and armed primarily with spear, shield and the ubiquitous all-purpose knife or seax (see below). Shields could be raised to create a testudo-like defence, some defence against a shower of arrows or throwing spears.

Both sides would advance slowly to contact, usually at the half step, a sloppy shield wall was a splintered one. Each local commander had his men around him, a brotherhood, trained and formed, their weapons honed to razor-edged perfection. They fought as a team, ready to deliver opportunistic blows left and right. The wall itself need not be entirely rigid, men needed space to wield weapons once the action had begun. Missile troops fought at the periphery, archers shooting over the heads of their comrades, specific marksmen detailed to seek out targets of opportunity. Bringing down a jarl or lendmann could dramatically change the outcome. Convention dictated that once a leader fell, his followers must fight around his body to the end.

One of the most famous clashes of the era, somewhat after Eirik's day, is the Battle of Maldon fought on 11 August 991. Ealdorman Byrhtnoth, rather ill-advisedly, allowed a Viking force, possibly led by formidable Olaf Tryggvason, to cross an island causeway and fight in formation on the mainland. All very sporting but it ended badly. The ealdorman, who was well advanced in years, became an early casualty and a large contingent of his *fyrd* promptly defected, but his surviving household men slogged it out to the last and made the Norwegians pay dearly for their victory:

Then some Viking warrior let go a spear from his hand,
flying from his fist so that it went too deeply

through the noble thane of Æthelred.
One stood by his side, a young warrior not fully grown,
a boy in the battle, who very bravely
pulled the bloody spear out of the warrior,
the son of Wulfstan, Wulfmær the young,
let go the exceedingly hard spear go back again;
the point travelled in, so that he who had laid his lord
previously onto the earth was wounded sorely. (149-58)[8]

This epic poem echoes Homer, it puts you in the thick of the action and that's not really somewhere you want to be. Living history, however you strive for accuracy, is a very far cry from the real thing, but it does give you an idea, however diluted. The sensory confusion and physical exhaustion are real enough, mail, if far lighter and less constrictive than plate armour, is still heavy, (say 15–20 kilos), and rapid dehydration is debilitating.

To go back to numbers involved. As mentioned, this can never be satisfactorily answered. We have no note of the extent of forces engaged for any of Eirik's battles. We dare to assume these would not be large, from several hundred to perhaps 1,000–2,000. Medieval chroniclers are notoriously vague or downright unreliable with a marked tendency to exaggerate both the number of combatants on the field and the final death toll.

Take Stamford Bridge (25 September 1066), the generally agreed figures, insofar as there is any agreement, give Harold II and the English as many as 10,000, Harald Hardrada with Tostig and a mainly Norse army rather fewer. The battle was both long and bloody. We could assume that the victors might lose up to ten per cent of their strength with the vanquished losing a great deal more, perhaps up to 25 per cent or worse. The *ASC* asserts that a mere two dozen ships out of several hundred which had arrived were enough to transport the Norse survivors[9].

When the Viking Great Army (see chapter four) invaded, it was thought Ivar the Boneless may have commanded as many as 300 ships, which, with an average crew of say 30+ would give him a force 9,000 strong, a very substantial army by the standards of the day. Debate has since been fierce as to whether this was the case, or whether the contingent was very much smaller, as few as 500. Evidence from the Viking base at Repton pointed very much towards a radical scaling down, but more recent work at Torksey suggests that higher numbers may indeed have been present.

If you were wounded and left on the battlefield, your chances of survival were slim. You would be fortunate to succumb to a single stroke:

> In the winter of 873–874 a member of the Great Army met a gruesome end at Repton... He was around 35–45 years old and a big man, almost 1.8 metres (six feet) tall, but in the battle he suffered a massive blow to the skull and, as he reeled from that, the point of a sword found the weak spot in his helmet – the eye slit – gouging out his left eye and penetrating the back of the eye socket, entering his brain. While he lay on the ground, a second sword blow sliced into his upper thigh, between his legs, cutting into the bone at the top of his leg and probably slicing away his genitals.[10]

In Eirik's day battlefield medicine was in its infancy even if, in Europe, Galen's works were being rediscovered. This reclaimed knowledge would take some time to permeate through to Scandinavia, out on the cold, distant fringes. Aside from shamanistic and herbal treatments (many of which have been shown to be far from ineffective), cleaning wounds, anointing, bandaging and bone-setting were widely practised. Then as now, a man's chances of survival would depend on how quickly he could be got off the field. If he was left, then a *coup de grace*, shock or blood loss would very likely do for him one way or another.

Forensic examination of skeletons shows that some wounds, often quite serious, were survivable and that treatment had been effective. In the tight brotherhood of the individual unit, men would look out for each other as best they were able. We hear of shields being placed over prone wounded to minimise the risk of further injuries. Frequently, there might be pauses during fighting to recover and treat casualties.

In one of the sagas, a warrior suffers a downward slicing cut to the shoulder. This was a familiar blow which could open a man like a tin or sardines, usually fatal. Yet, in this instance, although the stricken man's lungs were exposed by the force and precision of the strike, he was able to be treated and the hideous gaping wound bound. He certainly survived the initial trauma and was casevaced from the field. Nonetheless, his overall chances of survival wouldn't be promising.

One established diagnostic test for abdominal injuries was the 'onion test'. The casualty was fed a broth of leeks and onions. If the physician could detect the smell of onions from the wound, this clearly indicated the intestines were penetrated and that death would follow. Crude certainly, yet likely to have been a practical diagnostic tool.

One of the most popular images in contemporary understanding of Vikings in battle is that of the berserker. Opinion varies as to whether these famed madmen were real or a storyteller's elaboration. There are contemporary references, one of the earliest being a skaldic verse penned in the late ninth century by one Thorbjorn Hornkofli to honour Eirik's father Harald Fairhair:

I'll ask of the berserks, you tasters of blood,
Those intrepid heroes, how are they treated,
Those who wade out into battle?
Wolf-skinned they are called. In battle
They bear bloody shields.
Red with blood are their spears when they come to fight.
They form a closed group.
The prince in his wisdom puts trust in such men
Who hack through enemy shields'[11]

Snorri, admittedly writing some centuries after the event, also refers to these wildcat warriors: 'His (Odin's) men rushed forwards without armour, were as mad as dogs or wolves, bit their shields, and were strong as bears or wild oxen, and killed people at a blow, but neither fire nor iron told upon them. This was called *Berserker gang*'[12].

We view the berserker as a fanatical warrior who fights in a trance-like state, frothing at the mouth, shield biting; furious, heedless of blows and wounds, a human Exocet. The name may derive from one who wore a bear shirt or bearskin[13] or, as Snorri suggests, was literally 'bare shirt', fighting unarmoured. Battle fury isn't limited to wild-eyed Norsemen, the red mist is a feature of warfare since Cain killed Abel; Māoris perform their fearful hakas and the wild keening of the highland pipes heats the blood. As recently as 1915, at the Great War battle of Loos that September, Piper Daniel Laidlaw VC so stirred his reluctant comrades when he played fearlessly and heedlessly across No-Man's-Land that they rushed forth from their trenches.

Berserkers may have originated as followers of early hunting cults as they identify, it seems, with the bear, wolf or wild boar. Before battle they whip themselves into a collective howl of fury, possibly with the aid of hallucinogenic substances. If they survive and the blood cools, they slump deflated and exhausted.

There are suggestions such doomsday fighters were in fact criminals, condemned men already marked for death, given a last chance of self-sacrificial redemption to save their and their families' honour. Unleashing this wolfpack on the battlefield would be primarily psychological, to unnerve and terrify an opponent, especially an enemy force made up of militia. If they did exist in this role then their appearance and indifference to wounds and death could be seismic. Their legend still drives modern fictional accounts:

> I had never seen a berserker. I have heard all the tales since, about them being shapeshifters, turning into bears, or that they got their name from wearing bearskins, or that it was really wolf pelts… Some say they chew strange herbs or drink bark brews to get into the state of it, but the truth is that a berserker is a frothing madman with a blade, a man who does not care if he lives or dies so long as he gets to you and kills you. and the only way to kill one is to cut the legs off and hope he can't crawl as fast as you can run.[14]

We can easily imagine Gunnhild, Eirik's commanding wife, fighting as a Viking Amazon or shield maiden (*skjaldmaer*), immortalised in the character of Lagertha (played by Kathereyn Winnick), in History Channel of Canada's *Vikings* series referred to earlier. But there's little or no historical basis for a cult of female warriors. That some women, as the skalds may allege, did take up arms seems reasonable, but not in the numbers TV producers and their viewers might like to imagine. There are references in various sagas and in later accounts, but none of these may be regarded as entirely reliable.

Eric Bloodaxe the Viking: 'I Shall Die Laughing'

That there were women on early medieval battlefields is clear – they performed several vital functions – as water carriers, paramedics and looters of the dead – and were regarded by both sides as non-combatant. This wasn't chivalry but expediency. Did Eirik's armies include female warriors? We cannot say, but I think it unlikely. For one thing, women were Norse society's breeding stock and therefore not to be expended as spear fodder.

The kind of forces Eirik deployed for his battles (accepting we know little or nothing of the detail), would be primarily professional fighting men, his own retainers and those of the lords who followed his banner, a mailed elite only swelled, when necessary, by levies drawn from freemen and farmers. Eirik, we know, engages in raiding, most of his contemporaries did. The *Orkneyinga Saga* makes frequent references to farmers who spend most of the season in profitable raiding, this includes senior nobility as well as *hersirs*. Raiding was a part of life, natural as the farming cycle.

Vikings fought wars at several levels, one of which the late Paddy Griffith[15] defined as 'saga warfare', small-scale internecine conflict, often between rival clans, low intensity but endemic and likely very bloody. As an alternative to litigation or to satisfy personal or family honour, there was always the duel. This was a judicial process; men could fight as an alternative to the courts, bad news for lawyers. This was the *holmgang* (old Norse, *holm-ganga*) from the notion of 'going to an island', where the duellists retired to an agreed islet as their arena – to flee was to lose.

In the Arthurian cycle, Tristan is challenged by the Irish champion Morholt after the hero has killed one of his *hird*. Both parties row their coracles to the designated rock and prepare to fight. The Irishman sneeringly reminds Tristan to make a good job of tying his dingy up as he'll be needing it to run away in. Wordlessly, the hero pushes the boat out (literally) sending a clear message to his opponent – only one of them will be returning. And it's not Morholt.

This is, of course, what we expect of our paladins, referring a matter to arbitration or applying for legal aid doesn't have quite the same ring. A true warrior must defend his honour and uphold his right with his sword, otherwise he's just another rustic. Turning the other cheek may be both worthy and noble but, in a warrior society, it smacks of cowardice. Since man (or woman) first had the idea of creating an alloy of tin and copper and calling it bronze, the sword has enjoyed this mystique, the badge of the warrior and gentleman, his status, his oath and his honour. The Vikings accepted all that. Their tales aren't about inclusivity and group hugs, they're about blood and iron, that's why we still read them.

Typically, the fight would take place say three to seven days after a challenge, very bad form if either of the parties failed to appear. The challenger, if he baulked, could be outlawed, whilst the challenged would automatically forfeit his claim and judgment go to his rival if he did the same:

> If someone speaks insults to another man ('You're not the like of a man, and not a man in your chest!' – 'I'm a man like you!'), they shall meet where three roads meet. If he who has spoken comes and not the insulted one, then he shall be as he's been called: no right to swear oaths, no right to bear witness, may it concern man or woman. If the insulted one comes and not he who has spoken, then he shall cry *Niðingr!* three times and make a mark in the ground, and he is worse who spoke what he dared not keep. Now both meet fully armed: if the insulted one falls, the compensation is half a wergild, if he who has spoken falls, insults are the worst, the tongue the head's bane, he shall lie in a field of no compensation.[16]

It was all very Marquis of Queensbury[17]. Both combatants accepted the rules of engagement as recited by the challenger. These might include a list of the weapons to be used, who could make the first strike and what forfeiture might entail. In Norway, it could be the loser literally lost everything, the victor scooped the lot, so this wasn't an activity to be engaged in lightly. Battle was *a outrance*, to the death, and killing your opponent wasn't unlawful, so didn't risk the sanction of outlawry. Echoes of this process lingered well into the time of the later duel of honour. The eighteenth-century Irish 'Code Duello' was a manual that laid out ground rules for the combat – though by then, most were fought with pistols.

Duelling grounds could be chosen by the parties, or places hallowed by tradition. The actual cockpit was delineated by the spread of an oxhide or perhaps a voluminous cloak, which produced sides of say three metres or so, with an outer cordon just beyond, the corners of which were fixed by hazel wands. This was the ring and retreating beyond its bounds was to lose or be branded a poltroon. Normally, each duellist was allowed three shields, attrition being very high in so narrow and intense a meeting. Animals, perhaps a bull, might be sacrificed by the victor. Despite the levels of risk and careful ritualisation, the system was very much open to abuse when professional fighters or even berserkers issued challenges, purely in the hope of making a kill and enjoying the spoils. One of these ruffians, however, miscalculated badly and found himself up against Egil Skallagrimson's fearsome blade, (or rather blades).

The contentious hero, no stranger to duelling, was in Norway, heading along the west coast via Romsdal. He and his company were offered hospitality at a fine estate called Blindheim owned by an affable and prosperous farmer named Fridgeir, a nephew of Egil's friend Arinbjorn. Hospitality was a serious obligation, a main artery of family and wider affinity. Egil was well looked after and their host's mother, Gyda, sister to Arinbjorn, was anxious for news of her brother.

Egil was moved, as he often was, probably stirred by drink, to pen one of his verse quips, but he noticed the home crew were subdued and Fridgeir's lovely young sister seemed positively distracted. Adverse winds kept Egil at Blindheim – meanwhile the girl kept crying. Fridgeir was too proud to ask for help, but his mother wasn't. She confessed to Egil that the family were depressed because a hefty thug, Ljot the Pale, had demanded the young woman's hand in marriage.

Fridgeir had refused and the bully, a noted berserker, had challenged him. Even though he was no swordsman, honour forbad Fridgeir from shying away from the fight. This was due to take place on nearby Valdero Island the very next day. Gyda asked Egil to accompany her son, adding some serious muscle to the defence. The big man agreed instantly, after all he would be doing what his great friend Arinbjorn would have done if he had been there. Egil delayed his group's planned departure and spent the day consuming his host's ale. Backup might be an obligation but didn't necessarily come free of charge.

Next day, a pallid dawn broke over the featureless island while Fridgeir made ready, clearly without any great enthusiasm but bolstered by Egil's bulk and reputation. Both parties reached the location and designated ground where a ring of stones marked the killing space. Ljot was as big as his boasting, practising his berserker howls to overawe his inexperienced opponent. Egil wasn't impressed and the bully, carried away by his own spin, challenged him as a proxy. Killing so renowned a fighter would massively enhance his prestige. Bring it on was the reply.

Egil didn't need long to prepare. He hefted the shield he carried, drew his sword, the admirably named 'Slicer', with a second blade, 'Adder', still scabbarded. He stepped up to the mark, Ljot was fumbling. It had clearly just dawned on him he'd stepped out of his league. Finally, both men were in the ring and the berserker was immediately in trouble. He was soon wishing he'd stayed in Sweden. Egil was fast and precise, his blows coming like lightning bolts, driving his outclassed opponent backwards and round in circles. Ljot was shunted clear out of the arena. He asked for a rest. Egil allowed it. Little good it did him. The venerable brawler soon closed for the kill, made his thrashing opponent stumble and drop his shield. Egil took Ljot's leg off above the knee and he 'dropped dead on the spot'. Fight over, Egil allowed Fridgeir to claim the loser's property[18]. The champion's renown, already glowing, is burnished even brighter – though Eirik, had he been there and given the bad blood between them, would have been shouting for Ljot!

Saga warfare was not so usually gentlemanly. We read of ambushes, betrayals and murder committed at all levels of society. The Jarls of Orkney as their saga tells us (see following chapter) were frequently at feud, none more deadly than that between the mighty Thorfinn and his rival Rognvald Brusason, who is finally hounded out whilst hiding on a beach, given away by the yapping of his pet dog which he had refused to abandon. It cost him his life.

Frustratingly, we don't know if Eirik ever fought a duel, he clearly had both the physique and temperament, but while a challenge could be made regardless of the status of the parties, one of royal birth would prefer to nominate a champion we would imagine. However tempting the scent of a brawl might be, the risks were just too great. If we think the whole business both archaic and barbarous, two delegates from the French National Assembly fought a duel of honour with swords as recently as 1967![19]

At the opposite end of the military spectrum is organised campaigning, led by the king himself. Here, the ruler mobilises not just his own household but the full or nearly full resources of his realm. Eirik, when he took on and beat his fractious brothers, would have almost certainly ordered a full mobilisation. Here, the ruler is creating an army for a specific campaign objective, in Eirik's case it's a dynastic war and these became a template for wars throughout Europe up until the Age of Reason.

Such an army needs a logistical supply chain. It will likely need ships. It will certainly demand continuity of supply and a 'tail' of attendant craftsmen, armourers, swordsmiths, bowyers, shield-makers et al, as well as sutlers and all incidental trades. These people must be sourced, hired/mustered and presumably paid. Perhaps the greatest of all such major campaigns at the very end of the Viking era is Duke William of Normandy's successful invasion of England in 1066, a masterpiece of logistics.

As a scaled-down version, the king may just rely on his household warriors with perhaps those of a few leading subjects; 'short, sharp shock' warfare where the monarch is aiming to cow or compel recalcitrant vassals or possibly chastise another minor ruler. There may be a defined outcome, or the campaign can be purely punitive.

This is a far cry from individual raiding enterprises, primarily conceived and carried out at local level and featuring one or maybe more ship's crews. This is the classic going *A-Viking*, where there is no specific military or political objective, participants are driven by a lust for plunder with a dash of glory, but mainly for the loot. These categories aren't mutually exclusive, loot greases the wheels of any campaign, and nothing bolsters morale better than a bulging pack.

If we look at Ivar the Boneless' 'Great Army' that descended on England in 865, this represents a fusion of purely opportunistic raiding with defined political objectives directed by a commander-in-chief. Yet the army itself never really equates to a fixed continuum or one with a defined political objective. It rather translates raiding into an extended campaign of conquest, fixing upon targets as they arise. Leadership isn't fixed either, various captains rise to prominence as others, having got all they needed, step back to consolidate – but they're mainly not going home, consolidating conquest with colonisation.

As a rule, Viking generals couldn't afford to spend too much time on complex or protracted manoeuvres. Their logistical tail wasn't certain enough and resupply in landscapes where, at best, most barely attained subsistence level, was just too unsure. Besides, once men had filled their packs with portable spoils, their enthusiasm for further, riskier, campaigning would be apt to ebb away.

Battles would be of quite short duration – Brunanburh being an obvious exception, as the chroniclers note. Men fighting in full armour quickly become dehydrated and prone to heatstroke. A man, however fit, would be unlikely to heft his shield and weapons for longer than say 15 to 20 minutes before he would need rest and hydration, and we don't know if Viking drill was sophisticated enough to allow a front rank to retire as the second filters through to take their place. It's quite likely professional, elite units might well have trained for this, but not the raw militia.

How did battles end? This is probably less clear cut than it appears. We have a view that one side would be decimated or worse and that the victors would enjoy a howling triumph. I suspect it was very rarely as neat or decisive. By the time fighting ended, all survivors would be utterly exhausted, that draining of the soul as the red mist thins. Most would be glad simply to be alive and attending to wounded comrades would be an obvious priority. Battles were fought on foot, even if warriors rode to the field, and an organised, mounted pursuit was probably quite rare. Hastings was a one-off in that Duke William's mounted knights could harry fleeing Saxons into the thickening autumn dusk.

A skilled commander, even if he lost, might be able to extract a significant part of his forces. Edmund Ironside, despite his disastrous defeat at the hands of Cnut at Assandun in October 1016, (mainly a consequence of the slippery Eadric Streona's treachery), still managed to salvage much of his army and continue the war. If a commander died on the field, then that would likely signify the end or nearly the end of the fight, such as at Maldon or Stamford Bridge, even if the surviving elite stayed to fight to the last. When King Harold II fell at Hastings, this was too much for most of the surviving *fyrd* and the marker for Duke William's seismic victory.

During civil wars in Scandinavia, the victor might show magnanimity, better to win round old enemies than breed fresh blood feuds. Even such hard cases as King Olaf and Harald Hardradi could show clemency. This was strictly policy, not humanity. As ever, we don't know about Eirik. We know he fought and killed two of his brothers but how he dealt with their surviving affinities we don't know. If he had any sense, he'd have tried to win them over. We know he certainly wasn't popular, his rule too harsh and arbitrary, opening the door for his other brother Hakon's comeback.

Battle wasn't the only test – the era featured many sieges. Norsemen conducted lengthy leaguers of Paris in 845 and again 40 years later. London suffered a protracted siege during Aethelred's unfortunate rule through 1013. But as far as we know, Eirik was neither besieger nor besieged. He would doubtless be familiar with the evolving art of positional warfare but seems to have had no practical experience or cause to learn.

Strategy was instinctive, learned or copied. Viking rulers didn't have a handy local Vegetius to rely on and were probably ignorant of such classical resources (though not necessarily, given the breadth of Norse trading connections). Strategy was defined by circumstances and constrained by resources. Individual prowess, skill at arms, and heroic defiance were all part of the grist that fed skalds, but pragmatism was supreme. Thor was brave and bold, but Odin was wise, wily and downright slippery. Eirik's strategic objectives throughout his very long, if ultimately unsuccessful career, were invariably focused on gaining and retaining political power. At the end he runs out of time and space. Other than to cling to whatever power he could, we can't even say with any certainty what he was doing at Stainmore just before the final curtain fell.

Weapons. Steel sinews of war. I mentioned Gordon Honeycombe's 1973 novel *Dragon under the Hill*, set on Lindisfarne, the remote and magical landscape brilliantly evoked, inviting comparison with Robert Westall's equally atmospheric *The Wind Eye*. In the former tale a boy hero, also named Erik, dangerously disturbs a Viking Howe in the dunes and makes off with a hero's sword. There are dire consequences.

In Westall's novel, one of the time-travelling characters finds himself on Lindisfarne just as the Vikings hit in 793. These Norsemen, a significantly unimpressive bunch of not very bright thugs, are destroying the monastery, but our modern hero easily defeats their champion using unarmed combat skills. Written in 1976, the novel came out before much of the current evidence of Viking physiognomy was revealed through forensic archaeology.

Swords have been the badge of the high-status warrior since the Bronze Age. Arthurian legend is almost defined by Excalibur. In 2012, my eldest daughter carried her great-grandfather's sword at her passing out parade from Sandhurst. She wouldn't be called upon to fight with it, defence cuts haven't bitten quite that deep, at least not yet; but the status holds good.

We don't know the name of Eirik's sword. He will have owned several and they would have had names and characters. These things mattered. For a warrior the sword was his principal offensive tool, axes were good, too, but spears were still the relatively poor relation. That said, the Norsemen tended not to forge their own blades but to buy them in from Frankia, recognised as best quality and ideally of pattern welded construction[20]. Not all were reliable, as the sagas tell us of blades which would bend or even shatter on contact, very embarrassing for the user and quite likely to have dire results.

By Eirik's day, improved smithing skills meant blades were stronger, more flexible, with an elegant taper towards the point so that they could be used for the lunge as opposed to purely slashing blows. Average length tended to be around 90 centimetres; a longer blade would be unusual. Names were inlaid into the fuller (a channel which runs down the length, intended to lighten and improve heft, not a blood gutter as often suggested), to reinforce the martial character of the weapon. Hero Sigurd's dragon-slaying blade was named *Gramr* ('Fierce'). Egil, as we've seen, carried a brace, *Slicer* together with *Adder*. Others were branded as *Bloodaxe*, (a tribute to Eirik perhaps), or *Serpent's Tongue*.

Vikings loved bling and, as a good sword represented a significant cash outlay, hilts were lavishly decorated, plated with tin, copper, silver or even, in very high-status examples, gold. Those of Eirik's day show a uniform pattern of short thick quillons (cross-guards) with trilobate pommels (the piece that crowns the tang), which has an additional practical function of contributing to heft and balance. Not as depicted in many movies, a relatively short grip shows the weapon was intended to be used single-handed, in conjunction with a shield. A double-handed grip would impart little advantage and unbalance the heft. Scabbards were of wooden framing and often lined with wool – this contains lanolin, a natural oil which would inhibit rust. As a rule, the sword was carried suspended from a waist belt or, less often, a baldric (never slung across the back!).

Axes were a terror weapon in themselves, especially the long-hafted, double-handed model which would become the staple of later elite units such as King Harold II's Housecarls. These 'Danish' axes could inspire severe consternation (and wreak havoc) among even seasoned Norman mounted knights. These weapons comprised two main variants, of which the earlier was the bearded version. Here, the lower section of the curved cutting blade was longer and could be hefted to catch the shield edge of an opponent dragging it aside, opening him up for a killer stroke. Later, after Eirik's day, this prototype grew and transitioned into the broad axe.

Spears weren't really a gentleman's weapon, though we saw how Egil's brother Thorolf neatly eviscerated his opponent Hring at Vin Heath/Brunanburh. His spear was called Ron and would have been of the heavy broad-bladed *hoggspjot* variant, a substantial polearm designed for thrusting with an elegant but very functional leaf-shaped blade. According to Geoffrey of Monmouth, King Arthur's spear at the battle of Badon was also so named: 'A spear called Ron graced his right hand: long, broad in the blade and thirsty for slaughter.' Lighter spears, some with barbed points, were used for throwing. The barb made for a ghastly wound and was extremely difficult to extract, increasing the ever-attendant risk of infection.

Shields were constructed in composite fashion from thin morticed planks of timber. Linden wood was a favourite, and the edging could be of leather or iron, heat shrunk onto the wooden boards to impart greater strength. Average width tended to be around 60 centimetres, with a dished iron boss fitted with an internal grip. This seems harder to heft than internal straps but in fact makes the shield far more agile, enabling the warrior, strong and accomplished enough, to use his shield to block, parry and beat. They could of course be painted with designs to suit the owner, a form of early heraldry or a way of invoking the favour of the gods, always a wise precaution.

Good shield drill was an invaluable survival tool. One standard gambit was for an attacker to feint to the defender's head but then switch to a low swinging cut, aiming for ankle or hamstrings, or just slashing the lower leg. Numerous dead from the later, high medieval battle of Visby on Gotland in 1361 had been felled by such blows. Once you were lamed and down, you were as good as dead.

Knives were handy as well. I've mentioned the ubiquitous seax, long- or short-bladed, sometimes fashioned from a recycled sword blade which had previously shattered, leaving a salvageable portion. These were carried by all classes in society, though the elite would have far more finely finished examples, decorative as well as practical. In a melee, the seax was a handy backup weapon and could, in a seriously tight press, be more effective for thrusting than a sword.

Mail made a great deal of difference, generally impervious to a sword or knife slash, strong against the thrust. Mail is crafted from 6-millimetre rings drawn from steel wire, each riveted together to create a flexible, figure-hugging armour. Making one was a daunting job, infinitely laborious, since hundreds of rings are required. Inevitably, it was expensive so not for the average conscript dragged from his plough. These 'woven breast nets' such as Beowulf's warriors all possess, were treasured in themselves, given as gifts, and eagerly stripped from battlefield dead.

When you pick a mail shirt up it seems both heavy and unwieldy but when you put it on it is transformed, generally made to order it will conform to your body shape and move as one with you. Once you've got used to the weight, you stop feeling it. It's warm though, with a heavily padded canvas or hide gambeson beneath. This would soak up the force of a blow and prevent the shock from translating into broken bones and as a handy bonus, keep the mail conforming to your shape.

There are lots of ways you can die in battle, none of them appealing. Your head is naturally the most vulnerable point, and we see many head injuries as cause of death on skeletal remains. Anyone who could afford it would have a helmet, as vital to the warrior as mail and shield. Very few helmets from Eirik's era survive. One that does is the one which came from the 10th-century *Gjermundbu* grave[21].

Discovered by accident during field clearance in 1943 and broken into nine fragments, the helmet was beautifully restored by a University of Oslo team. It is constructed from four plates or ribs, with a rounded profile, spiked and with a most distinctive brow band and even more distinctive nose and eye guard – giving it its unique 'spectacle' appearance. Eirik would have worn something very similar, if probably rather more ornate. He was, after all in charge, if only for a while.

Eirik, being high born, would have trained extensively with the sword. A blade differs from other weapons in that it can be effectively used for both attack and defence. Its mastery demands a high level of skill, coordination, strength and dexterity. Mastery can only be achieved and maintained by training and practice. Primarily, a sword is intended to serve as an offensive weapon, with a double-edged blade (generally if not always), it is intended for the cut, to deliver fast, strong blows.

Most historic combats would have ended in under a minute, the drawn-out duel involving much prancing and posturing is Hollywood fiction. With a long killing edge, it's more versatile than the axe, which has a relatively short lethal length. When using the sword effectively, it is relatively easy to feint and so switch the direction of any attack. The point can achieve extended range with just a small flick of the wrist and be delivered at speed, yet with far less effort than spear or axe would demand.

The cross guard is very effective for taking control of an opponent's weapon and executing circular parries. When in a close grip or bind, the closer the bind point is to the cross guard, the more control or leverage the swordsman can exercise. This is dubbed a 'strong' bind, a 'weak' bind means the warrior lacks a full measure of control and must apply greater force to gain leverage. Good swordsmanship minimises effort and husbands energy. As the old maxim dictates, 'sweat saves blood' but with swords you aim to conserve both.

Depending on how well the warrior controls the bind, he can employ his sword to force gaps in his opponent's defence. A two-stage process, force the opening and then move in with a lightning attack. Speed is everything. As Egil demonstrates in his duel with Ljot, speed enables you to take control of the fight from the outset and deny your opponent any respite.

In defence, the sword can be deployed to parry effectively and hold an opponent's blow, and it is superior in delivering swift counter strikes than most other weapons. It's fair to say the sword is most efficient at medium range, far less so at close quarters. This may be where the seax comes in. But the skilled fighter will always attempt to keep a respectable distance from his enemy, be ready to give ground, be adept at swift, responsive blocks, feints and beats, soak up the momentum of attack and avoid narrowing the range to disadvantage.

Using your shield in tandem with a sword is a reliable way to exploit openings in an opponent's defence. I've already commented on using the shield as an offensive weapon, blocking can deflect the enemy's blade, opening him up for a counterstroke. It can be used as a bludgeon to keep him off balance, as a blind so he can't see the angle where your attack is coming from.

Good swordsmanship is an exercise in whole body coordination and reflex. Practice makes the moves instinctive. If you have to take time to ponder, you're as good as dead. If your feet are in the wrong place, your weapon will be too. Feet should be braced well apart, forming an 'L' shape, knees slightly bent, and adjusting the stance as you shift your weight. Stance is a weapon, your whole movement is a weapon, the sword is merely the tip of this weapon, you are the weapon. That way you win and get to live, at least long enough to face the next challenge.

If you prepare to strike by holding your sword beneath the shield's rim, you give yourself an opportunity to strike at your enemy's belly and thighs or of delivering that sweeping cut which slashes through his vulnerable calves. But you must be close, so you're exposing yourself to a fast riposte from a suitably skilled and responsive opponent. It's a lethal form of chess.

Such readiness demands years of constant practice and intensive training, building muscle strength and developing the right mindset, weighing your opponent to discern his weaknesses. Egil gets this when he fights Ljot, who is even bigger than he. Essentially a bully, Ljot is accustomed to using his bulk and animal ferocity to take control of a fight. Egil denies him this with a controlled but sustained offensive, so he is forced onto the defensive where his skills shortage soon becomes fatally evident.

Eric Bloodaxe the Viking: 'I Shall Die Laughing'

The best weaponry in the world is no good unless you know how to use it. With training goes motivation. We speak of Vikings as warriors and individual prowess was supremely prized, but in the field discipline and unit cohesion were what mattered. In battle, the integrity of the shield wall demanded that individual units coalesce into a composite force, not easy when, in all probability, most had only trained at local level. An overall commander relied wholly on his officers, whose control over their individual warband would be what determined the day once both sides came to contact.

Training began at an early age. Paladins like Eirik or St Olaf are reputed to have begun their Viking careers whilst seemingly impossibly youthful. But you would start young and in the near certain knowledge that living to a ripe old age and dying in your bed was an unlikely outcome. *Orkneyinga Saga* specifically comments on those jarls who made it to old age. Raiding was of course primarily a commercial activity, but it was sound training, forging men into a fighting unit, building the trust that comes with brotherhood. This translates very neatly onto the battlefield.

'I am the God Thor, I am the War God, I am The Thunderer!
Here in my Northland,
My fastness and fortress, Reign I forever.'

Henry Wadsworth Longfellow:
The Challenge of Thor (1863)

Four

WOOD-WREATHED SHIPS

> It was a paved track, a path that kept them
> In marching order. Their mail shirts glinted,
> hard and hand linked, the high-gloss iron
> of their armour rang. So, they duly arrived
> in their grim war graith and gear at the hall,
> and, weary from the sea, stacked wide shields
> of the toughest hardwood against the wall.
>
> *Beowulf*
> (lines 319–325, p. 12).

Norse-Gael hero Onund Treefoot (he'd been careless enough to lose a limb in battle against the formidable Harald Fairhair), off a Hebridean island called 'Bot' (Bute), with five sail, took on a stronger squadron of eight. Onund cruised with his ally Thrond, the pair opposed by two captains, Vigbiod and Vestmar. These Norwegians had chased the rival squadron and caught up with the Hebrideans off Bute. But Onund had chosen these waters with care:

> And when the Vikings saw their ships, and knew how many they were, they thought they had numbers enough, and they took their weapons and lay waiting for the ships. Then Onund bade lay his ships between two cliffs; there was a great channel there and deep, and ships could sail one way only, and not more than five at a time. Onund was a wise man; and

he made the ships go forward into the strait in such a manner that they could immediately let themselves drift, with hanging oars, when they wished, because there was much sea-room behind them. There was also a certain island on one side. Under it he made one ship lie; and they carried many stones to the edge of the cliff, where they could not be seen from the ships.

Vigbiod led his ships in to the attack, deriding his foeman's disability. The fight was joined in earnest and, in the narrow strait, neither could win the advantage. Onund chose his moment, allowing his flagship to drift toward the cliff as though in retreat. As the longship closed for the supposed kill, his shore party emerged at the lip of the overhanging precipice and rained down their deadly cargo of stones. Depleted and discomfited the Norwegians sought to disengage but found the constriction of the channel and the adverse current both major impediments.

Thrond engaged Vestmar and Onund closed with Vigbiod. Now the boaster was put to the test as the two men clashed amidships. Onund had jammed a ship's timber under his false limb to provide stability. His attacker hewed at shield and blade, but his point stuck fast in the log. Onund delivered a classic killing cut to the shoulder and his assailant fell, severed arm jetting blood. Disheartened, the remaining attackers crammed into the rearward craft and made a run for it. Onund could not resist the understandable temptation to taunt his dying foe who lay rolling in the gunwales, his blood lapping the timbers, reminding him that the one-legged warrior had triumphed and come off without a scratch.[1]

Our saga sources attribute such piratical activity to Eirik starting, if the skalds are to be believed, before he had even reached his teens. Aged only twelve, precocious even by Norse standards, he cruises the Baltic, striking Saxony, Denmark and Frisia. It's impossible to overstate just how vital ships and shipbuilding were, not just to Bloodaxe but to the whole Viking Age. Their elegant and deadly craft were the raider's perfect tool, 'float like a butterfly, sting like a bee', or perhaps more like a swarm of enraged hornets. Dragon ships evoked terror wherever they struck.* To understand Eirik we need to understand how these ships were built and sailed, and how naval clashes were fought.

For many years two famous Viking vessels preserved near Oslo, the Osberg[2] and Gokstad[3] attested to this triumph of technology. Such ships are the principal source of archaeological evidence for the methods of construction used. In 1962, a further rich haul of five sunken boats was made off Skuldelev, in Roskilde Fjord, Zealand ('The Skuldelev Ships'). The vessels were built primarily for war, developed over the tenth century, sometimes referred to as '*drekkar*' (dragon) ships, a reference to the carved prow. The Gokstad ship is described as a '*skuta*' or '*karve*' – a more all-purpose craft that could be employed for civil or military use.

The bespoke man o'war was longer and sleeker (thus the 'longship'), than its fuller-bellied cousin. It possessed a shallow draft and greater reliance upon oars. Size might be defined according to the number of oars or 'rooms' (the space between the main deck beams). The average size of Viking craft seems to have been 16–18 'benches', thus making a total of 32 or 36 oars. 20–25 benches gradually became more commonplace, more than 30 was rare. The celebrated warrior-king Olaf Tryggvason's giant warship the *Long Serpent* held 34 benches, a veritable leviathan of the late tenth century.

Gokstad (*c.* 850–900) is 76 feet (23 metres) in length with a beam of 17½ feet (5.5 metres). Every vessel would usually have a small, raised deck area at prow and stern with a lower planked floor between. A canvas awning was rigged to shelter the crew whilst in harbour or riding at anchor. Many illustrations show the warriors' shields hung over the gunwales at sea, though most modern authorities agree this is fanciful. Such a shield-array would have hampered the oars and was probably reserved for ceremony or to inspire awe. The targes were hooked in sockets cut into a continuous rail and were almost certainly displayed as a war-panoply as the ship closed to contact with the foe.

---

* Viking ships were not all men o'war and came in a variety of designs. Larger merchant men with greater draught, the *knarr*, relying primarily on sail, as did the smaller merchant craft or *byrding*. The smallest warships are classified as Karve, going up through the *snekke*, *drekkar* and *skeld*.

Rather than fixed timber benches (no trace of which has been found), it is suggested that the seamen's chests were employed as seating for the rowers, though the Vikings might have preferred to keep their gear in hide kitbags that could be used as mattresses. Oars were bespoke, cut to match the lines of the vessel, but averaging some 16–18 feet (5–5.5 metres) in length.

A lone crewman could handle a single oar but, if the ships were geared for battle, then two rowers or perhaps three could be employed – this meant both more spears for the melee and a greater speed through the water. For the decisive encounter at Svoldr (1000 AD) the *Long Serpent*, allowing for a full complement or oarsmen and additional marines, might have crammed 300 souls onto the decks.

Once out of sight of land the sail would be hoisted and this provided the means of propulsion for the bulk of the voyage, perhaps, with favourable winds, as fast as 11 knots. When contact was imminent, the sail (possibly wool or linen), was taken in and the mast lowered – typically half the length of the ship in height. Steering gear was in the form of the steer board (starboard) oar, which was finished with a removable tiller arm. The carving of fantastical animal heads on prow and stern posts was an ancient art, pagan and deeply symbolic.

Oak, then native to Scandinavia (now due to the requirements of the Norse ship-building industry almost completely gone), was the favoured wood, though if this was scarce (and reserved for the keel), substitutes such as pine, ash, birch alder, lime and willow were used. The keel was laid first, with prow and stern posts being fixed next. Rows of strakes were then nailed to form the hull sections, each board projecting over the one next below ('clinker-built'). Joints were caulked with tarred rope. Such was the shipwright's art that these slim-waisted vessels assumed a wondrously sleek line. Oar holes were bored in the topmost strake, sealed with small covers to resist ingress of water when she was under sail. The ribs only went in as the last structural component, bound (thus offering a measure of elasticity to the frame) rather than nailed to the strakes[4].

For Norsemen, the sea was their natural element, and many battles took place upon it. In the inhospitable terrain of Scandinavia or the equally difficult ground of highlands and islands, broad water highways were the natural areas of contention. Longships were built and bred for war, yet sea-fights were relatively static affairs with little scope for superior seamanship, fought in the manner of an encounter on land. The opposing fleets would form line of battle, possibly spear- or wedge-shaped formations with the heaviest forming the tip. We know that Eirik fights at least one major fight at sea, though detail is exceedingly sparse. It's possible he fought others.

Vessels were roped together, gunwale to gunwale, to form one large fighting platform, prows of the longer vessels, often armoured, jutting out toward the enemy. Higher sided merchantmen could be employed to stiffen the flanks of the static squadron, their height conferring an advantage. Primitive rams or iron points '*skeggs*' ('beards') could be used for holing, though these seem to have been more for defence than offence. Manoeuvring to strike was rare. The fighting platform had the advantage of providing a single space, help could be sent quickly to any area under threat; losses could be made good, dead and wounded dragged clear. At least on land you can make a run for it, but on water there's no chance to flee. If you attempt to swim, assuming you can, the weight of your mail will certainly drag you down – ask King Olaf.

The action would be confined to calm, sheltered water. Prior to contact there would be the usual jostling for position. Commanders would scan the opposing vessels for size, the critical height of gunwales, the number of fighting men. Not all marines would wear mail in a sea-fight; it was heavy, difficult stow and encumbered a rower very considerably. Size of the opposing vessels was more important than overall numbers. A few big ships was preferable to a horde of smaller boats, they were higher, a better fighting platform and less vulnerable to the vagaries of wind and tide. It would be the weaker side which formed a defensive raft. The attackers would close in, seeking to grapple and board. As a 'pre-emptive strike' the weaker squadron might bunch and concentrate on targeted enemy vessels, possibly seeking to kill or capture an enemy admiral.

Shearing the enemy's oars was one tactic. As masts were lowered prior to action, propulsion depended entirely on the oars. Loss of these left the foe immobilised. Contact was invariably preceded by a deluge of missiles: arrows, throwing spears and axes, a rain of stones. Lighter vessels circled like hungry dogs, acting as marksmen, sniping enemy officers, or pushing reinforcements into the fight. Hostilities would commence at a distance, as the ships formed up, long-range shooting designed to pick off key figures on enemy decks.

Once both sides were locked together, the battle became one of attrition. Heavily armed warriors in the melee, a shield wall at sea, the decks soon crowded with dead and dying, literally awash with gore. On land, either side, finding themselves hard pressed, can seek refuge in flight. At sea there is no hiding place, no sheltering forest, only small boats to gather survivors.

Shield to shield, blade to point, combatants would remain locked in a murderous embrace until one side broke or they simply fought each other to a standstill. Once either could claim the victory, dead would be heaved overboard, wounded enemy dealt with, sent splashing after. For the victors, captured enemy vessels were fine prizes, hopefully laden with spoil. Winning boats defined victory. Once a vessel had been cleared, victorious attackers would likely secure their prize and investigate the contents before, if at all, returning to the fray. Keeping control was a commander's nightmare, yet he could never relax, victory was never certain until the final blow was struck.

Specialised marine equipment did not really exist as such. Men used the same weapons they would wield on land. Their woollen tunics and leggings, cowhide shoes or boots and perhaps fur-lined cloaks would help to keep out ice-laden northern winds. Vikings liked to show off, so extravagantly striped breeches, fine woven tunics with rich coloured hems were commonplace. The Viking was often something of a peacock, much concerned with his appearance. Just because you were aboard ship was no reason to let standards slide; hair was worn long, plaited and often dyed.

What did Eirik look like as he stood on the deck of his flagship? We can gather from the skalds he was a tall, physically imposing man; it would not be unreasonable to assume he took after his father in looks. He must have had charisma and presence; he could hardly have led otherwise. We can also assume his war gear combined both opulence and function. We possess no detail of his sea-fights and must rely on accounts of others to glean any insight. Though it relates to Olaf Tryggvason's last stands in the battle of Svoldr, the following extract from his *Saga* carries the essence of a set piece sea-battle of the era:

Wood-wreathed Ships

Earl Eric was in the fore-hold of his ship, where a shield wall had been set up. Hewing weapons – the sword and axe – and thrusting spears alike were being used in the fighting and everything that could be used as a missile was being thrown. Some shot with bows, other hurled javelins. In fact, so many weapons rained down on the *Long Serpent*, so thickly flew the spears and arrows, that the shields could scarcely withstand them, for *The Serpent* was surrounded by longships on every side. At this King Olaf's men became so enraged that they ran on board the enemies' ships so as to have their attackers within reach of their swords and kill them. But many of the enemy ships had kept out of *The Serpent's* reach to avoid this and most of Olaf's men therefore fell overboard and sank under the weight of their weapons.[5]

The Saga relates how an archer shoots at Earl Eric, arrows thudding into the boards. The earl instructs one of his own bowmen to return the compliment, splitting the shooter's bow. Olaf's men, thinned by missiles, cling desperately to their decks, spearmen on the raised decks fore and aft doing the greatest damage. Amidships, where casualties are highest and the king's men are weakest, Earl Eric leads a party of fourteen broadswords onto the blood-washed deck.

Fighting is savage and prolonged, but reinforcements from the foredeck drive the boarders back. As the battle rages Earl Eric tries again, his boarding party fighting to gain a lodgement. So thinned are the defenders that portions of the deck are empty of all but the heaped corpses of the slain. Gradually, the attackers gain the upper hand, forcing Olaf and his survivors back toward the prow. Surrounded and outnumbered, the king's men sell their lives as dearly as they can. Most who try to leap overboard are killed as they jump. Olaf himself is the last to go over the side. His heavy mail drags the king under to his watery grave.

As early as 617 AD, a band of pirates, *Spuinneadair-mara* (sea-robbers), most likely at this early date sailing from Ireland or Man, raided the monastery of St Donan on Eigg. The pirates were gracious enough to permit the saint to conclude mass before putting him and fifty-odd monks to the sword. This was the beginning of a long tradition. Corsairs such as fearsome Svein

Asleifsson from Orkney, see chapter one, were active off the west coast as late as the mid-twelfth century.

Orkneyinga Saga makes much of Svein, who had a long and colourful career before finally coming to grief in Dublin. His galleys would over-winter on Gairsay then sweep down the long coastline in spring, return for harvesting then set out again in the early autumn. Svein was prolific even by Norse standards, but his combination of farmer cum pirate (and political wrangler), was not uncommon. Eirik would have instantly recognised the type, he merely practised on a larger scale. Svein came after Eirik, but he was just the kind of bruiser Eirik would have recruited, typical of the more adventurous and ambitious *hersir*.

Once, while cruising, Svein scooped a lovely prize of two fat English merchantmen laden with fabric and wine. This, the 'Cloth-Cruise', became legendary. Having consumed the alcohol, the valuable cloth was utilised to effect repairs to the ship's sail. On his final cruise, as noted, Svein ran out of luck. He attempted a raid upon Dublin but was outfought and killed by the inhabitants. Other Norse pirates Thormund Thasramr, or Thormond Foals-Leg, Holmfast and his cousin Grim, infested the natural harbours of the Hebrides. Piracy filled pirates' coffers and enlarged a king's war-chest. Eirik understood that.

Egil's Saga tells us that Eirik fitted out an expedition to go raiding in 'Permia'. This was the remote area around the White Sea and the furthest extremity of Norse awareness, a wild and savage place but potentially offering a rich haul in furs and much prized walrus ivory. Egil's brother Thorolf joined this muster and served the king as standard-bearer. Even though King Harald was still alive, Eirik was already ruling Hordaland and Fjordane, either jointly with his father or as a sub-king. The saga tells us Bloodaxe won a great sea battle by the River Dvina but doesn't tell us against whom, presumably local forces. Whoever he fought he beat. During this cruise he met and married Gunnhild, daughter of Ozur Snout. She was 'outstandingly attractive and wise and well-versed in the magic arts'. She and Thorolf hit it off straightaway – the royal couple's relationship with Egil would be rather less cordial.*

---

* *Egil's Saga*, 37, p. 64 – frustratingly the skald simply refers to sagas about Eirik himself and gives us no details of the fight.

Eirik may or may not have later become embroiled with local politics further north, in the Orkneys (*Okkneyar* or 'Seal Islands'). As we saw, Harald Fairhair had extended his sway here and brought the local lords under his thumb. This didn't imply that peace was likely to endure. Rognvald of Orkney, his line originally backed by Harald, fell into dispute with his powerful uncle Thorfinn. The Earl drew supporters from Orkney, Shetland and Norway whilst the wily and experienced Thorfinn raised forces in Caithness, the west and the Isles. Rognvald had a smaller squadron, some 30 capital ships, whilst his uncle amassed twice that many lesser craft.

After battle was joined, Thorfinn received a significant and timely reinforcement of half a dozen larger craft under Kalf Arnason (one of those responsible for the demise of King, later Saint, Olaf). This intervention was none too soon, for Thorfinn was hard pressed: 'Each of the Earls encouraged his men as the fighting grew fierce, but soon Thorfinn began to suffer heavy losses, mostly because the ships in the two fleets differed so much in size. He himself had a big ship, well fitted out, and he used it vigorously in attack, but once his smaller ships had been put out of action, his own was flanked by the enemy and his crew placed in a dangerous situation, many of them being killed and others badly wounded.'[6]

Thorfinn was in serious difficulties. His lighter, predominantly Scottish craft were completely outclassed. These larger, more stable vessels with their critically higher gunwales made a far better fighting platform. His vessels, minnows by comparison, were simply picked off (probably there was accompanying attrition through desertion). Feeling the cold breath of defeat on his neck, Thorfinn, prepared for flight, hacked through the grappling ropes and extracting his wounded. His one remaining hope was Kalf, who had been a mere spectator thus far. Responding to the Earl's entreaties the Norwegian brought his ships into the fray.

The effect was immediate. His larger vessels, with their markedly higher gunwales, cut a swathe through Rognvald's fleet. With victory seeming so certain, it was suddenly snatched away. Part of his fleet, the Norwegian element, cut their losses and made a run for it, leaving their Orkney and Shetland allies in dire straits. Within a short time, the verdict was reversed. Kalf's longships presumably struck in line and against the flanks of Rognvald's fleet. A knockout blow.

Their arrows and javelins fell into the packed ranks and wreaked havoc, literally transfixing the Earl's marines. Men so confident of victory were snatched away by the arrow's song. The attackers would throw stones down onto the decks below, using the advantage of their higher gunwales. Those grey waters of the Pentland Firth became crowded with bobbing carcasses, a mess of broken spars and cordage. It was now Rognvald's turn as his flagship came under pressure, and the final victory went to Thorfinn.

Despite this triumph Thorfinn's position was far from safe. Rognvald returned to indulge in a spot of hall-burning, a favoured Norse custom, his warriors downing ale as the flames crackled around the high posts of Thorfinn's dwelling. Any celebration would have been premature for the quarry escaped in the smoke and presently returned the compliment, Rognvald was less fortunate. Under Thorfinn, now undisputed ruler, the power of the Orkney earls reached its apogee and the northerners retained their semi-independence from both kingdoms until 1196, when Harald Maddadsson agreed to do homage to William the Lion, King of Scots.

A later Earl Rognvald was also obliged to fight for possession of Orkney. He was a client of another King Harald of Norway and had done the king good service in a recent civil war. The Islands were held at this time by Earl Paul, a son of the Hakon who had murdered Magnus (soon to be canonised). To stiffen the war fleet he was building, Rognvald hired the formidable Frakokk and her grandson Olvir. The cost of their hire was to be a half share in the captured province. Olvir and his active grandparent recruited men from the Scottish mainland and the Western Isles. Their squadron comprised around a dozen craft 'mostly small and poorly manned'. This unimpressive flotilla sailed at midsummer to meet with Rognvald. Aware of his enemies' intentions, Earl Paul had not been idle, amassing ships and recruiting crews.

As his fleet pulled east of Tankerness, they spied Olvir's dozen ships making straight for them, rowing eastwards from Mull Head. Paul put his vessels into a defensive array, lashing them together in the usual way. At the same moment, he received an offer of aid from Erling of Tankerness, a local landowner and his sons. The Earl felt his decks were already too crowded and set these willing reinforcements to work collecting stones for missiles.

force together throughout the autumn until he heard that Rognvald and his men had cleared out of Shetland.⁹

For Man, a further estimate suggests a dozen ships in total. When the King of Man wisely submitted in 1264 (admittedly long after Eirik's day), following the Norwegian King's reverse at Largs and the collapse of the Norse position, he had ten sail at his command (five carried 24 oars and the remainder half as many). Given that the Orkney earls exercised at least nominal sway over the Hebrides for the best part of a century from the 980s onwards, then ship-service was very likely the favoured form of dues. This, of itself, would not differ greatly from previous obligations to earlier Scots or Pictish magnates. The Isles and the west coast were relatively impoverished areas, where farming gave a poor yield, so the level of obligation was probably diluted.

As a further illustration of battles at sea, Orkneymen were again active in the maelstrom of Norwegian politics in the late twelfth century, sailing in support of a pretender named Sigurd. These so-called 'Islanders' were opposed by the ruling claimant, King Sverre and his indigenous followers, known as 'Birchlegs'.* In the spring of 1194, the King moved to deal with the opposition fleet. His initiative caught the Islanders unprepared, nine of their capital ships being dispersed, though their remaining craft still had the vital advantage of size. The magnate Hallkell called upon the Orkneymen to adopt a standard defensive platform, lash their ships together and prepare to use hurling stones and then arrows as the enemy sought to close.

King Sverre, who was attempting his manoeuvre in the half light of the spring dawn, ordered his captains to mark their craft with linen bands tied around the prows so that, in uncertain light, they might tell friend from foe. He was aware the enemy enjoyed the advantage of higher gunwales, so he urged his men to hit and run, using speed and manoeuvrability as a counter to size and weight, wearing the enemy down with missiles before closing to grapple. The odds weren't favourable. The King had a score of his small ships and even with numbers of their muster absent the Islanders

---

* 'Birchlegs' (Norse *Birkebeiner*) were rough types from the broad central belt abutting Sweden. These were so poor they had to make leggings from birch bark – hence birch-legs.

could still count fourteen sail in their line. 'In the morning, at dawn, the Islanders lay tent-less; and next they loosed their cables and rowed out from the bay. They laid cords between their ships, both fore and aft, and rowed all in line, and intended to look for King Sverre. But because it was dark, they did not see anything before King Sverre's ships were running at them; and both sides raised the war-cry.'[10]

According to plan, the Orkneymen drew their ships together. At this point they were relying solely upon oars for propulsion and the coming together of hulls splintered many. Soon, they were lashed into a solid fighting platform. The Birchlegs came on fast, speeding from the opaque light of dawn, their hulls skimming the water. A shower of missiles greeted their appearance, but the Norwegians held firm.

Sailors protected themselves with their shields, like the old Roman testudo, darting and lunging, showering the heavier vessels with volleys of darts and javelins. This was their type of fighting, the business second nature. 'Then they rose up under their shields and made a second affray; some threw stones, some shot, and they laid their ships so close that some thrust and some hewed. The Islanders received them manfully; they had now the advantage of their higher gunwales. They came with grappling hooks against the king's ship; and they slew the forecastle-men and took the standard, and cleared very nearly all the ships, to the front of the mast.'[11]

As the fight came to close quarters the Islanders clearly established an advantage but, when they sought to board, King Sverre rallied his survivors and they met the attackers amidships with spears and blades. The struggle was desperate. Men hacked and hewed. Points flickered over the shield wall, short seaxes sought out belly and groin. Men bled and died in the press, their corpses piling up on the slippery decks. Gradually, the Norwegians began to press their enemy back, many were driven off and obliged to scramble back to their own ships. Whilst the Islanders took several of the smaller ships, the larger vessels fought free, though Sverre was paying a heavy price in casualties.

Crippled by his losses, Sverre was constrained to withdraw, his craft breaking contact. Sensing victory, the Islanders cut their lines and prepared to give chase. It was now they began to miss their broken oars, ships starting to drift on the swell, cohesion of the platform lost. Again, the Birchlegs, perceiving this confusion, returned to the attack, cutting out individual galleys and laying alongside, three or four to one.

The outcome hung in the balance when the mainlanders received a sudden and very welcome reinforcement. A large and sturdy vessel, a hundred fresh marines, all well harnessed in burnished ring mail, laid into the scattered Islanders, unleashing chaos. The Birchlegs took one ship after another. As they cleared the decks of one enemy, they fitted spare oars and turned against the rest. The victory, and it was crushing, went to Sverre: 'It is the talk of men that the battle has never been, in which men have conquered against so great gunwale-odds as there were in Floruvagar.'[12] Eirik would have been familiar with sea fights such as these.

> Time went by, the boat was on water,
> in close under the cliffs.
> men climbed eagerly up the gangplank,
> sand churned in surf, warriors loaded,
> a cargo of weapons, shining war-gear
> in the vessel's hold, then heaved out,
> away with a will in their wood-wreathed ship.
> Over the waves, with the wind behind her
> and foam at her neck, she flew like a bird,
> until her curved prow had covered the distance.[13]

There is another use for a ship.

Flaming arrows ignite the ship-borne pyre and the hero ascends in a brilliant blaze of heat and light, only ashes are left to scatter on the water. This is our classic image of a Viking funeral, skald and, latterly, film-maker's gift. Eirik was denied such a send-off, he died on land, bloodied, hacked and dumped in a lonely ditch. He should have had such a spectacular end, but he did not:

> Soon with a roaring rose the mighty fire,
> And the pile crackled, and between the logs,
> Sharp quivering tongues of flame shot out and leapt,
> Curling and darting, higher, until they licked
> The summit of the pile, the dead, the mast,
> And ate the shrivelling sails, but still the Ship,
> Drove on, ablaze above her hull with fire.[14]

Five

NORTHANHYMBRE

> Men went to Catraeth, keen their warband.
> Pale mead their portion, it was poison,
> Three hundred under orders to fight.
> And after celebration, silence.
> Though they went to churches for shriving,
> True is the tale, death confronted them.
>
> *Y Goddodin* verse viii.

Egil's Saga is one of the liveliest accounts we have of life in the Viking Age. It provides a great deal of what might now be termed gratuitous violence. In a set-piece fight, he duels with another called Atli at an assembly over a land dispute:

> After that they prepared themselves for the duel. Egill came forward wearing a helmet on his head and carrying a shield in front of him, with a spear in his hand and his sword Dragvandil tied to his right hand. It was the custom among duellers to have their swords at hand to have them ready when they wanted them, instead of needing to draw them during the fight.
>
> Atli was equipped in the same way as Egil. He was strong and courageous, an experienced dueller, and skilled in the magic arts. Then a huge old bull was brought out, known as the sacrificial bull, for the victor to slaughter. Sometimes there was one bull, and sometimes each of the duellers brought his

own. When they were ready for the duel, they ran at each other and began by throwing their spears. Neither stuck in the shields; the spears both fell to the ground. Then they both grabbed their swords, closed in and exchanged blows. Atli did not yield.

They struck hard and fast, and their shields soon began to split. When Atli's shield was split right through, he tossed it away, took his sword in both hands and hacked away with all his might. Egil struck him a blow on the shoulder, but his sword did not bite. He dealt a second and third blow, finding places to strike because Atli had no protection. Egil wielded his sword with all his might, but it would not bite wherever he struck him. Egil saw that this was pointless, because his own shield was splitting through by then.

He threw down his sword and shield, ran for Atli and grabbed him with his hands. By his greater strength, Egil pushed Atli over backwards, then sprawled over him and bit through his throat.

Egil rushed to his feet and ran over to the sacrificial bull, took it by the nostrils with one hand and by the horns with the other, and swung it over on to its back, breaking its neck.

Eirik's violent demise at Stainmore was the last stanza in his own saga, if we had such a saga. But it's also the final stanza in a much longer epic, an independent kingdom of Northumbria. Ivar the Boneless's conquest was more a shift in management than fundamental change – there was still a northern kingdom free from southern rule. After 87 years that would end altogether with Eirik's death, the final verse of an ancient song several centuries older than the Viking Kingdom of York. It's very much a tale of war and warlords but also of priests, philosophers, scribes and artists.

'Let loose the hounds/ Of war The whirling swords! / Send them leaping/ Afar / Red in their thirst for war / Odin laughs in his Car / At the screaming of the swords!'[1]

Those Norse kings who preceded Eirik are as much a part of that free northern history as they are of Norse sagas. By Eirik's day those indigenous 'roaring northerners' descended from an already very old Northumbria would, given a choice, have preferred an independent Scandinavian ruler to one imposed upon them from the House of Wessex. In the end they lost, as Eirik lost – he 'came too late and stayed too long'. But just so we get the song right, we have to go back to the first verse.

Those of us who live here still see the North as different, very different, to the south (and for me that starts once you get clear of York). It *is* different. The landscape, the climate, the toponomy and the accents are not the same. Gaze at the orgulous mass of lordly Bamburgh rearing up on its basalt outcrop (the same whin stone as Hadrian's Wall). It's not just a wonderful view, grey rolling waves colliding with a tundra of dunes, it's a symbol of ancient overlordship. Warlords from Lancelot (possibly) onwards. Perhaps the ultimate irony is that after 1890 or so it experienced its grand makeover from William Lord Armstrong, the arms magnate! This martial tradition continued, if with a distinct shift in emphasis.

'Northumbria' today exists only in commercial branding. Northumberland is a much smaller region than its illustrious predecessor, probably about the same size as Bernicia (see below). A recently established local distillery has called itself Ad Gefrin after Edwin's Palace and has established itself successfully as part of a long tradition. Links between the north east of England and Scandinavia remain strong. My Norwegian relatives, like so many of their fellow Skandis, forayed relentlessly over the North Sea to raid retail bargains from Eldon Square and the Metro Centre.

After his accession in 117 AD, Emperor Hadrian fixed a new frontier line between Tyne and Solway, even though his successor temporarily shifted this line further north to the Forth/Clyde isthmus. It soon reverted and the long, lonely stetches of his great wall remained garrisoned, the north-west frontier of Rome, for at least another three centuries. George Macdonald Fraser in his seminal *Steel Bonnets*, has fictional Romans marching back towards Italy sometime in the year 410 and looking over their shoulders as the cold north is consumed by the mists. They ponder what a waste of time it had all been. He says then they'd have been quite wrong.

Rome never quite did go away. The line or its spectre stayed potent for a long time after, it affects us still – Northumberland's huge Roman tourist industry being a wholly unintended but welcome legacy. We know forts such as Birdoswald and

Housesteads endured as local townships, garrisoned by militias. Such a line once drawn cannot be easily undrawn. The Wall with its array of matching cantonments, milecastles and turrets, its decaying civilian settlements, was part of the fading echoes of what must in retrospect have seemed like a golden age; empty echoing markets that once bustled, the tombs of people who'd come from all corners of Rome's vast imperial fief. Their successors must have felt like failures.

After Rome came Arthur (or at least we like to imagine so), and the old frontier reverberates with Arthurian connections. 'This last, dim, weird battle in the west' – Tennyson described the final battle between Arthur and Mordred in those terms. There were three of these 'futile' fights, when Celt fought Celt instead of uniting against common enemies. One, as described by W. F. Skene,* was the battle of Arfderydd, which occurred near Arthuret on the English West March. Here, according to the *Annales Cambriae*[2]: 'The Sons of Eliffer [fought] Gwenddolau son of Ceidio; in which battle Gwenddolau fell'[3]. The date is given as 573 and we know from the *Annales* that these two sons, Gwrgi and Peredur, were both dead by 580[4].

It was for the site of this fight that Skene, lawyer cum antiquarian, was searching in the nineteenth century, and he relied on local oral tradition for its location, linking Liddel Moat and the parish of Carwinley with the fallen hero. Nobody is quite sure who these combatants were, but Skene felt – and this seems plausible – that they were successors to the Novantae tribe of Galloway and Selgovae from Dumfriesshire. This puts the dead king's ground north of Rheged,** perhaps part of what later become the British Kingdom of Strathclyde.

One of the players was the loser's bard/priest/druid Myrddin, Merlin. Whether this was Arthurian Merlin or another we don't know; date-wise he appears far too late, but the idea is appealing.

---

* William Forbes Skene (1809–1892) was an eminent Scottish lawyer (the firm he founded continued until it merged in 2008), historian and antiquarian with a special interest in the early Medieval Era.

** Rheged, a Brittonic-speaking region borders of which have never been adequately mapped and now sadly relegated to the branding of a shopping mall outside Penrith. For a detailed account see, Williams, T., *Lost Realms* (London, William Collins 2022), pp. 215–253.

Battle casualties were around three hundred and the dead were dumped into some handy marshy ground. The horror was too much for the temperamental druid, who lost his wits and fled into the woods. Even with Gwenddolau killed, his war band (or the survivors), fought on for another six weeks, which suggests a campaign consisting more of extended skirmishes, most likely fought over territory. But both factions would have done better banding together and focusing on Saxon intruders, all set to gobble up their petty realms.

Ida was a Saxon war leader who had taken over the infant state of Bernicia in 547: 'This year Ida began his reign, from who arose the royal race of Northumbria; and he reigned twelve years and built Bamburgh.'[5] He probably came not from the continent but from an earlier settlement farther down the east coast. From its inception, his new mini kingdom embarked on an era of relentless expansion, (For detailed genealogies of the kings of Bernicia and Deira, see appendix two).

This shouldn't imply that the Angles had it all their own way: their expansion wasn't uncontested. Largely relegated to the land of myth and shopping malls is that principality of Rheged, the capital of which may have been Carlisle (Roman Luguvalium) and whose kings claimed descent from the late Roman governor and imperial pretender, Magnus Maximus[6]. Even the boundaries of this Brittonic realm remain a mystery. Nonetheless, its most celebrated ruler, Urien[7], was a favourite hero whose praises were sung by bards Taliesin and Llywarch Hen. He defeated the Angles in a series of battles and succeeded, for a while at least, in penning them up in their coastal fortresses.

'Hussa reigned seven years, against whom four Kings made war, Urien, and Rideric, and Guallian and Morcant ... and he shut them up three nights in the island of Metcaud (Lindisfarne) and during that expedition he was slain, at the instance of Morcant, through envy.'[8] Disunity – a tragic flaw of the Britons – jealousy and an assassin's stroke ended Urien's brilliant reign. He was murdered by the mouth of the Low Burn near what is now Beal, presumably at the instigation of his supposed ally, Morcant.

With Urien assassinated, his crown passed to his son Owain, known as 'Chief of the Glittering West'; he was a hero worthy to succeed his father. Owain, too, became a favourite of the bards, whose verses chronicle the death-throes of Celtic Britain. Owain is credited with a great victory over the Angles at *Argoed Llwyfain*[9] when the Saxon prince Fflamddwyn is said to have suffered defeat and death. Ultimately, he, too, failed to stem the tide and died at the battle of Catraeth (Catterick?) around 593, an end made glorious in the poet Aneirin's epic, Y *Gododdin*[10].

Though Rheged vanished, other British kingdoms survived. Saint Patrick wrote to the Damnonii, secure in their rocky fastness at Dumbarton (future capital of Strathclyde), ruled by Coroticus or Ceredig; the sainted traveller lambasted them roundly for trafficking in slaves. North of the Britons lay the kingdoms of Picts and Scots. The former, who made up the majority, were descendants of those tribes who had rallied to Calgacus, leading his stand against Agricola.

Their origins were obscure; Irish legend chronicles the Picts' first arrival as invaders from distant Scythia, an interesting if unlikely conjecture. It does appear that there were two distinct Pictish kingdoms. As early as 310, Cassius Dio refers to the Caledonii as living north of the Maeatae, who had earlier disturbed the reign of Commodus. In 565, Columba visited the Pictish King Bridei in his fort, or dun, near the future site of Inverness.

These Anglians were an aggressive race, sprung from Saxon stock, imported as mercenaries in the service of Rome and latterly of those Romano-British chiefs they were soon to supplant. Warlords with a good track record attracted hardened warriors – household men who were expected to follow their leaders to victory or to death. In fact, for one to return home when the chief had gone down was the greatest dishonour, a tradition that would echo down through to Maldon and Hastings.

Recruitment was not determined by ethnicity: a trained and experienced warrior could always find employment. In return for absolute loyalty and good service he would expect – indeed demand – substantial rewards, typically silver arm rings and above all, land. A warrior could become a landowner, a *thegn*, but he was still bound to his lord. The greater success the lord enjoyed, the more men he could recruit. Of course, they would expect to be rewarded in turn, so peaceful cooperation with neighbours offered few incentives. Latterly, the church, with its own insatiable demand for land, increased the burden on kings, even as unworldly an ecclesiastic as Bede saw the risks in this (see below).

When Ida of Bernicia died, several successors came and went remarkably quickly. Eventually, Aethelfrith, possibly an illegitimate grandson, took control. In his eventful lifetime he would transform this small, insignificant principality into a super-power whose reach stretched as far north as the Forth and beyond, west into Northern Ireland, south to the Humber and across to the Welsh marches. Despite his being pagan and demonstrably violent with it, Bede approved of him: 'At this time Ethelfrid (Aethelfrith), a most worthy king and ambitious of glory, governed the kingdom of the Northumbrians and ravaged the Britons more than all the great men of the English.'[11]

Owain and the Gododdin (successors to the Votadini, who had furnished the Romans with a buffer state north of Hadrian's Wall) were first to be dealt with. Aethelfrith carried Northumbrian banners into the Lothians and established influence that would endure for over four centuries. By then he had demanded and got a wedding with a princess of Deira, the Anglian kingdom centred on Durham or perhaps York. He married the king's daughter, then disposed of her father and sent her brother, Edwin, into precarious exile. This Edwin would become an obsession – a special project.

Aedan mac Gabran, ruler of Dalriada, was his next opponent. These Dalriadic Scots were recent immigrants who had filtered across the Irish Sea in relatively small numbers, probably not beginning to arrive until after the fall of Rome. By the year 500 AD, their chieftain Fergus Mór and his two brothers had established toeholds in Kintyre, Lorn, Islay and Jura. Their capital was Dunadd. This 'Fort by the River Add' is a wondrous site still, a kind of West Scottish Mycenae, thrusting like a primeval fist above a flat alluvial plain.

Alarmed by Northumbria's rapid and violent rise, the Scots and their affinity invaded, aiming for a pre-emptive strike. The clash occurred at 'Daegsastan', which might be Dalston in Cumbria, Dawston in Teviotdale or even Dissington in south Northumberland. It was a hard struggle. In the first contact the Northumbrian vanguard, led by the King's brother Theobald, was badly cut up and he himself killed. Aethelfrith counter-attacked with his centre, and for a time both sides held their ground as casualties mounted. Finally, the discipline and staying power of the better-drilled Anglian warriors began to tell and the Scots army disintegrated; Aedan fled but his losses were high. 'From that day until the present,' wrote Bede, 'no King of the Scots in Britain has dared make war on the English.'[12]

Aethelfrith hadn't finished. As his empire expanded, the Welsh princes became alarmed. In 616, he marched south-west to Chester where he won another dazzling victory: 'Ethelfrid ... made a very great slaughter of that perfidious nation.'[13] Bede was prepared to overlook the king's cutting down of a group of Welsh monks who had come out to pray for their side! At last, his pathological hatred of Edwin, or perhaps just fatal overconfidence – maybe he had started to believe in the myth of his own invincibility – got the better of him, and he faced his detested brother-in-law, with his sponsor Raedwald of East Anglia, on the banks of the River Idle.

This was a battle too far and though he did considerable damage to his opponents, killing the other king's son, his smaller force and he along with it were annihilated. Earlier, Raedwald had had doubts and considered just handing Edwin over, but God (in the person of Raedwald's queen) interceded, removed his fears and put heart into Edwin: 'Thus Edwin, pursuant to the oracle he had received, not only escaped the danger from the King (Aethelfrith) his enemy but by his death, succeeded him in the throne.'[14]

Edwin, to Bede's great joy, introduced Christianity into Northumbria, and his reign became a kind of mini Golden Age: 'This Edwin, as a reward of his receiving the faith, and as an earnest of his share in the heavenly kingdom, received an increase of that which he enjoyed on earth, for he reduced under his dominion all the borders of England ... a thing which no British King had ever done before.'[15] Of course, this may be a dash of hagiography and a not-so-subtle hint to his contemporaries that godliness and prosperity went hand in hand.

Bede's World in Jarrow has on show a grand model of Edwin's palace complex of Ad Gefrin. Today, the archaeological site stands just north of the B6351 in North Northumberland, commemorated by a fine roadside memorial. This wonderfully evocative place, under the shadow of Yeavering Bell with its impressive hillfort, was where Paulinus preached and baptised many converts in the River Glen. Excavation carried out by the late Brian Hope-Taylor in the nineteen-fifties and early sixties revealed a mightily impressive citadel of vast timbered halls and ancillary buildings, strongly evoking King Hrothgar's Heorot:

> We took our places at the banquet table. There was singing and excitement: an old reciter, a carrier of stories, recalled the early days. At times some hero made the timbered harp tremble with sweetness, or related true and tragic happenings; at times the king gave the proper turn to some fantastic tale, or a battle-scarred veteran, bowed with age, would begin to remember the martial deeds of his youth and prime and be overcome as the past welled up in his wintry heart.[16]

Most enigmatic of the finds were traces of a raised timber amphitheatre or grandstand, almost certainly some form of civic structure – an open-air debating chamber, theatre and performance space perhaps, or used as a cattle auction area, or maybe a combination of these and more. Bede was in no doubt, and just in case his readership hadn't got the message he rammed it home: 'It is reported that there was then such perfect peace in Britain, wheresoever the dominion of King Edwin extended that, as is still proverbially said, a woman with her new born babe might walk throughout the island, from seas to sea, without receiving any harm'[17]. The missionary would demand according to the old Saxon Baptismal Vow or 'Abrenuntiatio Diaboli' ('Renunciation of the Devil'):

> Forsachistu diabolae?
> (Do you forsake the devil?)
> & respondeat. Ec forsacho diabolae.
> (and he/she responds I forsake the devil)
> Concluding response:

> And I forsake all the devil's works and words, Thunor and Woden and Seaxnot and all those devils who are their followers.[18]

If you drive westwards along General Wade's military road towards Greenhead, you'll pass a large wooden cross on the right not long before the road swoops down to Chollerford. This is

Heavenfield, in old English *Hefenfelth*, where King Oswald routed the Welsh and restored the kingdom of Northumbria to its rightful owner (himself) in AD 633/4.

He needed God's help, as things were in a very poor state. A potent alliance between Christian Cadwallon of Gwynedd and pagan Penda of Mercia had resulted in the defeat and death of sainted King Edwin at Hatfield Chase (near Doncaster) on 12 October 633[19]. Their victory exposed Northumbria to widespread pillage. Then, the reeling kingdom was divided into two regions – old Bernicia and Deira. Eanfrith, Oswald's brother, was quickly disposed of by Cadwallon, and Osric of Deira rapidly went the same way[20]. With classic showmanship – and we shouldn't lose sight of the fact that Bede is a superb storyteller – cometh the hour, cometh the man, in this case 'Oswald, a man beloved by God'.[21]

Oswald, along with a surviving brother Oswy (who would succeed him after 642), had been in profitable exile amongst his kin, the Dalriadic Scots, where he had built up a reputation as a formidable fighterer – *Whiteblade*. King Domnall Brecc, Oswald's Scottish overlord, was happy for him to return home and try to win back the crown of his father Aethelfrith. The Scots king would not technically lend military support as he was allied to Cadwallon (though not to Penda) but he did provide the brothers with a strong war band to ensure their safe passage back to Northumbria's ravaged borders.

Once home, Oswald rallied the Northumbrian militia or *fyrd*, his war band swelled by Scottish fighters who, even if they were disobeying their king's explicit instructions (as he may well have anticipated, or even intended), could legitimately claim they were fighting for Christ and St Columba. Abbot Segine of Iona was ranged with Oswald's affinity and this validation by the Celtic Church carried a great deal of weight. Indeed, Oswald might have brought a squad of monks with him to provide spiritual gravitas … one hopes they were unaware of how many of their brethren his father, Aethelfrith, had killed at Bangor.

The exiles came down the valley of North Tyne, by which time Cadwallon, still at York, became aware of the threat and immediately marched north. He advanced up Dere Street, then branched left along the line of the Wall at Stagshaw. Oswald had occupied a strong defensive position above Chollerford, flanked by the Vallum. During the long watches of the night before battle, Oswald received a visitation from Saint Columba (our very own Cuthbert provided similar inspiration later for Alfred on Athelney). This was most heartening, as the saint promised God's strong arm would be with them: a huge boost to morale, given that Oswald was greatly outnumbered. These portents mattered: his polyglot, ad hoc force would need all the motivation it could find. Oswald's war council was easily convinced and his army advanced to contact.

It seems the Welsh were not expecting this. Maybe Cadwallon was lulled by too many easy victories, but this time the clash of shield walls (wherever it actually occurred) was decisive. After a short sharp shock, the invaders broke; their front, hemmed in by Vallum and Wall, was far too narrow for their greater numbers to tell. The broken army was chased back down the length of the Denise Burn in a running fight. They had won no hearts and minds in Northumbria and probably plenty of locals were willing to lend a hand now their enemy was beaten. It is possible that Heavenfield was just the muster point and that the actual fight occurred further south, over the river crossing at Corbridge.

Cadwallon was amongst the dead and Northumbria was reunited under a new king, one who would soon be recognised as *Bretwalda* – King of Kings. As Bede exulted: 'The place is shown to this day and held in much veneration where Oswald, being about to engage, erected the sign of the holy cross and on his knees prayed to God that he would assist his worshippers in their great distress'[22]. Today, by the roadside stands a replica of the cross with a chapel beyond.

Was Eirik over two centuries later aware of all this? It is possible, if it can't be proved, that his Norse predecessors would seek to legitimise their own tenure by linking their rule to a hallowed past. They would be daft not to. By Eirik's day the threat from the south was sufficient to cast a veneer of common inheritance over the Norse occupation, which 80 years after Ivar and his Viking Great Army, suited everyone.

St Oswald failed against Penda, being defeated and killed by him in 642, 'in a great battle, by the same pagan nation and pagan king of the Mercians'[23]. Oswald's younger brother, Oswy, succeeded him and (remarkably for a Northumbrian king in this heroic age), died in his bed at the age of 58. It was Oswy who finally settled his family's account with ageing Penda in 655: 'The engagement beginning, the pagans were defeated, the thirty commanders and those who had come to their assistance were put to flight and almost all of them slain.'[24]

Northumbria had now reached the dazzling zenith of its power, ruling or dominating the whole of what became the Anglo-Scottish borderlands. Oswald and Oswy were also influential in importing Celtic Christianity from Iona, which became established and flourished on the coastal archipelago of Lindisfarne. Also known as Holy Island, Lindisfarne is cut off twice a day from the mainland by a long rolling tide which has frequently caught out the unwary on the narrow finger of causeway (now equipped with a refuge tower where over-optimists can watch their cars drown and ponder on how they'll phrase this to their insurers). It is two different places: when the tide is out it's a tourist Mecca, but when the tide is in, it is transformed into something very different, quiet, shut off and shut in. Roman Polanski filmed his *Macbeth* there in 1972. I have a family connection on my mother's side. The graveyard is full of my Kyle relatives and a number still live in the village.

First Aidan and then Cuthbert led a community of Celtic monks there. They were devout, austere, 'of the people' in a way that the far more worldly Bishop Wilfrid of Hexham could barely recognise, their rigid piety and poverty clearly annoyed him. These Northern saints are with us still. They hallowed the ground, and that later medieval monastic remnant is a place of pilgrimage: 'The Isle of Lindisfarne ... which place as the tide flows and ebbs twice a day, is enclosed by the waves of the sea like an island; and again, twice in the day, when the shore is left dry, becomes contiguous to the land.'[25] Their Saxon structures were timber – all the better to burn down the Vikings might have said – and built on the higher Heugh overlooking the medieval monastery. There is the same aura of sanctity at Cuthbert's retreat, nearby Inner Farne – the sort of meditative sanctum where you'd really understand what austerity implies.

Oswy facilitated the great Synod of Whitby in 664, where the procedural breaches with Rome were papered over in Rome's favour and Bishop Wilfrid clearly got the upper hand. Celticism was marginalised but did not disappear; Cuthbert was a mightily important political figure, much favoured by Oswy's son and successor Ecgfrith. This last of Northumbria's heroic line seems to have been bold and aggressive to the point of rashness. He ravaged the Irish, 'sending Beort, his general, with an army into Ireland, who miserably wasted that harmless nation ... in their hostile rage [they] spared not even the churches or monasteries.'[26]

The disaster that a confederation of Picts and Scots and Britons from Strathclyde inflicted on the hitherto almost invincible Northumbrian army at Dunnichen Moss (Nechtansmere), amongst the Sidlaw Hills in the spring of 685 was a momentous victory for them and proof of Ecgfrith's gung-ho folly. This Anglian *Götterdämmerung* put an end to the systematic inroads onto Scottish soil which had threatened to turn the Pictish kingdom into a Northumbrian client.

In 1985, on the 1300th anniversary of the fight, it was hailed as the most decisive battle in Scottish history. Bridei mac Bile, who beat Ecgfrith, brought all the Picts beneath his own colours and moved against the Scots of the western seaboard, attacking Dunadd. His descendant, Oengus Mac Fergus (752-61), finally defeated the Scots and established Pictish hegemony. For Northumbria, this was bad news.

Ecgfrith had had nothing but contempt for the Picts, a disregard born out of earlier easy victories. Apparently, quite early in his reign, a Pictish confederation had rebelled against the Northumbrian yoke, only to be cut up when the Angles stormed their base. Ecgfrith's cavalry, possibly aided by disaffected Pictish allies, slaughtered their lightly armed opposition in a lightning attack, 'filling two rivers with the corpses', according to the Anglian Chronicler, Eddi[28].

A classic case of familiarity breeds contempt: 'that same king, rashly leading an army to ravage the province of the Picts, much against the advice of his friends ... was drawn into the straits of inaccessible mountains and slain'[29]. Bede is making a further point here: if you don't listen to your bishop, in this case Cuthbert, you're headed for the rocks. Though Ecgfrith was succeeded by his half-brother Aldfrith, the long decline of Aethelfrith's grand empire had begun.

Northanhymbre

Northan-Hymbre in old English was all those lands or provinces lying north of the Humber Estuary; and Eirik's kingdom was, in its day, even though he only ruled directly over the southern half – ancient Deira – substantial. Boundaries were never fixed, for one thing there were no maps as such, but in Oswy's reign its northern border probably lay along the line of the Tay. To what extent kings first of Bamburgh and then of York exercised sway over what is now southern Scotland wasn't that fixed either.

It wasn't until well after Eirik's day that the line of the River Tweed came to be recognised as the frontier line between the earldom of Northumbria and the emerging Scottish kingdom. Malcolm II of Scotland won a great victory over the Northumbrians at Carham on the river in 1018, which finally ended any trace of English sovereignty beyond. A very bad day for the Northumbrian clergy, who not only lost their revenues from the Lothians but perished in large numbers attempting to cling on to them.

By 948, the year Eirik first arrived in York, Scandinavian influence, dominant since Ivar the Boneless's conquest four score years before, was focused on what had been ancient Deira, the southern half of old Northumbria. The northern rump, Bernicia was still ruled by client kings holding their very limited sway from Bamburgh. This frontier pale was a handy buffer zone for the Kings of York, who needed watchful eyes both north and south. Bishop Alcuin, berating the local elites for allowing the first raid on Lindisfarne to happen, referred to 'this fair land'. I am of this Northumbrian soil, so may be a bit biased, but he's right. Eirik held a fair kingdom.

Eirik probably enjoyed better weather, his short tenures straddle the period between two early medieval warm periods (say 450–900 & 1000–1250). There's a great deal of debate around this amongst climatologists, but if you journey up into the northern closed-in section of Upper Coquetdale in North Northumberland there are clearly visible traces of early medieval terraces, indicating cultivation that would not be viable today, even with modern agricultural methods.

At its height, the kingdom probably stretched from east to west coast with outposts of influence in Northern Ireland. The flat plains of the Lothians with its rocky coastline swelled uphill to Carter Bar and the straddling mass of the Cheviot Hills. South of

Berwick the coastline becomes far sandier, Northumbria's Lordly Strand with the archipelago of Lindisfarne pointing into the cold, restless waters of the North Sea. A kingdom of seabirds – varieties of terns, black guillemots, shags and legions of gulls – sweep and screech above the restless winds and long golden beaches.

West of the coastal flatlands, upland dales, Coquetdale, Redesdale and Tynedale, slash through the higher ground. South of the Tyne the land is gentler, though the long spine of the Pennines creates an east/west watershed. In geological terms this is a landscape over five hundred million years old: Here are rocks that tell the tale of the convergence and collision of the ancient Laurentian, Avalonian, Baltican, Armorican and Gondwana tectonic plates and the compressive and extensional forces that resulted. I've no idea what any of that means but those distant seismic upheavals have formed a distinctive landscape or set of landscapes with bony ridges of high ground, the Cheviots in the centre of the English side, the Southern Uplands over on the Scottish. Old high hills, scoured by the winds from chilled lands north and east and with the lilt of curlews haunting the emptiness.

South of Cheviot you find the altogether sharper edges of Simonside and south again the hard rampart of the basalt Whin Sill, which carries Hadrian's Wall and, much further east, the great bulk of Bamburgh Castle. These uplands are slashed by the dales, North Tyne, Rede, and Coquet which spill out onto the coastal plain and former coal measures.

Further west into England and the Eden Valley is very different. Cumberland is softer, somehow mellower. Sandstone here is a pleasing shade of red and the small villages between Brampton and Longtown look nothing like their Northumbrian counterparts In February 2020, after monsoon rain, the river had swelled to a mini-Amazon, its great red waters spreading over flat alluvial fields and Carlisle, badly flooded before, rightly trembled but happily, was spared. South and east, the Vale of York is a richly endowed landscape, before Rome it was the territory of the lordly Parisi and Rome made York, their Eboracum, a major provincial centre. To the Saxons this became Eoforwic, then Scandinavian Jorvik (see next chapter).

We think of the Viking city as a hub of trade and industry, but most lived by subsistence agriculture, growing only just sufficient to feed themselves. There was a significant dependence on livestock and farmers would move their beasts into the uplands during spring and summer, living in shielings while warmer weather lasted. Urban centres, beyond York and to a lesser extent Durham, were virtually unknown. Of this patchwork of sub-regions, probably only the Yorkshire Wolds would have supported a larger population density – this area had been cleared and settled certainly since the Bronze Age. But those great border valleys such as those of the Tweed, Teviot, Till and Eden are also deeply fertile, some of the best farming land in Europe.

If, after 685, Northumbria was no longer heroic, it was just embarking on its 'Renaissance' or 'Golden Age', lasting from the mid-seventh to mid-eighth centuries. Despite its political and military decline, the northern kingdom produced a magnificent treasure-trove of art, becoming renowned throughout Europe as a centre of excellence. This period coincides with the life of, arguably, Northumbria's most famous son, the Venerable Bede (in 1899 he was canonised as Doctor of the Church St Bede the Venerable). Happily, in a note to his *Historia Ecclesiastica*, he gives us some biographical details. Born in 672 (or perhaps the year after) at Monkton in Durham, he entered Benedict Biscop's monastery of Wearmouth aged seven. At twenty he followed Bishop Ceolfrith to Jarrow and St Paul's, remaining there all his life, adding to the already impressive library (it held somewhere between three and five hundred texts).

His classical credentials were impressive: he spoke Latin, Greek and probably Hebrew. He was a man of his times, devoted to an allegorical mode of interpretation yet possessed of vast wisdom, deep humanity, and a ready wit. So profound was his influence that he has been dubbed 'Teacher of the Middle Ages'. His output was prolific, but his most influential work is his five-volume *Historia Ecclesiastica Gentis Anglorum*, which covers English history from Caesar's expeditions up to his own time, and while he does lean heavily on earlier sources such as Orosius, Gildas and Prosper of Aquitaine, he includes much original material. This is a milestone not just in the history of Northumbria and the borders but of Britain, a welding together to produce something which is truly English.

In death he travelled much further than he had during his lifetime. Dying in 735, he was first interred at St Paul's then finally moved to Durham around 1022 where he was laid with St Cuthbert in the choir of the great cathedral. Three and a half centuries later his remains were reburied in a splendid monument within the Galilee Chapel. This, like so much else, was vandalised during the Reformation and Bede's bones relegated to a simpler grave. It wasn't until 1831 that his present and glorious tomb, constructed from carboniferous limestone, was built.

St Cuthbert, from his original resting place on Holy Island, did his own fair share of roving. For a while he rested at Chester-Le-Street before his final interment in Durham. A number of locations have been called Cuthbert's or Cuddy's Caves. There's one near Doddington and another at Holburn, in the Kyloe Hills between Belford and Lowick.

I prefer the latter. While the term 'magical' might be is overworked, it still applies here. You walk uphill then branch right into modern woodland, pointed by a cup and ring stone. The cave is a lateral hollow overhung with frowning sandstone, like a vast frozen fist. If this place had once been a Mesolithic shelter, you would not be surprised. Viewed from the western approach though an avenue of trees, it has the sanctity of some ancient temple. All of this would be part of Eirik, the ostensibly pagan Norseman's inheritance. He, a foreigner, became the last paladin.

Bede's home, St Paul's in Jarrow, is still a remarkable site. Founded in 681 by Bishop Biscop on land granted by King Ecgfrith, it's the other half of the Jarrow/Wearmouth monastic complex – 'one monastery in two places' as Bede describes it. The late seventh-century square-sided chancel is a Saxon survivor with much later re-building. What remains of the monastic buildings is much later, secularised during the Reformation but, it's said, Bede's original chair remains in the wonderful chancel, which certainly preserves a distinct feel of ancient sanctity. It's also rumoured there's a vault below which might just contain the mortal remains of Ecgfrith himself, repatriated after his unfortunate Scottish excursion of 685[30].

Ecgfrith's *Gotterdammerung* drew a line under Northumbria's steady expansion, from now on that tide was firmly on the ebb. His half-brother and successor Aldfrith was no warrior, learned and erudite but, as Trotsky observed, you may not be interested in war, but war is always interested in you. The echoes of Nechtansmere continued to reverberate. The Picts, Scots and Strathclyde Britons firmly asserted their independence, shrugged off any vestiges of Northumbrian domination and sharpened their swords. In 698, Aldfrith's satrap or client in the Lothians Bhitred (Behrt?) was killed. It's possible his son and successor Osred also fell to northern spears in 716.

By the mid-eighth century, the Northumbrians under Eadberht were again active on their northern borders, battling the Picts while coping with opportunistic Mercian attacks from the south. Thereafter Picts and Northumbrians seem to have learned how to coexist and it appears the influence of the church may have been a significant factor in this rapprochement. From the early to mid-ninth centuries, the Picts were eclipsed by their Scottish neighbours, who established a viable kingdom that steadily and inexorably flexed its swelling muscles. Northumbrians would from then on, until their final disaster at Carham in 1018, be on the back foot. How strongly this fluid northern frontier was ever fixed or defended in any depth is unclear. This contrasts sharply with the situation further south where the consolidation of a powerful Mercian state created a very real menace. Here the Northumbrians dug in, making the most of rivers and the near-impassable fens with fortified outpost settlements or *burhs*.

In summer 2013, the Lindisfarne Gospels were 'home', on display in Durham. It was a once in a lifetime chance to see this astonishing work of art, one of the most important survivors of the early Middle Ages. Eadfrith, latterly Bishop of Lindisfarne, may have spent as long as a decade copying and illuminating the Gospels. This was around the year 700, and the work was bound in unpretentious leather. The current version is a Victorian gothic fantasy.

This was just as well. The Anglo-Saxon Chronicle records that the portents for the year 793 were unfavourable: 'There were excessive whirlwinds, lightning and fiery dragons were seen flying in the air'[31]. For the inhabitants of Northumbria at least, this dire forecast was accurate. In that year the community of Lindisfarne was the first to taste the fury of the Northmen. They came out of a bright clear sky, sunlight chasing the movement of the oars, three long, sleek ships of a kind never seen in these coastal waters. They were elegant and graceful, seeming to skim across a placid sea, but the great square sail was decorated with pagan imagery and a dragon's head reared from the curved prow. They 'lamentably destroyed God's Church on Lindisfarne through rapine and slaughter'.[32]

Those men who swept ashore were tall and well proportioned, clad in gleaming ring mail. The monks were killed without pity or comment. Anything of value was methodically looted and piled up; any likely girl or boy was seized to be sold. In the brief fury of the sack, lay and clergy were pillaged, settlement and monastery consigned to the flames, the place stripped and emptied. That the Lindisfarne Gospels escaped the raiders' attentions verges on the miraculous – the great work was probably saved by its unostentatious binding.

Such scenes were to be enacted and re-enacted along the coasts of England, Scotland and Ireland as the sea-rovers made their presence felt. The sudden and terrible swiftness – the emerging of these pagan warriors in their rapier craft, springing from the very vastness of the oceans – is a powerful one but probably misleading. The Norse raiders were, of course, good sailors but long voyages over open water were risky: island or coast-hopping was preferable. After 865, coastal raiding gave way to conquest (more on that in the next chapter) and the ancient, tottering kingdom of Northumbria was the first of the Saxon homelands to be dismembered. Despite many adventures, the Gospels survived.

Raiding wasn't just an opportunistic exercise in vandalism and larceny, it was a worked-up tactical doctrine. Attacks were planned and executed with deadly precision. The Norsemen possessed a first-rate intelligence gathering system. Re-supply, the umbilical of success, was essential. Island-hopping provided opportunities for re-victualling at small harbours and staging posts, or by raiding, the *strandhogg*. Making free with handy flocks or herds of cattle would be accompanied by the lifting of local teenagers for the slaving business. Where no useful harbour presented itself, ships could just be beached, ideally on an island or river-loop where a defensive stockade could be thrown up: loss of their ships was crippling to the sea-raiders, and they would go to great pains to ensure secure anchorage.

Though these Norsemen first struck Northumbria in 793 and for several seasons following, these were hit and run raids with slaves and booty as main prizes. It was a long while, not quite a full century, before the Vikings came back to stay, led by the sons of legendary Ragnar Lodbrok ('hairy breeches'). He may or may not have existed but Ivar the Boneless (see next chapter) certainly did, and his ambitions extended far beyond mere banditry. He came to conquer.

Between those times Northumbrians and Scots still found plenty to fight over. Just on the northern fringe of the border marches, in the Lothians, is the village of Athelstaneford. It stands on a short east/west ridge and covers a route over the (Scottish) River Tyne; it's not too far from mighty Traprain Law. Since Aethelfrith's day, Northumbria had maintained influence over this region, stronger at some times than others, probably not with any direct form of vassalage but some if its rulers were Northumbrian clients.

King Oengus (Angus) II, ruler of Pictland, led a foray during 832, a savage spoiling which prompted instant reprisal. King Athelstan of Northumbria hurried north with a sizeable war band and caught the Picts just north of Athelstaneford, surrounding their camp with superior numbers. Fervent prayer seemed the best tactic and Oengus vowed to honour God and everyone else, especially St Andrew, if they would just spare a moment to save him.

During the night St Andrew came good and promised victory next day beneath his talisman. Spiritually sustained and enthused, the Picts sallied out and launched a surprise attack of their own, presumably at dawn, and won the day. Athelstan and his thegns were cut down, the army bolted. This may be the origin of the Saltire, the cross of St Andrew, as a national flag, though there's little or nothing left on the probable ground today; marker stones said to have been on the field have long since vanished[33].

'Such,' he said, 'O King, seems to me the present life of men on earth, in comparison with that time which to us is uncertain, as if when on a winter's night you sit feasting with your ealdormen and thegns a single sparrow should fly swiftly into the hall, and coming in at one door, instantly fly out through another. In that time in which it is indoors it is indeed not touched by the fury of the winter, and yet, this smallest space of calmness being passed almost in a flash, from winter going into winter again, it is lost to your eyes. Somewhat like this appears the life of man; but of what follows or what went before we are utterly ignorant.'[34]

Northumbria had certainly shrunk from its earlier grand proportions and new, powerful external pressures were mounting. Viking raids fractured the apparent serenity of a monastic-inspired Golden Age. In 844 King Raedwulf went down fighting Norse intruders, and a rabidly fractious internal polity undermined stability (see appendix three). While, as N. J. Higham points out, regicide, murder, forced abdication and exile were common enough throughout Anglo-Saxon England, in Northumbria these became the norm. Whilst the exact chronology isn't completely clear, the pattern certainly is. What the players themselves didn't get is that others across the reaches of the cold North Sea were watching and waiting. Ivar's Army wasn't just a bigger raid, it was a very carefully planned strategy executed at just the right moment.

History would shift after 867 and the Viking menace moved up several gears from being nuisance attacks to a full-scale invasion. This would be the genesis of Eirik's later opportunity but, at the same time, it was the very threat posed by the Viking Great Army that would propel the rise of Wessex and herald the end of any northern hegemony.

Bede, farsighted as ever, saw where a part of the problem of Northumbria's fractious and unstable polity lay during his day. In a letter to Bishop Ecgberht written in 734, the great churchman cautions that progressive alienation of royal estates, leeched off for monastic settlement, was undermining the traditional power of kings to swell their war bands and keep warriors satisfied by parcelling out lands. This left young men with limited prospects and too much time on their hands and a 'Versailles' culture could only lead to infighting and mayhem. This is quite radical coming from so senior and respected a clergyman, the leading thinker of his age. Quite obviously, he was right.

Speaking of survivors, one is the Jorvik or Coppergate Helmet. It dates to the latter part of the eighth century, a couple of hundred years before Eirik Bloodaxe though it may well still have been in use at that time. High status kit is expensive and can have a seriously long shelf life. It was discovered during archaeological investigation prior to the construction of a new shopping mall in

May 1982. A JCB driver, backfilling one of the trenches discovered the helmet, close to where traces of Viking Age occupation had come to light. It emerged out of a small, wood lined pit, accompanied by shards of antler, stone, glass and iron.

Only a small number of such protective headgear, say half a dozen or so, have ever been found from this era and this is by far the best preserved, superbly put back together and conserved by the British Museum. It is constructed from iron and copper alloy, the skull crossed by two-banded brass crests, back to front and side to side. It's these which contain the inscription. Aesthetically satisfying, the banding nonetheless offers additional deflective protection. The Jorvik Helmet wasn't just for show.

The brass crest ends with a decorated beast's head at the base of the pronounced nasal guard. Brass eyebrows flanking the nasal also finish with a flourish of animal heads. The nasal itself is fashioned from a brace of intertwined creatures, whose bodies and limbs interlace. It screams warlord! Good news is we at least know who this warrior was – his name was Oshere. Sadly, that's all we do know.*

The gallery also houses the equally splendid Gilling Sword. Nine-year-old Garry Fridd, playing on the banks of the Gilling beck, West Gilling, by Richmond, saw the blade in the water. This was in April 1976 and the eagle-eyed youth won a Blue Peter Badge for his discovery. Probably a century later than the helmet, it has a broad double-edged blade, distinctive down swept quillons with silver mountings on the hilt.

All this deep historic past would form part of Eirik's inherited burden. The business about being King in York wasn't just a legacy from Ivar the Boneless. It went much deeper. It was about a separate northern identity, based on the great Kingdom of Northumbria and the Scandinavian kingdom was as much a continuation of that as it was a sea change. At the outset, the Northmen came as raiders, pillagers and slavers. Then they came as conquerors but

---

* IN NOMINE: DNI: NOSTRI: IHV: SCS: SPS: DI: ET: OMNIBVS: DECEMVS: AMEN: OSHERE:XPI. 'In the name of our Lord Jesus, the Holy Spirit, and God; and to all we say Amen / Oshere / Christ'. Alternatively: 'In the name of our Lord Jesus Christ and of the Spirit of God, let us offer up Oshere to All Saints. Amen'. Oshere is a male Anglian name and XPI are the first three letters of the word Christos Χριστός (khristos) in Greek.

never fully as occupiers. They blended and coalesced into a new or refreshed northern identity, very distinct from its southern, Wessex-centred counterpart. The Kingdom of Northumbria hadn't died, it had merely progressed. Eirik had no blood connection to Oswald or Oswy, but he was their successor. In time, the enemy was no longer Norsemen but the English.

'Now mourn for ever, / Saxon and English, from the sea's margin / To the western forest! The wall is fallen, women are weeping; the wood is blazing. / And the fire flaming as a far beacon. / Build high the barrow his bones to keep! / For shall be hid both helm and sword. / And to the ground be given golden corslet, / And rich raiment and rings gleaming, / Wealth unbegrudged for the well beloved. / Of the friends of men first and noblest, /To his hearth comrades help unfailing, /To his folk the fairest father of peoples. / Glory loved he; now glory earning. / His grave shall be green, while ground or sea, / While word or woe in the world lasteth.'[35]

Six

'NEVER GREATER SLAUGHTER'

> Since Brutus came to Britain many kings and realms have come and gone... What with the love of petty independence on the one hand, and on the other the greed of kings for wide realms, the years were filled with swift alternations of war and peace, or mirth and woe... A time of unsettled frontiers, when men might rise or fall suddenly, and songwriters had abundant material and eager audiences.
>
> J. R. R. Tolkien
> *Farmer Giles of Ham* (1940)

Brunanburh, the morning after.

Michael Livingston says of this fearful battle that 'Englishness came of age.' Whether it was fought in the west or east is still a matter fiercely debated. Even in an era punctuated by battle, Brunanburh was exceptional – 'never greater slaughter, a day for the ravens to feast.'

Mankind has spent a fair proportion of recorded history trying to create an earthly version of Hell. At the time this field would have ranked as one of our better efforts. You'd smell the place before you saw it, a stink of putrefaction and of suffering, as though so much anguish could be somehow distilled into an odour.

Burial parties would be at work. They'd tie cloths over their faces, scented against the stench. They'd dig great yawning pits and would perhaps lay bodies in neat rows, like fishermen after a good catch. Rigor Mortis would have had set in, so the pioneers would be using spades and axes to break stiffened limbs, the crack sharp in that rancid air.

Some faces you might recognise even in the sack-like indifference of death. Twisted, contorted, bereft of limbs, without faces, dressed only in ribbons of their own blood, gouged, hacked and smeared, en who like Aneurin's warriors from the *Goddodin* had gone to war in the full splendour of their youth.

Corpses would be stiffening in the strengthening sun, some shifting as they swelled. Down the line one might burst noisily, exciting the carpet of flies which lifted briefly then swooped down for the feast. The stink went up yet another notch.

For Eirik, his ancestry was both blessing and curse. Harald Finehair was going to be a very difficult act to follow. No Norwegian since Ragnar Lodbrok (if indeed, he ever existed), had accomplished so much and garnered such great renown. Yet, Harald, for all his triumphs, had not created a stable platform for unhindered succession. He had fathered too many ambitious sons, whose very multiplicity was a gift to the fissiparous jarls lurking ever resentful in their dark glens. There were so many brothers/half-brothers.

The story of how Hakon the Good became king Athelstan's foster-son is related in some detail in the *Fagrskinna*:

> The next summer King Harald sent a ship west to England, and got his best friend, Haukr hábrók (Long-Leg), to command it [possibly Halfdan Long-Leg, one of the King's sons, of whom more later]. King Harald put into his charge a boy who had been born of his bondwoman, Þóra morst‡ng. She came from a family in Mostr in South H‡räaland. This boy was called Hákon, and his mother claimed that he was the son of King Haraldr. Haukr came west to England and met King Aäalsteinn in London and came into his presence when the meal-tables had been cleared away and greeted the king. The king bade him welcome. Then Haukr said, 'Lord, King Harald of the Norwegians has sent you fair greetings, and he has also sent you a white bird, well trained, and asked you to train it still better in future.' He took the child from the folds of his cloak and set him on the king's lap.

The king looked at the boy, while Haukr stood before the king and did not bow to him. He had at his left side a keen sword under his cloak, and all his men were similarly equipped, and there were thirty of them altogether. Then King Aðalsteinn said, 'Whose is this child?' Then Haukr replied, 'He belongs to a slave-woman in Norway, and King Harald said that you were to bring up her child.' The king answered, 'This boy does not have slave's eyes.' Haukr said, 'The mother is a slave, and she says that King Harald is the father, and now the boy is your foster-son, King, and is entitled to the same care from you as your own son.' The king answered, 'Why would I bring up a child for Harald, even if it were his wife's child, much less a slave-woman's child,' and with one hand he reached for a sword which lay beside him, and with the other hand seized the child.

Then Haukr said, 'You have just fostered Harald's son, King, and set him on your knee, and you can murder him now if you wish, but you will not be able to get rid of all King Haraldr's sons any the sooner for that, and it will still be said in future as it has been until now, that the man who brings up another's child is of lower status.' After that Haukr turned away…And in this way, they went to their ship, and there was a favourable wind blowing from the land out to sea, and they made the most of it and sailed to Norway. And when they came before the king, he thanked Haukr warmly for his mission. But King Aðalsteinn had Hákon brought up there in his court, and he has since been called Aðalsteinsfóstri (Athelstan's foster-son). From such dealings between the kings, it could be seen that each of them wanted to be considered greater than the other, but no undue disparity in their dignity arose from this cause, and each of them ruled his kingdom until his dying day.[1]

Eirik, the author of *Fagrskinna* states, had much to commend him: 'After King Harald, Eirík blóðøx succeeded to the kingdom, while Hákon was west in England. King Eirík was married to Gunnhildr, who was called konungamóðir (Mother of Kings), daughter of Æzurr toti (Teat) or lafskeggr (Wag-beard) from Hálogaland in the north' (almost certainly untrue).

Eric Bloodaxe the Viking: 'I Shall Die Laughing'

King Eirik was a big, strong man and a bold warrior, handsome in appearance, persuadable, harsh in temperament, greedy for money, improvident, blessed with victory, and a great warrior. His wife Gunnhildr was a fine-looking and highborn woman, not tall, with a profound mind, talkative and of grim temper, not steadfast in friendship, rather eager for money and lands. They had several children, who were named thus: Gamli, Guäbormr, Haraldr, Erlingr, Ragnfrøär, Sigurär slefa (Slobber). Ragnhild was their daughter, who was married in Orkney [more of her later].

This period was short, yet it seemed quite long enough to the people, for they considered that the king was persuadable, and the queen malicious. That was manifested in the fact that Eiríkr caused to be killed Bj‡rn kaupmaär, Óláfr digrbeinn and others of his brothers. Many people said that he must want to get rid of his brothers and have sole control of the kingdom and so raise up his sons to power after his day, and because of that he grew unpopular with all the population.[2]

Historia Norwegiae tells a similar tale:

The eldest of these [sons of Harald Fairhair], Eirik Bloodaxe, obtained the kingdom after his father and took a wife from Denmark, Gunnhild, cruel and double-dyed in wickedness, daughter of the Danish king, Gorm the Stupid, and his very clever wife, Tyra. By this Gunnhild he got six sons, namely Harald Gråfell, next Gamle, third Sigurd Ljome, fourth Gunnrød, fifth Erling and sixth Gorm.

When Eirik had reigned for a year and had suited no one owing to his wife's overweening arrogance, on the advice of the Norwegian magnates he was divested of the realm by his brother Håkon, the foster-son of the English king, Æthelstan, and departed as a refugee to England. There he was well received by his brother's foster-father and was cleansed at the baptismal font; he was appointed earl, commanding the whole of Northumbria, and was most acceptable to all, that is until his villainous wife, Gunnhild, appeared on the scene. As the Northumbrians could not brook her pernicious fury, they straight away flung off the intolerable yoke imposed by this pair. And while Eirik was pursuing a viking expedition in Spanish territory, he suffered an armed attack and met his end; Gunnhild however returned with her sons to her brother Harald, the Danish king.*

Snorri, we know, is not entirely reliable, yet Egil's Saga does contain a mass of detail about Eirik which certainly has a ring of authenticity about it. He and Egil were contemporaries and their relationship, if largely antagonistic, seems very real. Egil first mentions Eirik when he speaks of King Harald Fairhair's declining years: 'Eirik, Harald's son, who was nicknamed Bloodaxe, was still young then. He was being fostered by Thorir the Hersir. The king loved Eirik most of all his sons.'[3]

Egil's brother Thorolf, after a successful cruise, had scooped up a handy vessel with 12 or 13 oars, graceful, elegant and lovely to behold. They had called in to see Thorir and couldn't help noticing how fondly the young Eirik was admiring their prize. Thorolf's companion Bjorn points out it could be a plan to give the craft to the prince to put themselves in the old king's good books. Eirik was very pleased with the gesture: 'You will not think the pledge of my friendship much of a reward for it, but that is likely to be worth more, the longer I live'[4]. True to his word, Eirik does speak up for Thorolf when he confronts King Harald over his supposed animosity towards Thorolf.

Relations with the sons of Skallagrim become soured at a later feast where both Eirik and Gunnhild are present. This took place on Atloy Island where the king had a large estate. Egil was also there in the company of Olvir, Thorir's foreman and general enforcer. The farm manager was a man named Bard who managed the land on King Eirik's behalf. Olvir and his crew, including Egil, were summoned to dine in the king and queen's presence. So far so good, but Bard kept plying his guests with drink so that Olvir and most of his sailors quickly became drunk; but Not Egil, whose capacity was legendary, and he sank every draught Bard pressed on him.

---

* The chroniclers really don't like Gunnhild, Eirik receives a get out of gaol card as his misdeeds can all be squarely blamed on his viper of a consort, see *Historia Norwegiae*. p. 83.

We don't know the cause of this swelling animosity, but Bard connived with Gunnhild to add poison to the next round, but Egil was too quick for them and smashed the horn before trying to extricate Olvir, who was practically unconscious by this point. Bard was stupid enough not to let it go, he pushed his luck that bit too far and Egil stabbed him to death. This was unfortunate for Bard but a mortal insult to King Eirik, who immediately sent out a search party to look for the big fellow.

Egil got clear but not until after he had killed another couple of the King's men. Although Thorir did persuade Eirik to accept compensation for his losses, the blood spilt poisoned the well and there could be no friendship between the two men, though Snorri points the finger of blame clearly at Queen Gunnhild. Egil, the Icelander, is no longer welcome in Norway. Thorir the Hersir perhaps rather nervously goes to see his former royal protégé when Egil stays with him. The king is quite calm, 'although things would have been different if someone else had taken Egil in'[5]. Gunnhild, predictably, isn't happy.

It doesn't get any better. Some years later Egil, forever contentious, becomes embroiled in a property feud. Eirik, as king, is asked to adjudicate and appears in the saga to be quite reasonable in his approach, despite his dislike of Egil. Once more, Gunnhild pours fresh poison into her husband's ear: 'How peculiar of you, King, to let this big man Egil run circles around you. would you even raise an objection if he claimed the throne out of your hands?' She hasn't finished, declaiming how intolerable any favour shown towards the Icelander would be. Eirik does rather appear as the much put upon husband and Gunnhild's intervention leads to chaos. Egil, for whom diplomacy was never a priority, simply challenges the other side to a fight.

Eirik, whose patience, so far exemplary, is beginning to wear thin, not helped by his wife's open meddling, warns Egil off. If he's than keen for a fight Eirik will ensure he gets one. At the end of the day there's no fighting but Egil, ushered away by his own faction before he drops them in even further, is dragged off still spitting loud defiance.

Reaching their ships, the disappointed litigants clear off as fast as their oars will move them. Just as well. The king, now thoroughly enraged by Egil and humiliated by his wife, sets off after them, vowing he'll stop Egil's fractious tongue for good. The pace of the hunt quickens as the king races to cut his prey off. A confused set of naval actions follows. Egil hurls a spear, killing Eirik's helmsman, Ketil the Slayer (now the slain), but the king catches a group of the big man's deckhands and puts them all to the sword. Despite the heat of the chase, Egil gets clear. Relations with the king have gone from bad to worse. They're not destined to improve.

When King Harald finally dies, Eirik scoops the pot. All he must do is hang on to it. The inhabitants of Vik preferred the new king's brother Olaf, whilst those of Trondheim preferred another sibling, Sigurd. Eirik settles his account with both in battle near Tonsberg. These momentous events took place during the same summer as Egil and his adversary Berg-Onund fell out at the *Gulathing*. Despite the threat from his brothers, Eirik hadn't forgotten Egil, who was now formally outlawed.

Fearing Egil would attempt to settle his score with Berg-Onund, the king left him extra men with one of his foster sons Frodi, accompanied by Eirik and Gunnhild's young son Rognvald, 'a promising and attractive lad'. Egil was indeed resolved to deal with Berg-Onund and, after adopting a cunning ruse, surprised his enemy. The pair duelled, an exchange of throwing spears was followed up with swords and Egil ran Berg through. Frodi and another man called Hadd rushed to Berg's aid, only to perish on Egil's blade.

In time-honoured fashion, Egil and his crew proceeded to pillage Berg's settlement and relieve the deceased of any stock and valuables they could find. En route by ship to their target, Egil's craft was blindly intercepted by Prince Rognvald's small boat, only six oars per side. Egil rammed and boarded, killing the entire complement. The boy wasn't spared. Afterwards Egil had his men set up a totem – 'here I set up this scorn pole and turn its scorn upon King Eirik and Queen Gunnhild.'[6] Snorri doesn't tell us what the king and queen made of this or the callous murder of their son. If Gunnhild had hated Egil beforehand, this must now have turned to the deepest and bitterest loathing. And Gunnhild knew how to bear a grudge.

Eirik meanwhile had even more pressing concerns. Hakon The Good, his other half-brother who had been fostered by

Athelstan of England, returned with an army and was able to drum up significant support in Norway, establishing himself as king in the Trondelag. A showdown looked set for next spring, but the Norwegians were deserting Eirik, tired of his perceived tyranny, and he was obliged to take to his heels along with Gunnhild and their surviving children. Eirik sailed away from Norway and would never go back. His story moves across the North Sea to the Kingdom of York. He probably wasn't much missed, certainly not by Egil.

Once again, we get a fine description of Hakon from the author of *Fagrskinna*:

> FrHákon inn góäi (the Good) ... was like his father in good looks, stronger and bigger than his forefathers had been. Þórálfr Skólmsson was considered as strong a man as Hákon, but no third was their match in strength. Hákon was of gentle temperament, thoughtful of wise counsel, with a good memory, cheerful, sincere, wise, with more courtly accomplishments than other men in all feats of arms, in terms of strength and skill.
>
> His foster father the king loved him more than anyone else, and so did all people to whom his name was known. Aäalsteinn gave him a sword with a hilt of gold, and Hákon tested it severely by hewing into a millstone with it, and it pierced all the way to the centre hole. After that it was called Kvernbítr (Quernbiter). That sword Hákon carried to his dying day.[7]

He was certainly bad news for his half-brother. Eirik's travails were about to begin. Once again, *Fagrskinna* offers more details:

> One year after King Harald had died his passing became known west in England, and that same summer, on the advice of his foster-father Aäalsteinn, Hákon went to Norway. Bad weather overtook them at sea, and the troop was separated; some perished, but others got to Norway, and those who landed closest to where King Eirík was went to see him and told him that his brother Hákon must have been lost at sea. This story the king laid before Gunnhild, and said it had

turned out well, so that he had no need to fear Hákon as a threat to his kingdom. She answered in this way: the prince has reached Firäir. Because of her magic arts she knew that Hákon was alive and had brought his ship safe to Norway.

He behaved wisely and cleverly, made no demands, made friends with everyone, got on good terms with his counsellors, remembered old men with wise counsels, shared gifts among laymen and young people, trained alongside them in sports and amusements, displayed his attainments amongst assembled people in many ways. For these reasons every man praised him; reports sprang up about him which flew into everyone's house.

After that all longed for him, but they feared the tyranny and lawlessness which had set in among the inhabitants of the land, and they all blamed Gunnhildr; there was no one who argued against her being responsible for that. That winter passed without Hákon having the title of king, but in the summer the bonder put great pressure on Eiríkr's rule, and increased Hákon's power, and accepted Hákon as king over them; he was nearly twenty years old when he came into the country. After that the bonder turned against Eirik and were no longer willing to endure Gunnhild's wickedness.[8]

According to this author, Eirik goes straight to Athelstan upon his arrival in England and negotiates his tenure in Northumbria. This is plainly wrong as Athelstan was dead by the time Eirik is likely to have arrived, so a period of a dozen years is unaccounted for. *Fagrskinna* alleges that Eirik went raiding around the costs of Britain after he is made king of Northumbria and finally comes unstuck during one of these expeditions. I think we can discount this as well, Eirik's twin tenures as king of York were too brief and too fraught to have left much time for such adventures – though these would certainly not have been out of character.

Heimskringla states otherwise: 'He [Eirik] sailed first to Orkney and took many people with him from that country; and then went south towards England, plundering in Scotland and in the north parts of England, wherever he could land.'[9] Did Eirik spend those intervening years in Orkney, or was he to all intents and purposes a peripatetic pirate?

Eric Bloodaxe the Viking: 'I Shall Die Laughing'

Orkneyinga Saga paints another and quite complex picture. For once, Eirik wasn't the problem. It was rather two of his brothers/half-brothers: 'When they grew up the sons of Horald Finehair turned out to be very arrogant and caused a lot of trouble in Norway, bullying the King's earls, killing some of them and driving others from their estates. Halfdan Long-Leg (who we encountered previously?) and Gudrod Gleam, King Harald's sons by Snaefrid, attacked Earl Rognvald of More, killed him and assumed his authority.'[10]

Now Rognvald of More had been a loyal supporter of King Harald who raged against his sons' savagery and sent a naval squadron to deal with them. Halfdan took to his own ship and fled, but Gudrod stayed to face the music. Harald paid the blood-price for the murder of Earl Rognvald and married his daughter, Alof the Fecund, to Thorir, the dead man's elder son and handed him the earldom. Halfdan Long-Leg wasn't done and returned to Orkney, sparking a civil war. Jarl Einar (Turf-Einar, youngest of Rognvald's sons), proved a very determined foe and eventually defeated Halfdan at sea. The incomer was captured in the wrack of the fight and made to endure the horror of Blood Eagle[11]. Though the truth of what Blood Eagle really was is impossible to establish, he never re-offended!

Halfdan's surviving siblings in Norway were enraged and swore vengeance, but the old king saw that nothing came of it. Harald himself later mounted an expedition to Orkney and chased Einar across to Caithness. A deal was brokered, Einar bought his way out of royal disfavour. Once re-established as earl, Einar enjoyed a long and peaceful tenure, achieving the notable distinction of living into old age and dying in his bed.

Orkneyinga Saga never claims that Eirik ruled in Orkney, and it is highly unlikely that he ever did, but Snorri credits Eirik with extensive raids against Scotland and Northumbria. He also claims that it was Athelstan who made overtures, hoping to end the enmity between Eirik and his foster-son Hakon. If Athelstan did so before his death in 939 then this could just fit. It may be, and this is pure speculation, that Eirik continued his raiding career to fill his war chest. Cash was an essential component of would-be kingship. So, when the opportunity finally crystallized, he was ready.

Snorri suggests that Eirik did accept the governance of Northumbria during Athelstan's lifetime, 'but as he had little land

'Never Greater Slaughter'

and a large following, he ran short of money, which is why he spent the summer plundering, while staying in his kingdom over winter'. This jars with our current understanding that Oswulf I (934–954), son of Eadwulf I, was ruling Bernicia at this time while Olaf Guthfrithson held on, if very precariously, to York. None of this seems likely. We may dare to surmise that Eirik, for a dozen years after his retreat from Norway, lived as a Viking freebooter in the old style, possibly based on Orkney. After all, his father had exercised overlordship of the place. If so, it further seems he played no part in his half-brother's mayhem. This doesn't mean negotiations may not have taken place. As with so much of Eirik's career we're left in the realm of heroic assumptions.

According to Snorri, Eirik comes unstuck during Athelstan's brother and successor King Edmund's reign. Edmund was 'less friendly towards the Norwegians, not liking King Eirik's rule over Northumbria'.[12] Then the Icelander veers significantly off-track. He states that Eirik, after Edmund's succession, sails his squadron northwards to Orkney where he is joined by two local notables Earls Arnkel and Erlend, sons of Turf-Einar (Halfdan Long-Leg's nemesis). The trio, having collected more ships in the Hebrides, then go on an extended raiding spree to Ireland, Strathclyde and finally to England (Snorri doesn't say where in England).

Here, their sport is interrupted by Olaf (Guthfrithson?) who engages Eirik's raiders in a pitched battle inland. The raiders put up a tremendous fight but are overcome by sheer numbers. This is where, according to Snorri, Eirik is killed along with 'six other kings, one called Guthorm... Earls Arnkel and Erlend died too.'[13] Is this some rather twisted account of the fight at Stainmore? Again, it's not possible to say but the details of losses suggest some form of historical basis (see chapter nine).

The skald goes on to say that with Eirik dead, Queen Gunnhild and her sons decamped to Orkney, now ruled by the wonderfully named Earl Thorfinn Skull-Splitter. He says 'Queen Gunnhild's sons took over power in the islands and used them as their base in winter, spending the summers on Viking expeditions.'[14] Same family business, just a new management generation, but this does suggest some form of prior connection. Once Gunnhild hears of war between King Harald of Denmark and her half-brother-in-law Hakon of Norway, she glimpses an opportunity and heads across the North Sea, but not until she's seen her daughter Ragnhild safely married off to Thorfinn's son Arnfinn. We must really feel sorry for the groom.*

To understand just what was meant by this Norse Kingdom of York we have to backtrack over 70 years and follow in the footsteps of Ivar the Boneless.

When Kev Cockayne greets you at Jorvik in York's bustling, very contemporary Coppergate, he's wearing fine maille and we're impressed by him, by Jorvik and by the armour. Most of the crew are in period clothing – we're Viking anoraks so this makes us happy. At the risk of being seen plugging a specific site, Jorvik is unique, it offers a fully immersive 360-degree tour through the heart of the Viking city, directly beneath its 21st-century successor, proof that the past never really goes away, it just gets built over.

We talk of Eirik and the York he knew or might have known (see next chapter), a Jorvik that was a British Iron Age township, major Roman garrison centre and an Anglo-Saxon capital. Eirik is always the ghost at his own table, but the superb gallery hosts a remarkable collection of Viking Age artefacts and the remains of those who lived there[15].

Even at this date there was a marked north/south divide. Later medieval chroniclers of the fifteenth century would shudder at the mention of these *boreales bobinantes* (literally 'roaring northerners') whose incursions into the more 'civilised' south were likened to barbarian invasions: 'The whole speech of the Northumbrians, especially that of the men of York, grates so harshly upon the ear that it is completely unintelligible to us

---

* Ragnhild proved to be very much a chip off the old block. She soon tired of Arnfin, did away with him (method unspecified) and married his brother Havard the Fecund, who inherited the title. Not for that long, Ragnhild was soon winning over the new earl's nephew Einar Buttered-Bread. Einar was flustered, then flattered and soon persuaded. Husband number two had to go. At Havard's Field, the new beau took on and killed his uncle. Much good it did him, he became hated and Ragnhild denied any complicity, sending for another nephew, Einar Hard-Mouth. He was a bit tougher to persuade but did attack and kill the other Einar. She didn't marry him though, preferring another of her first husband's surviving brothers, Ljot. Einar Hard-Mouth was angered by Ragnhild's conniving but his attempt at insurrection ended in defeat and death. I'm sure Ragnhild's father would have been proud of her. (*Orkneyinga Saga*, pp. 33–35.)

southerners. The reason for this is their proximity to barbaric tribes and their distance from the kings of the land who, whether English as once or Norman as now, are known to stay more often in the south than the north.'[16]

York was the capital of Northumbria, a kingdom first troubled by Viking raids after 793, during a century lightened culturally by 'The Golden Age' but darkened by internecine strife, palace intrigue compounded by waning political influence, together with the rise of competing states such as Mercia and Wessex. Across the North Sea another threat was looming, far more potent than any previous menace.

Those Sons of Ragnar Lodbrok were about to pounce. We don't know if Ragnar existed, perhaps he did, he certainly should have done and whether Ivar the Boneless was indeed his son or merely one who adopted a handy and glorious lineage we can't say. Did King Aella hurl Ragnar to his death in a pit of vipers thus creating a perfect casus belli, a 'just war' for his sons to pursue, or was this all an accretion of legend or clever ninth-century spin? What happened next was very real and would irrevocably shape the history of these islands. Ivar would begin a tale that Eirik would complete.

'And this same year came a great host to England and took winter quarters in East Anglia, and there they were provided with horses, and they made peace with them,' so cautions the Anglo-Saxon Chronicle. This sounds like an offer the Anglians could not refuse – give us horses, fodder and food and we won't burn your house down, not this time. This heathen army's target wasn't East Anglia but Northumbria, and the Vikings were clearly acting on good intelligence:

> In this year [867] the host went from East Anglia over the Humber to York in Northumbria; and there was a great dissension of the people amongst themselves; and they had repudiated their king Osberht and accepted Aella, a king not of royal birth; and it was late in the year when they set about making war against the host, nevertheless they gathered great levies and went to attack the host at York and stormed the city [21 March 867] and some of them got inside; and immense slaughter was made of the Northumbrians there,

some inside, some outside, and both the kings were slain and the remnant made peace with the host.[17]

Simeon of Durham confirms the magnitude of this catastrophe:

> In those days, the nation of the Northumbrians had violently expelled from the kingdom the rightful king of their nation, Osbryht by name, and had placed at the head of the kingdom a certain tyrant, named Alla [Aella]. When the pagans came upon the kingdom, the dissension was allayed by divine counsel and the aid of the nobles. King Osbryht and Alla, having united their forces and formed an army, came to the city of York; on their approach the multitude of the shipmen immediately took flight. The Christians, perceiving their flight and terror, found that they themselves were the stronger party. They fought upon each side with much ferocity, and both kings fell. The rest who escaped made peace with the Danes.[18]

Aella apparently did not die in the fighting. He might have wished he had, but there is the suggestion in the *Saga of Ragnar's Sons* that Ivar captured the surviving kingly contender whom he and his siblings held responsible for the horrible (even if well-merited) death of their notorious father. Aella became a victim of the exquisitely vile ritual of the Blood Eagle. There is significant doubt about this whether it happened here or indeed if it every happened at all, there's no chronicle evidence, only poetic, and that very limited.

Assuming it did, then the victim was forced to lie prone, face down whilst his back was incised, ribs exposed and then these broken and drawn back so the lungs ('wings') could be pulled free of the shattered ribcage and laid out in a ghastly parody of flight. To finish the show, he could then be flung from a high place to see if he could indeed fly. Aella died[19].

Whatever Aella's actual fate, his death and that of his fellow ruler marked a watershed in the history of Northumbria and indeed of England. York was now a Norse kingdom. This would endure till Eirik met his mysterious and bloody demise at Stainmore nearly 90 years after. Ivar's successful invasion would be the prologue to Eirik's entrance. Ivar, presumably to secure some element of legitimacy, placed a puppet called Egbert on the throne. This maintained a façade of legitimacy as the Northmen tightened their grip and pondered fresh targets. Ivar's ambitions obviously extended far beyond Northumbria's borders.

There was policy in this. We can debate the actual size of this Viking Great Army, much ink and professorial ping pong has been devoted to this; some say the force could be numbered in hundreds, others in thousands. Dawn Hadley and Julian Richards have looked thoroughly and analytically at this, considering known camps such as Repton and Torksey[20]. Their conclusions favour the idea of a rather larger force, certainly one comprised of several thousand fighting men.

Viking Age Northumbria was really focused, in geographical terms, on the ancient sub-kingdom of Deira, leaving Bernicia to local satraps whose prime functions were to pay taxes and keep an eye on their Scottish neighbours. York was a forward base for fresh conquests. A year after having taken Northumbria, the Army turned its predatory attentions towards Mercia, capturing the major fortress of Nottingham. Mercians and the men of Wessex, old hatreds forgot, laid siege to the place but couldn't break in or starve the invaders out. By 869, the Army was recuperating and rebuilding its energies at York.

The next year, 870, they turned on East Anglia, whose earlier appeasement now came back to haunt them. King Edmund was defeated and martyred. With the soon to be saintly Edmund's kingdom now in the bag, it became Wessex's turn. This 'Last Kingdom' proved a rather tougher nut and Bagsecg, one of the Army's generals, died at Ashdown, a battle fought early in January 871:

> ... King Ethelred and Alfred his brother fought against the entire host at Ashdown; and they were in two divisions; in the one were Bagsecg and Halfdan, the heathen kings, and in the other were the jarls. And then fought the king Ethelred against the division of the kings, and there the king Bagsecg was slain and Alfred, his brother, against the division of the jarls, and there Jarl Sidroc the Old was slain and Jarl Sidroc the Young and Jarl Osbern and Jarl Freena and Jarl Harald, and both the hosts were put to flight and there were many thousands of dead.[21]

Eric Bloodaxe the Viking: 'I Shall Die Laughing'

Despite such a huge victory, King Ethelred with his brother Alfred – to be known as 'The Great' – remained hard-pressed, as the Army seemed to have no difficulties in recruiting new men from Scandinavia. When Ethelred died, Alfred succeeded his brother, and by the end of the year he was grateful to agree to a truce. This bought him breathing space, for the Viking Army spent most of the year 872 consolidating its previous gains in Mercia. Within a space of two years, luckless King Burhred was harried into exile and left skulking in Rome. Ceowulf, a more pliant quisling, was set up in his place. All was not quiet on the northern front as, also in 872, the Northumbrians expelled the puppet Egbert and Archbishop Wulfhere of York, seemingly seen as another collaborator, but the invaders soon reasserted their authority.

In 875, the Army split peaceably, with Halfdan and a sizeable contingent returning north. He next cemented his grip on the old rump of Bernicia and generally made his presence painfully known north of the border, reminding Strathclyde Britons, Picts and Scots who was in charge of the marches now: 'In this year went the host from Repton, and Halfdan went with a part of the host into Northumbria and took winter quarters on the River Tyne; and the host overran that land, and made frequent raids against the Picts and against the Strathclyde Britons.'[22]

This shows policy on two levels: firstly, he was stamping his will upon the whole Kingdom of Northumbria while at the same time winning hearts and minds. Attacking the Scots et al would help boost his popularity and promote acceptance by the old Saxon aristocracy. Making Northumbria both secure and strong played well to a local audience who might, in time, forget they were the conquered. Nonetheless, it seems to be this episode which prompted the further migration of St Cuthbert's remains, accompanied by St Oswald's head, which would eventually lead the monks to Durham via Chester le Street.

Simeon of Durham tells us that Halfdan used Tynemouth as his logistical base. This makes good sense as the promontory site offers just the type of easily defensible enclosure the Vikings favoured. *ASC* informs us, quite cryptically, 'And in this year Halfdan shared out the lands of Northumbria and they were engaged in ploughing and in making a living for themselves.'[23] This note, brief as it is, is momentous, for now the Norsemen were acquiring or appropriating land and settling down as farmers. We can surmise that Halfdan parcelled out the estates of the many local gentry killed at York as payment to his own warriors. But he's clearly signalling that he didn't come just for the loot but to settle. Northumbria is now a Norse state.

This was, of itself, a fundamental change. Nicholas Higham certainly thinks so[24]. He also asserts that Halfdan divided his territory into three 'Ridings' as an administrative measure, aimed at ensuring he had a ready levy of warriors at hand. This then was not a cultural invasion like later settlers emigrating to the promised land of the New World. Halfdan's paladins were mostly younger, land-hungry fighters, keen to win lands by the edge of the sword. A mass immigration of peasant classes, *bonder*, from their homeland wasn't needed. Peasants were already in plentiful supply, all they needed were new masters. It's probable these men sought spouses from amongst the local landowning classes, reinforcing their legitimacy and blending blood lines.

Halfdan might have guaranteed the existence of a Norse state, but it did him little good. In fact, he lasted barely a couple of years before being killed (it seems) in a tussle over dominion in Ireland (more on the Irish connection below), or possibly as the consequence of a botched raid in south-west England. As the powers of the Anglian kingdoms of Northumbria and Mercia crumbled beneath the Viking onslaught, Scottish kings used their growing influence to interfere in the affairs of northern England. Opportunists like Ivar, allied to a (possible) half-brother/cousin, Olaf of Dublin, who had grown rich through the slave trade, were always able to play off various sides at once.

Scotland's King Constantine had been trying and failing to bring Strathclyde under his control, but that great stubborn rock of Dumbarton laughed off any siege. Ivar has a proposition. He and Olaf will reduce the fortress, hand it to the King and take their fee in slaves. Ivar isn't called 'Boneless' if this means cunning as a snake for nothing because he has worked out the Rock's Achilles' heel. The Norse besiegers simply find and cut off the defenders' water supply. They are forced to surrender, and three thousand wretched Britons, cream of the crop only, find themselves on the market.

Halfdan's success, as well as being brief, was also personal. When he fell, the cohesion he had built crumbled. This vacuum allowed a distinctly Saxon entity centred on Bamburgh to re-emerge and assert itself as independent of Viking York. New petty princes, Ecgberht II and Eadwulf (d. 913), established links with English realms to the south. Halfdan's hegemony marks the high water mark of the independent Norse kingdom, which some time thereafter is finally forced onto the defensive. Cumberland was lost to the Strathclyde Britons, perhaps abetted by the rulers of Bernicia, who might have preferred British to Norse neighbours in the west.

By the closing decades of the ninth century, Northumbria as a cohesive state had ceased to exist, once again split into the two ancient provinces of Bernicia (Saxon) and Deira (Norse). By now, after wanderings in the ecclesiastic wilderness the community of Lindisfarne had established itself at Chester Le Street, (the old Roman fort of Conagium). The church held extensive landholdings and effectively formed a buffer between the two statelets. The community would eventually migrate to Durham and the County Palatine would coalesce. Prince Bishops of Durham would be significant players during the medieval period and three long centuries of Anglo-Scottish Wars.

From York, the Norsemen looked mainly south to their cousins in East Anglia and the eastern flank of partitioned Mercia, the Danelaw. They could also look to the north-west where their influence extended over much of what is now Lancashire. Even now, the old aggressive and opportunistic instinct of the Viking Great Army still flared when opportunity arose. These Northumbrian Vikings were very active participants in a blitz against the West Saxons which began in 893: 'In that year ... the Northumbrians and East Anglians had given oaths to King Alfred, and the east Angles six preliminary hostages, yet contrary to the pledge, as often as the other hosts [Viking marauders from the European mainland] sallied forth in full force, then went they either with them or alone on their own account.'[25]

The old glory days of easy pickings were long gone, and Alfred was by now a master of war. He positioned his own substantial forces between the two main invading forces and kept them apart. As the Norse split up to raid and harry, so the Saxons formed up to confront them. Alfred's garrisons were well manned, and he rotated levies from his *fyrd* to ensure he always maintained adequate forces in the field[26].

When the Norse decided to get out while they could, replete with spoils, Alfred's cavalry cut them up at Farnham and chased the survivors, minus their ill-gotten gains, clear back to their ships. Meanwhile, the York and east Anglian Norse – whose king ASC tells us had been wounded[27], boarded their own vessels, cruised south and then west, picking up another 40 sail and laid siege to one of the coastal forts guarding Devon.

Alfred riposted with his habitual gusto and marched his forces westwards, pausing at London to bolster his ranks. By now the leading Viking headman Haesten (or Hastein) had concentrated his forces within an earlier fort he had thrown up at Benfleet. Possibly while many of his warriors were engaged on separate forays, the West Saxons attacked and stormed the camp, capturing all the invaders' baggage and their families. Alfred, perspicacious and far-sighted, opted for conciliation, restoring Haesten's sons to him – one of whom on his conversion, Alfred adopted as his godson. A noble gesture, but the wily old Norseman was soon up to his old tricks, again based at Benfleet.

Northumbrian and East Anglian Vikings had joined forces with a second invasion force based in Essex. The combined army now sailed via the Thames to the Severn and headed upriver. This thrust didn't go unchallenged as several of Alfred's ealdormen mustered their available forces, stripped garrisons as need be and, reinforced by a Welsh contingent, blockaded the attackers at Burrington on the banks of the Severn. After weeks of leaguer, the Norsemen, facing starvation, launched a desperate sally and were badly cut up in the fight, a costly but palpable victory[28].

Despite these losses, surviving raiders got clear and back to Essex where they were yet again bolstered by Northumbrian and East Anglian elements. Next, they launched a well-directed tangential thrust at Chester, beating the Wessex men to the city gates. Much good it did them, Alfred knew that pressure, once exerted, had to be maintained. The Norsemen broke out of Chester and tried to establish a position in Wales but again threatened by hunger, had to retreat via Northumbria and East Anglia. By the time this series of campaigns ended, a full three years had elapsed and Alfred had seen the invaders off, though at quite considerable cost.

Plague and famine, war's old bedfellows, had also taken their toll. Still, the Northumbrians and their Anglian kinfolk weren't done, using their amphibious capabilities to harass Wessex to the extent that Alfred had to order the building of an English navy, and the potency of his new ships quickly became apparent. Throughout, the Northumbrians had used the Mersey crossings as a safe route away from pursuing Wessex levies, and this region would now form a frontier[29].

Even Alfred's death in 900 failed to open another window of opportunity. The plain fact was Alfred's own genius and the resilient defensive network he had established had halted the incoming tide. The Northumbrians had gained more recruits to their ranks from the hosts who had entered southern England, but Wessex was safe, and both sides needing a respite, they came to terms at Tiddingford in 906.

An entry in the Annals of Ulster for 902 records: 'The heathens were driven from Ireland, from the fortress of Ath Cliath (Dublin), by Mael Finnia son of Flannacan, with the men of Brega and by Cerball son of Muirican with the Laigin; and they abandoned a good number of their ships and escaped half dead after they had been wounded and broken.'[30] This was clearly a very bad day for the Norsemen in Ireland, and it would reverberate through England as well.

One of the survivors, a petty ruler named Ingimund, managed to inveigle a grant from formidable Queen Aethelflaed of Mercia (a daughter of Alfred), to settle in the Wirral region. Gratitude wasn't a noticeable Norse characteristic, and an Irish chronicler relates that the new face in town was soon stirring up trouble and casting envious glances at Chester. It seems likely that the Kings of York already had an administrative presence in this region, which lay on the margins of their extensive sphere of influence.

York may have already granted another escaper Ivar II (killed 904), haven here. Chester was recovered by Mercia three years later, but the deceased Ivar had been replaced by his brother Ragnald. This is supported by toponomy, several Norse place names appearing in the district[31]. These fresh immigrants made themselves useful in York's various fights against Strathclyde, the Scots and Bernicians. When King Eadwulf of Bamburgh died in 913, his demise triggered a Norse attack on the old Saxon rump. This apparent amity between the heirs of the Northern Army at York and the Norse expelled from Dublin marks a more cordial phase in a difficult relationship, hitherto far more fractious.*

We do know that Aethelflaed and her equally able brother, Alfred's son and successor Edward the Elder, forming a dynamic duo, had sought and obtained defensive alliances with the Celtic rulers farther north. They followed this up with a serious of punitive campaigns, pushing across the Mersey and obliging the men of York to accept the overlordship of Ethelred of Mercia (Aethelflaed's terminally ill consort). The Northumbrians struck back in 910 but were badly beaten at Tettenhall in the West Midlands, losing more than a few notables. From now on, York would be the attacked not the attacker.

Despite their summary ejection from Dublin, the new settlers demonstrated considerable vigour, pushing into what is now Cumbria and winning new lands – to the extent the Abbot of Heversham (in the Furness District), together with other dispossessed clergy, was obliged to seek sanctuary with St Cuthbert's community east of the Pennines. At sea, they defeated the Irish in 912 and saw off a hostile Norse squadron with their eyes on Man in the following year.** More Vikings out of Breton ports, who had been rebuffed in their attempts to raid Wessex, descended on Ireland and provided Ragnald with a timely injection of fresh muscle.

Emboldened and with larger numbers, Ragnald's cousin Sihtric instigated a successful bid to recover Dublin (917?). Then Ragnald

---

* Eirik would not rule in Dublin (perhaps) but the Norse presence in Ireland was of vital importance to the Kingdom of York. Raiding began there around 795, Rathin Island was the first place to be hit, then Inishmore, Sligo and Galway. Raiding picked up in tempo and frequency, Viking fleets overwintering along all the main rivers. By 841, their presence was widespread and all year round. A number of these *longphuirts* became fixed settlements: Dublin, Limerick, Waterford and Wexford. Monasteries were frequent targets and Norse war bands hired themselves out as mercenaries during the unceasing strife, which was already endemic. Such conflict sated a hunger for loot and slaves. Though Irish chroniclers not unsurprisingly painted these incomers as uncouth and rapacious heathens, modern research tends to paint a more nuanced picture.

** Man, with its prime strategic location straddling sea routes between Scandinavia and Ireland with easy access to both south-west Scotland and north-west England was a jewel to be coveted. According to the *Irish Annals*, they first made landfall there in 798 and within a generation had come to dominate the island. An abundance of Norse links survive today.

himself, accompanied by another cousin Gothfrith and with the bulk of the Breton Norse, wrested back control of Bernicia. This was a significant revival, but the Kings of York still couldn't hope to challenge the burgeoning power of Wessex.

Ragnald proved no friend to the followers of St Cuthbert, driving them off lands in Durham to reward his *hird*-men. Besides, he had more pressing problems. Aethelflaed, before her death in June 918, had reinforced her frontier *limes* along the Mersey – but her greatest triumph had been the successful storming of Derby, which unlocked the whole of that slice of the old Danelaw. Leicester's submission followed, but Mercia's own independence proved to be effectively over-reached when the heroine died. Her daughter held on for some months, but Edward of Wessex simply took over. The Norse at Nottingham were his next target, and it began to seem that York must be in his sights.

In the summer of 2018, it was 1,100 years since Vikings and Scots slogged it out at Corbridge. For a pleasant market village, Corbridge has an impressive history of mayhem: a later, better-known fight took place there during the Civil Wars in 1644. Of the earlier battle, we say 'Norsemen' and 'Gael', but it was never quite that clear-cut. Ragnald commanded a force of Norse and Irish from Dublin/Brittany, with probably a good few opportunists from Northumbria as well. The Scots, under King Constantine III, weren't all Scottish. Other Northumbrians, supporting Eadred of Bamburgh, anxious to recover control of Bernicia, were happy to join in.

As is usually the case with such conflicts, details of the fighting are sketchy, and we have no real idea of numbers involved. Probably, these weren't that great on either side, though we do know Ragnald divided his forces into four divisions or 'battles', three of which faced the Scots with a fourth deployed in ambush. Both sides would have adopted the classic shield wall formation, linden shields overlapping, a barrage of missiles ahead of the main clash. As ever, training, *esprit de corps* with effective command and control of sub-units were what counted. These Norsemen, former exiles on the make, were good at this, but their enemies had proved quick learners and Constantine's shield wall broke Ragnald's line. Fighting would have split up into a series of untidy brawls, sharp, savage murderous.

'Never Greater Slaughter'

It was only the timely intervention of his hidden reserve that stopped the rot for Ragnald. These men had been well hidden and led by Ragnald himself, they intended to deliver the *coup de grace*. It's axiomatic in war that no plan ever survives contact with reality. While the Scots were pushed back, they were not routed and got off in good order. It was effectively a draw. Ragnald did manage to grab and hang onto York, pre-empting any strike from Edward, whose northern charge was temporarily halted.

It was still an unequal fight. Ragnald had managed to close the gates, but the enemy was closing, and his resources were far, far greater. Edward threw up new burhs at Thelwall and Manchester to tighten the vice. Ragnald needed to take the fight to Edward and stir up smouldering embers within the Mercian Danelaw. His cousin Sihtric, clearly acting in concert, struck against English Mercia, thrusting across the Mersey Line, beating up enemy quarters but, perhaps surprisingly, failing to foment discord inside the former Danelaw. Ragnald accepted the inevitable, and in 920 he bent the knee to Wessex.

Both sides gained from the accord. For Ragnald the pressure was off, but he seems to have had to compensate the clergy for their earlier losses and Eadred of Bamburgh recovered the keys to his castle, denied since Ragnald's Pyrrhic victory at Corbridge. Edward, too, needed a respite, to consolidate his gains and tighten his grip on Mercia. Ragnald was probably also forced to give up Southern Lancashire, giving the King of Wessex control of the Ribble estuary[32]. It wasn't Ragnald's problem for long, as he died in 921 and cousin Sihtric immediately filled the vacancy.

Edward died three years later, to be succeeded by his son Athelstan. Sihtric took advantage of the hiatus to stir up resistance from within the Northern Danelaw[33]. Any hopes of a Norse revival were short-lived and, by 926, Sihtric had bent the knee. Consideration was an arranged marriage to King Athelstan's sister, a fully Christian ceremony, celebrated at Tamworth. Amity was very brief, for the very next year Sihtric repudiated both his wife and her faith. Luck wasn't with him, he died, and Athelstan marched in through the open gates.

Athelstan, as noted, brilliant and aggressive, clearly perceived York as ripe for plucking. The death of Sihtric of York in 927 gave Wessex the opportunity to intervene and Athelstan ruthlessly drove out the Norse pretender Olaf Guthfrithson, who fled to his compatriots established or reestablished in Ireland, usually not necessarily friends of York Vikings. With hindsight, this grab and hold seems rather bland and straightforward, but, as Higham points out, it 'disguises a usurpation more blatant even than that perpetrated by Edward the Elder in Mercia'.[34]

This is correct, as we only really get a view of this through southern chroniclers: 'In this year King Athelstan drove out King Guthfrith and Archbishop Wulfhelm went to Rome.'[35] Edward at least had a very clear blood relationship through his sister Aethelflaed, while Athelstan had no link to Sihtric other than his brief stint as a brother-in-law! For Athelstan, this was a neat and bloodless coup. He had completed his father and grandfather's lives' work at a single stroke. This doesn't mean the northerners were happy about it, very far from it, and this boiling resentment would prove to be Eirik's cue.

The Saxon King wasn't done. He commanded a summit at Eamont Bridge in Cumbria where Constantine, King Hywel Dda of Duheubarth, Eadred of Bamburgh and Owen I of Strathclyde all bent the knee. Athelstan was Master of Britain, Bede's old vision of an *England* now a reality, if by no means a secure one. Obviously, Athelstan was aware his new northern subjects were far from content, and he took steps to buy their loyalty. He showered endowments on the Minsters at Beverley, York and Chester-Le-Street, boosting Christ's presence in a kingdom with an innately hostile pagan heritage. He bought more acres in Lancashire, gave these to the Church of York and kept the mint there going – turning out coins that proclaimed the king's commitment to Christ. Faith is ever a remarkably effective tool of statecraft.

With the north east of England apparently secure, in 934 Athelstan conducted a *chevauchée* through Scotland, a show of strength. Quite why such drastic action was needed isn't clear. Possibly, as John of Worcester asserts, Constantine might have been stirring trouble, chafing under various onerous terms of the 927 accord[36]. The invasion force, supported by a naval squadron, pushed up as far as Caithness but never fought a battle. Constantine was too clever for that, but he was left smarting.

Olaf Guthfrithson stepped in with a proposal, sniffing the heady scent of stirring resentment. He began to forge a coalition of the disaffected, beginning with Constantine (who may have been his father-in-law), then drawing in Owen of Strathclyde. This was never a natural set of alliances; these men were all frequently at odds with each other, but Olaf was able to use the threat of English domination as cement to bind his allies and bend them to a common strategy.

If as we believe Olaf sailed from Dublin in August 937, then there seems a broad consensus that the decisive Battle of Brunanburh was fought during autumn, probably in October. The modern-day fight is over where the clash did in fact occur. There is an eastern and a western school, both equally convinced and assiduous in their scholarship. My own instinct for what it's worth is that the easterners, as trumpeted back in 1950 by Colonel Burne and reinforced today by Professor Wood, are right, but what we do know is that Athelstan won a major victory – after a very long, and costly struggle.

'In this year King Athelstan, lord of warriors / Ring-giver of men, with his brother prince Edmund / won undying glory with the edges of swords / in warfare around Brunanburh / with their hammered blades, the sons of Edward / clove the shield-wall and hacked the linden bucklers / as was instinctive in them from their ancestry / to defend their land, their treasures and their homes / in frequent battle against each enemy / the foemen were laid low: the Scots / and the host from the ships fell doomed. The field / grew dark with the blood of men.'[37]

What all commentators do agree upon is that the slaughter was prodigious and the pursuit merciless. Olaf and his survivors from Dublin slunk back in their ships, Constantine rushed back to Scotland, his son dead, a broken man. Owen's fate is not recorded. The Annals of Ulster tell us that five kings and seven jarls from Olaf's contingent never left the field. Athelstan, too, sustained significant casualties including two of his cousins and leading men Aelfwine and Aethelwine. It was truly a day for the bards to sing of and they did. 'On long biers were borne men drenched in blood.' (Y *Goddodin* verse xv.)

Athelstan's victory appeared to be complete, his foes trampled in the dust, his dream of a unified realm secure. But this was only temporary. On his death two years later, his sceptre slipped and an independent Kingdom of York re-emerged for a final envoi.

Eric Bloodaxe the Viking: 'I Shall Die Laughing'

Enter Eirik Bloodaxe. The enduring pretender waiting in the wings, probably already an anachronism, the last prop of a collapsing structure. The advance of Alfred's successors had doomed the independent kingdom of York. Alfred's halting of the Viking Great Army began a slow reversal and recovery. The fierce energy of Ivar and his successors began to fade and the English resistance became a recovery and then an expansion. Bede had dreamt of an England and the Norse attack, which might initially have been seen as the end of any such dream, had in fact lit the fuse which detonates its realisation.

Seven

A BAD COUNTRY FOR OLD GODS

They were always landing in those days, or being driven back to their ships, and they always brought their Gods with them. England is a bad country for Gods.

> Rudyard Kipling:
> *Puck of Pook's Hill* (1906)

Eirik must have liked Thor, if Odin's son failed to solve a problem it was because he'd not hit it hard enough, so a mite more brute force was needed. Thor patrols the margins; he keeps an eye out for opportunistic giants and whacks them with Mjollnir, his almighty sledgehammer. If none appear to chance their arm, he will mount a pre-emptive strike into their homeland Jotunheimar and find oversize skulls to break, he doesn't ever discriminate, he'll brain men and women with impartiality. He's huge and fierce but doesn't seem all that bright.

Happily, the giants are even thicker. One day starts badly for Thor when the giant Prymr steals Mjollnir. Thor has to bargain for its return and only the hand in marriage of the goddess Freyja will suffice. She won't cooperate though, so Thor has to investigate his feminine side and dress up pretending to be her. He takes slippery Loki along to do the talking. Prymr isn't altogether sure, but he goes along with the intended nuptials notwithstanding his bride's bulging biceps and capacity for conspicuous consumption. Stupidly tThe oversize oaf produces Mjollnir to formalise the wedding alliance, so his bride-to-be promptly seizes back his stolen property and brains Prymr. Consider that a divorce.

Egil and Eirik were never destined to be friends. Killing the king's men and then his son weren't tactics calculated to endear. The incipient blood feud was forestalled by Eirik's defeat and expulsion from Norway at the hands of his half-brother Hakon the Good, backed by King Athelstan, his foster father and certainly not one to miss an opportunity to shape events across the water. Neutralising any likely threat from Norway was little short of a masterstroke.

Arinbjorn the Hersir was one of Eirik's closest friends and foster brother, as well as foster father to the king's offspring. Eirik had rewarded his loyalty with extensive lands and he fled with Eirik to the relative sanctuary of Orkney. We've mentioned the exiled king's adventures there and the bequest of his daughter Ragnhild, more of a curse than a blessing. Arinbjorn was a lifelong friend of Egil, though so far there'd been no test of loyalty. That was about to arise.

Next, Egil informs us[1] Eirik raids in Scotland and then continues to strike at England's shores. Athelstan, no doubt thoroughly alarmed by the presence of such a rearing cobra on his borders, 'gathered a great force and went to face Eirik. When they met, an agreement was settled whereby King Athelstan would appoint Eirik to rule Northumbria and defend his kingdom from the Scots and Irish. King Athelstan had made Scotland a tributary after the death of King Olaf, but the people there were invariably disloyal to him. King Eirik generally stayed in York.'[2]

Now we run into chronological difficulties here as the accepted view is Eirik only arrives in England after Athelstan's death when his brother Edmund in on the throne – these problems are more fully addressed in chapter ten. There is also the thorny question, impossible to resolve, whether Eirik of York is even the same man as Eirik Bloodaxe. Meanwhile, Queen Gunnhild hasn't forgotten Egil, who murdered her son. She had 'a magic rite performed to curse Egil from ever finding peace in Iceland until she had seen him'.[3]

Due to a maritime embargo, presumably imposed by Hakon, ships weren't sailing between Norway and Iceland. Egil was getting bored and falling into a depression, as he usually did when there was no action to be had. Eventually, he fits out a ship for his late summer cruise. He avoids Orkney, still under the illusion Eirik is based there, but runs into heavy weather off the northern coast of England. His ship with its crew of 30 is driven before the wind, harried by the storm until they make a run for land off the Humber Estuary.

Their ship grounds in the shallows and all hands are saved, but the relentless wind and tide crushes the stricken vessel into matchwood. Egil is now a Viking without a ship. Bad news and good news. Locals tell him that Eirik is in fact now King of York, rather too close for comfort, but that Arinbjorn is living in the city and attending the king's court. As Arinbjorn was a friend to both, this held out the promise, however slim, of a useful ally.

His options at this stage were limited. He could make a run for it but how and where to? His wasn't the kind of face that could blend in. Better to brazen it out. Drawing his cloak over his helmet, Egil rode into the lion's den, *toujours l'audace*. He did have an ally in Arinbjorn, so, asking directions, made for his friend's house. Arinbjorn's servant informed his master, then at table, 'there's a man outside, huge as a troll.'[4] The host would not have been overjoyed to see his old friend pitch up suddenly in York. Trouble invariably followed Egil as day follows night. The interview takes place outside and Arinbjorn bluntly asks Egil why he's here.

This probably wasn't the end to his evening the *Hersir* had anticipated, but on hearing the tale of Egil's misfortune sets out straightaway to conduct his unexpected guest into the king's presence, his whole company armed. Arinbjorn knew only too well what a restless, volatile and wholly unpredictable dynamic drove both men, and he was now in No-Man's-Land. Friends can be as dangerous as enemies.

Needless to say, Arinbjorn goes in first. Eirik is also at table. Caught between two such dangerous tides, Arinbjorn must use honeyed words: 'I have brought someone here who has travelled a long way to visit you and wants to make a reconciliation with you. It is a great honour for you, my Lord, when your enemies come to see you so voluntarily from other countries, feeling they cannot live with your wrath even in your absence.'[5] This is a masterclass in diplomacy and a wonderfully apt re-imagining. Arinbjorn knows just how to pander to his ruler's ego.

He continues in this vein for a while, by which time Eirik has discovered who his unexpected guest is. Eirik bluntly enquires how Egil dare to approach him. The big Icelander is only too happy to join in the performance. He kneels humbly at the king's feet and trots out a praiseworthy verse as balm: 'I have travelled on the sea-god's steed / a long and turbulent wave path / to visit the one who sits / in command of the English land / In great boldness, the shaker / of the wound-flaming sword / has met the mainstay / of King Harald's line.'[6]

As ad hoc goes, this is pretty good, and Egil knows his life depends on it. Steely Gunnhild is watching on. Egil knows he's wasting his time appealing to her better nature, with her son's blood still on his hands. Eirik tells it as it is, warning the big man he's wasting his time. A rope is the best he can hope for. Gunnhild joins in, reminding her husband, if a reminder was needed, that this fellow is responsible for the deaths of several of the king's affinity and also for the callous killing of his young son: 'Where would anyone dare to treat royalty in such a way?'[7]

Arinbjorn steps in with more mellifluous words, almost certainly aware Gunnhild is looking at his head, too. She wants her uninvited guest disposed of there and then. Arinbjorn is bold enough to challenge the queen, reminding her killing at night is murder (daytime is fine). Eirik can't really dispute this, so he bids Arinbjorn keep custody of his guest until the next day when he will be granted a fuller hearing – this is a stay of execution, not a reprieve. Arinbjorn, true to his friend, reminds Eirik that Fairhair had unjustly killed Egil's loyal uncle Thorolf and that the Icelander had suffered several wrongs at the king's hands – it wasn't totally one-sided. Brave talk.

Assuming this exchange was real, and as ever with the skalds, we cannot know if it happened as Snorri relates, then this does give us an insight into Eirik's character. He is not a bloody-minded psychopath, ready to kill Egil out of hand – though he has certainly given him sufficient cause – and Eirik is probably not taken in by Arinbjorn's careful makeover of the facts. He knows Egil wouldn't be here if he had a choice. Yet he's prepared to listen, to be reasonable and rein in his consort's more basic instincts. This is no wild berserker but someone who can aspire to statecraft. He hates Egil, but Arinbjorn is an important member of his affinity. There are fine lines here.

A Bad Country for old Gods

Back home and time for a strategy meeting. Arinbjorn advises his house guest the best thing he can do is to craft an epic *drapa* in the king's honour and recite it on the morrow. This was potentially powerful magic. Skalds were important and kings enjoy adulation, even when the poet is accused of murdering a prince. If Egil is eloquent enough he might just get away with it. He is himself a famed Viking, so praise from him reflects even better on Eirik. Nobody mentions Gunnhild. She wants blood.

Next morning, despite the fact Egil's muse appears to have deserted him, the pair with an armed retinue appear before the king, again at table. Arinbjorn reminds Eirik of all the good service he has given and that he hopes this will add weight to Egil's plea for reconciliation. If that's not enough, custom would dictate that as the supplicant came of his own free will, he should be given a week's grace to leave the kingdom. Gunnhild suggests Arinbjorn leans far more toward his friend than his sovereign. The wily courtier counters by arguing that killing a commoner like Egil won't reflect very well on so noble a king. He's sharp and he's quick, as all good courtiers need to be.

Arinbjorn then nails his colours to the mast by stating he'll stand or fall by Egil. If Eirik wants to kill Egil, then he'll have to deal with his friend and that friend's affinity who, he doesn't need to add, are fully armed and right in front of him. Eirik is thoughtful but not abashed and Arinbjorn knows only too well he has just staked his own life on the outcome. Then Egil is inspired, his muse returns and he launches into a carefully wrought and beautifully delivered paean in praise of Bloodaxe (see appendix one).

If nothing else, Egil has massive presence and knows how to put on a good show. This is one of his best, as it needs to be. The performance of a lifetime. Eirik listens intently and then delivers his judgement – and it's a fair one:

> Arinbjorn, I have thought about the outcome of my dealings with Egil. You have presented Egil's case so fervently that you were even prepared to enter into conflict with me. For your sake, I will do as you have asked and let Egil leave, safe and unharmed. You, Egil will arrange things so that the moment you leave this room, neither I nor my sons will ever set eyes upon you again. Never, cross my path or my men's.

I am letting you keep your head for the time being. Since you put yourself into my hands, I do not want to commit a base deed against you. but you can be sure that his is not a reconciliation with me or my sons, nor any of my kinsmen who want to seek justice.[8]

This is more than reasonable and Eirik was undoubtedly risking his wife's further fury. Egil, quick to see a good thing when in front of his big nose, responded in verse: 'Ugly as my head may be / the cliff my helmet rests upon / I am not loath / to accept it from the king. / Where is the man who ever / received a finer gift / from a noble-minded / son of a great ruler?'[9] In short, he gets away with it and we are left with a favourable picture of the king. Snorri is in no doubt that Eirik of Norway is Eirik in York. Despite our understandable misgivings over the reliability of skaldic sources I'm inclined to agree. (See chapter ten.)

York: *Eboracum, Eoforwic Jorvik*, capital of Scandinavian Northumbria. Prior to that, after its formal founding by Rome in 71 AD, though already a tribal capital of the lordly Parisii, then administrative centre of *Britannia Inferior*. Latterly, chief centre of Deira and then of all Northumbria. It was long established before Eirik's day. Today, the Roman Tower is only a stone's throw from the railway Museum and the city's later reincarnation as a grand Victorian industrial hub, now a tourist mecca with selfie-sticks as numerous as were spears. It is still a magnificent and compact city, with a superb ring of medieval walls virtually intact and walkable. Clifford's Tower, the medieval redoubt, clings to its steep motte, a circular shell keep, recently beneficiary of a sympathetic makeover by English Heritage. The city also has a dark side[10].

Nothing above ground now remains of the Norse quarter, but Eirik would probably have recognised the Minster, there in its earlier guise during his tenures. Bloodaxe is only a footnote, even the Jorvik Viking Centre doesn't really have much to say about him. His legend though is there, he was the last of what York was, representative of a thriving, independent Anglo-Norse kingdom with roots all the way back to Rome. It owed nothing to Wessex.

Jorvik would still retain significant traces of the great Roman city, now beset by squatters. As mentioned, one of the Roman angle towers still survives in the grounds of the Yorkshire Museum.

In the mid-tenth century, much of the original enceinte still stood, girding an area of some 50 acres (20.2 hectares), located on the north-eastern flank of the Ouse – still navigable at that date, giving the city clear access to the Humber and North Sea beyond.

Those grand and lofty civic gates controlling access to the streets were still in use. But inside, the predictable lines of the Roman fortress with its neat and characteristic grid of well-ordered barrack blocks, stores, HQ complex and legate's fine villa, were long gone. So, too, was the layout of the *Vicus*, across the river. Decay, after the end of Roman occupation, had been followed by piecemeal regeneration[11]. York, as Eoforwic, became the capital of the Anglian kingdom of Northumbria, but Edwin, Oswald, Oswy and their successors lived in a truncated remnant, rustic timber and thatch patching buildings once graced by marble and vibrant frescos, straw strewn across intricate mosaics.

It seems likely that early Northumbrian monarchs appropriated the old fortress enclosure as a royal precinct with an adjacent ecclesiastical presence. The cathedral was certainly constructed during the first quarter of the seventh century, with a likely episcopal palace located close to the royal apartments and houses of leading gentry. A new street plan emerged, cutting up the old layout but linking to the Roman gateways. A further monastic complex may have grown up on the site of the former *Colonia*, but this is yet unproven[12].

Eoforwic was but a pale shadow of *Eboracum* but in parts a bustling and successful one. The river frontages were crowded with workshops and warehouses, commercial activity spread along the banks of both river systems. Total population is estimated to have been in the low thousands. By Eirik's day, things had changed. *Domesday Book* reveals that the population was probably nearer 10,000 with some 1,800 building plots. The city had spread out beyond the former limits of the Roman *urbs* and was divided into seven administrative districts or 'shires'.

Ancient defences were maintained and even strengthened. Along the north-east and north-west flanks, the old work of the legions survived, suggesting little spread in these directions. Additional ditches and new sod ramparts were added, a chiaroscuro of Roman and Saxon/Norse with traces of the ancient stones like monoliths still visible in the gaps. In other directions it was very different,

Jorvik had burst outward, some lanes marked where the walls had once stood, others hacked clear through. Riverine traffic swelled and Viking Age York became a major trading hub, once again a city, though this was not urbanisation in the ordered Rome sense.

Rome had built a bridge over the Ouse immediately before the south-west portal, but by Eirik's day this crossing had been shifted some 800 feet (250 metres) downstream, where it still is. A Viking Age bridge surely spanned the Foss as well, close to where the present bridge stands[13]. It was almost certainly the Norse kings who widened the defensible area by extending a line of ramparts outwards towards the rivers – both then wider and shallower than they are today. At present, we have no archaeological evidence to back this up, this lies beneath the line of the great medieval curtain wall. It's possible a further Norse enclosure defended the parish boundary of St Denys's, a vital bridgehead.

Despite all this later rebuilding, a significant legacy of the original Roman grid survives, especially in the central area, formerly the great legionary fortress. These include today's Stonegate, Petergate, Chapter House Street, Colliergate, Bootham, St Andrewgate, Church Street, Coney Street, Gillygate, and Lord Mayor's Walk. Eirik and Gunnhild, perhaps Egil and Arinbjorn, could have walked on these streets, rather more crowded, noisy and miry that any *Dux Britanniarum* would have liked. These aside, the rest of today's streetscape belongs to the Norsemen with just a few later Norman additions[14].

Quite what these streets looked like is best evidenced by the archaeological findings from the Coppergate site, which was certainly in situ by Eirik's time, established for a generation. Coppergate was a child of the Norse era, part of the city's mercantile boom. Timber-framed units were constructed gable end facing the street and combined trade and retail premises with domestic and family accommodation. A bit like living over the shop except you were to the rear and on the same level. It would have been very crowded, very noisy and dirty. Mains drainage had vanished with the eagles and the reek from tanneries would have mingled and meshed with the stink of human and domestic waste.

While we can speculate that most of this growth was organic, driven by commerce, it seems equally likely that a Viking administration set up after Ivar's successful acquisition would see available space divided up amongst his affinity. It was probably this takeover which prompted expansion. York was now plugged in to Dublin and other Norse entrepots and linked to the marine freeways of the Irish and North Seas, the Baltic, and into the warmer waters of the Mediterranean. It was a capital city in the truest sense and looked in every direction but south. Ivar and his line didn't extinguish the idea of an independent Northumbria, they reinforced, shaped and focused it. That sense of otherness, of being different to the south, did not diminish, it swelled.

Ivar and his followers were undoubtedly pagan, but the wily Northman realised he needed the church, the cement which bound early medieval society, an asset rather than a liability. Christianity in York might have reeled but the blow wasn't mortal, far from it, and Vikings were soon building churches. At St Mary's in Castlegate, a dedication stone was found during Queen Victoria's reign, a fusion of Old English and Latin that proclaimed '…[ard] and Grim and Aese raised this church in the name of the Holy Lord Christ, and to St. Mary and St. Martin and St. C[uthbert] and all Saints.'[15] The date is obscured, but Grim and Aese are Norse names and the style of the inscription suggests the tenth or eleventh century. Eirik may possibly have known Grim and Aese.

Domesday Book tells us about those seven 'shires' or urban districts but doesn't say what ground each one covered. One at least was administered by the Archbishop, all others directly by the crown. As might be expected, the church's fief spread around the Minster, an area which previously had made up the north-eastern quadrant of the Roman enceinte. Despite much hypothesis, the makeup of the shires remains 'an archaeological and historical enigma'.[16]

These river-front areas have benefitted from very limited excavation, but digging on North Street, site of a former pumping station, has exposed traces of the *Jorvik* waterfront. By the thirteenth century, this location was being called *Divelinestaynes*, or 'Dublin-Stones', where the Irish Sea traffic moored. This must be an old Norse connection, probably well known to Eirik and his contemporaries, part of what would have been a crowded, bustling port.

Constructing the Norman castle, which involved damming the Foss, would have significantly disrupted parts of the existing street plan and riverine frontages. Tantalisingly, no surviving traces of any Viking Age boats have come to light. There would have been boat builders and repairers active, and hopefully traces await the future archaeologist's trowel. We can be certain the York of Eirik's day was very much the capital of the north and a major international trading hub, second only to London. No wonder the Wessex kings cast such covetous eyes. No wonder, also, that the northerners were so keen to maintain the status quo.

This then was the prize Eirik also coveted, won twice and lost. He could claim that on his father's side he was descended from Sigurd Snake-in-the-Eye, allegedly a son of Ragnar Lodbrok and brother of Ivar the Boneless. Genealogically, this may be far-fetched, but it would be valuable propaganda. Even if it was dubious, the Northumbrians may simply have wanted to believe. A descendant of Norse Ivar was preferable to a scion of Alfred's Wessex. Core Anglian, Ivar's affinity and then Ragnvald's later transfusion had produced a robust hybrid vigour, sure of its own place and identity. The South was not welcome.

And what a prize. One source writing around the time of the first millennium claimed the city could boast 30,000 citizens. That's a very high number for the time and more recent analysis, assuming, say, an average of five persons for each of the 1,800 plots within the walls, would suggest a population of a third of that, though at any one time there would have been a host of visitors, sailors, tradesmen and travellers to swell the number. Thus, a total figure of 12,000 might not be unrealistic.

Whoever controlled such a hub with the rich Vale of York and wider hinterland was a prince of note, ruling from his palace in the heart of this Viking Age metropolis, getting rich from renders and customs dues. He would receive embassies from across the early medieval world, controlling a trading network that spanned England, Scotland, Ireland, Wales, the whole of Europe as far as fabled Byzantium and beyond. It was a complex society, hierarchical and rigid. The king was at the head of the pyramid but with the Archbishop very nearly on a par, a cabal of churchmen embedded in many offices. Secular nobility had their great houses clustered around the seat of power. We don't know much about them, still less about any of the ordinary citizens, crammed into their insanitary tenements, bustling, industrious and probably more cosmopolitan than we might imagine.

A Bad Country for old Gods

Evidence, again from *Domesday Book*, suggests that the all-important moneyers, those men minting the coinage, came from a variety of backgrounds and that certainly some of these owned substantial estates in and around the city. Their names point to a blend of English, Norse, Celtic and even those from a wider continental background. Although some 75 per cent of the moneyers active around the time of the Conquest seem to have Scandinavian names, this need not necessarily imply Norse parentage – Viking names had become popular[17].

This was the York which Egil, if his skaldic tale is true, would have visited, and his friend Arinbjorn would have had one of those lofty halls built by gentry owners, close to the palace complex. What might Eirik's apartments have looked like? It is suggested that the city had two such high status sites. Possibly, the Anglian kings had a royal manor close to the city and/or a central residence within the heart of the old Roman *urbs*, perhaps on the site of the *principia* itself.

Eirik's hearth probably stood more towards the northeastern flank of the original fortress layout. There's no visible evidence for this, but a series of main streets – Shambles, Colliergate, Goodramgate, Church Street and Petergate – all converge here towards what would have been the *porta principalis sinistra*. Just beyond the old gate lies King's Square – a Middle English rendering of Old Norse *Konungsgarthe* – King's Residence. The name is first recorded much later and there are no handy runes telling us 'Eirik was here' but we can surmise he probably was.

What did the grand residence of the Kings of Northumbria look like? We could perhaps assume that it might be some made-over remnant from Imperium, or a lofty and gilded timber hall like Hrothgar's *Heorot*, a 'hall of halls ... radiant with gold'. A recreated Anglo-Saxon hall, Thirlings, at Bede's World in Jarrow, shows how a rustic thegn's house might have appeared. Eirik's would have been a much grander version, appropriate to kingly status, solid and soaring oak frame with wattle infill, central great hearth with smoke eddying in the rafters; painted and gilded, a mass of intricate carving, heavy tapestries enriching plain walls, high table raised up on a dais, trestles ranged throughout. Like Hrothgar, the king's power would be judged by his board, the number of warriors and household men who took his silver, ready to fight his wars; impressive and regal, but very expensive to maintain.

Perhaps in such a setting, Egil, sponsored by his loyal ally Arinbjorn, came to plead his cause, to deliver that impromptu *drapa* that saved his neck. And Queen Gunnhild, resplendent on carved and gilded throne, glowered at her son's killer, plotted and wove her dark magic. Yet the story shows that however powerful the influence of his formidable queen, Eirik made his own decisions.

Northumbrians, as we Northumbrians often assert, are still a race apart. By Eirik's day, Ivar the Boneless's assault had been eight decades ago and his blood and that of his affinity had been well stirred into the indigenous gene pool. Of course, the Northumbrians had seen themselves as different to their southern contemporaries since long before any Viking incursions. The Kingdom of Northumbria had been its own space, an independent and for a period dominant society within broader England. Any notion of southern dominance had always been repugnant.

That existing Anglo-Danish population had received a jolt after 918 when Ragnald kick-started a new era of independence and brought in Norse-Hibernian blood to add to the mix. This would require a further adjustment and a fresh era of absorption. By Eirik's day, northern society was sufficiently cosmopolitan to recognise a son of Harald Fairhair as legitimate claimant in York. Norway trumped Wessex any day.

As N. J. Higham and other scholars have observed: 'In no part of mainland Britain were Scandinavian cultural influences so widespread and profound as in the Viking Age Kingdom of York.' The process chimed with 'deep rooted political separatism'. Norse words came to litter the language. My Norwegian relatives would say 'gar hjem' for 'going home' and we Geordies might say 'ganging heyem'. Not too hard to spot the connection. Settlements have Scandinavian place names. Runes recur like a living thread and later incisions strongly imply a local dialect which endured long after the Norman Conquest.

Those of my fellow Northumbrians seeking a Norse identity when they submit DNA are likely to be disappointed. That part of Northumbria, originally Bernicia, now roughly the County of Northumberland, successfully *resisted* Scandinavian influences, the

The Stora Hammars I image stone, one of four stones in Gotland, Sweden, dating from around the 7th century, showing the saga of Hildr, under what may be the rite of blood eagle, and on the bottom a Viking longship. (Courtesy Berig, Creative Commons 3.0)

Above: Hadrian's Wall, a vast obstacle, testament to Rome's single-minded achievement and presumably an object of wonder in Eirik's day, though its military and political function was long past.

Left: Aberlemno Stones, discovered over 60 years ago; this series of five monoliths, found in and around the village of Aberlemno in Angus, have pictorial representations from Pictish history and this one, it is believed, commemorates the destruction of King Ecgfrith of Northumbria and his warband at the Battle of Nechtansmere in 685.

Above: Bamburgh – crowning Northumbria's lordly strand – capital of the early kingdom of Bernicia and seat of the Northumbrian royal family, it remained a bulwark of border defence through the long centuries of Anglo-Scottish warfare and, fittingly perhaps, was restored by William Lord Armstrong, arguably the world's leading arms magnate during the late nineteenth century, (Eirik would surely have approved).

Right: Dunadd, the Fort on the River Add in Argyll, capital of the Scottish kingdom of Dalriada, a magical place opening up towards Kilmartin Glen, Scotland's answer to Salisbury Plain. I have always likened the place to a British Mycenae.

Venerable Bede (672/673–735); though he never left his beloved monastery in Jarrow, Bede was a great polymath, writer and thinker. It was he who first had the notion of a united England – Land of the Angles – which Athelstan two centuries later turned into reality. (Courtesy British Library, public domain)

The reconstructed Anglo-Saxon farm at Jarrow Hall (formerly Bede's World), the museum in Jarrow, South Tyneside, which celebrates the life of the Venerable Bede. (NeddySeagoon, Creative Commons 3.0)

Gard Haugesund – an ancient Christian cross, certainly erected before the end of the first millennium and located 75 metres south of the national Monument at Haraldshaugen in Haugesund, Norway. It is one of 60 stone crosses in Rogaland. According to local tradition this was erected in memory of Eric Bloodaxe. (Courtesy Wolfmann, Creative Commons 4.0)

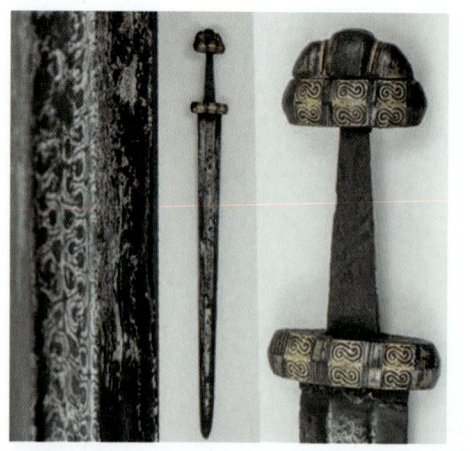 

Above left: An impressive array of Viking Age swords, these are in the Belgian Royal Museums of Art and History. There are many survivors charting the development of sword types and variations throughout the era. Most are of extremely high quality. (Courtesy Royal Museums of Art and History, Brussels)

Above right: The Gilling Sword, an iron blade with five silver bands on the grip and silver plaques on the pommel. The two-edged blade, is pattern welded, the pommel decorated with silver plates with geometric decoration. (Courtesy of York Museums Trust)

Viking axe-head of the later type, the Mammen Axe showing a deep broad-headed blade, with a two handed haft, this would become the dreaded weapon of late era housecarls as William's mounted knights would encounter to their considerable cost at Hastings in 1066. (Courtesy National Museum of Denmark)

Right: Typology of spears, showing the principal variants, less outwardly prestigious than the sword perhaps but a very effective tool in battle, as Egil's brother Thorolf so graphically demonstrates at Vinheath/Brunanburh. (Courtesy Project Forlog)

Below: A variety of facsimile seaxes. The seax was the backup weapon and general utility knife of the period carried by both genders and all classes of society, sometimes remade from a broken sword blade – it gave the Saxons their name. (Courtesy Viking Martial Arts)

Bottom: The Gjermundbu Helmet, excavated in 1943, the only truly complete Viking Era helmet found to date, with distinctive 'spectacle' defences to shield the wearer's eyes – and no horns! Housed in the Museum of Cultural History of the University of Oslo. (Courtesy Wolfmann under Creative Commons 4.0)

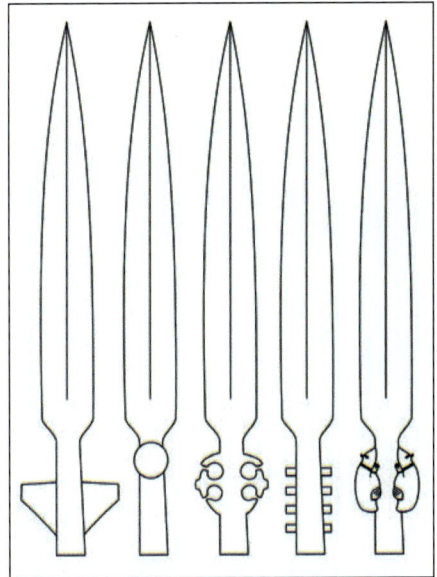

A haunted place, Lindisfarne Castle at sunrise. It is significantly younger than Eirik Bloodaxe, owing its beginnings to Henry VIII. (Courtesy Chris Coombe, Creative Commons 2.0)

Statue of Leif Ericsson, son of Erik the Red, brother to the darkly formidable Freydis, discoverer of Vinland whose name and exploits exemplify the restless dynamism of the Vikings and their indomitable spirit.

One of the five Viking era Skuldelev ships found there 20 kilometres north of Roskilde, Denmark, in 1962.

An example of a knarr (or knǫrr, pl. knerrir). This example is based on the Skuldelev I vessel recovered from the Peberrenden waterways near Roskilde, Denmark, dated to 1030. (Courtesy Alex Harvey, from *Forgotten Vikings*)

Above: The Sognefjorden looking from Vangsnes, home to a heroic bronze statue of the legendary King Fridjof who may have ruled over Ringerike and Sogn and whose likeness was in fact commissioned by Kaiser Wilhelm II, a year before the outbreak of the Great War.

Right: A nineteenth-century image of Eirik's Queen, Gunnhild, who generally doesn't get a good press, witch, sorceress and shapeshifter. Was Eirik just another hen-pecked husband? Yet she was the wife of a famous king and a mother of kings. (Creative Commons 2.0)

Viking propaganda. The sun cross – a cross inside a circle – is one of the oldest Nordic mythic symbols. The Nazis used a swastika variant of the sun cross as the 5th SS Panzer Division Wiking insignia (below). The division contained small contingents of foreign volunteers from Denmark, Norway, Sweden, Finland, and Iceland. The top picture is the same symbol and uses figures and scenes from Norse mythology to draw parallels with the Wiking volunteers themselves. (Courtesy of Willtron from *Voices of the Scandinavian SS* by Jonathan Trigg)

A silver penny of Eric Bloodaxe dating to the period AD 952–954, which would be the second reign. A small cross pattee on the reverse. Moneyer Ingelgar, mint of York. (Courtesy York Museums Trust, Rebecca Griffiths)

The Silverdale hoard, a collection of over 200 pieces of silver jewellery and coins discovered, appropriately enough, near Silverdale, Lancashire, England, in September 2011, The hoard includes Arabic, Anglo-Saxon, Anglo-Viking and Viking coins. The items were deposited together in and under the lead container in the photograph. It is dated to around AD 900, at the height of conflict between the Anglo-Saxons and the Danish settlers. (Courtesy the Portable Antiquities Scheme/the Trustees of the British Museum, Ian Richardson)

≈1cm

A silver-gilded Thor's hammer found in Scania, Sweden, date uncertain. The loop has a bird of prey face with a pronounced beak and eyebrows, and protruding eyes. It was probably made in southern Scandinavia or perhaps northern Germany. (Courtesy Ola Myrin, Statens historiska museum, Creative Commons 4.0)

Looking down from Stainmore – scene of Eirik's final Gotterdammerung, as wild today as it was in 954; not a lot has changed, a landscape of legend. (Courtesy Trevor Littlewood, Creative Commons 2.0)

A Bad Country for old Gods

Norsemen didn't leave their DNA much north of the Tyne. At any point, the actual number of Norse immigrants was small. These were warrior bands, young unmarried men who would be unlikely to subsequently import a gaggle of dependents. They intermarried and bred with locals. Their influence naturally was greater than percentages would suggest of course, as they formed a dominant elite, kings, higher gentry, household men and warriors in the shires.

Halfdan's settling of his fighting men in former Deira has been likened to Normanization after the Conquest. These new men may have been relatively few in number, but their authority and influence were disproportionally high. Higham notes that Danish '-by' names proliferate in lowland Yorkshire, generally within 'a day's ride of York'. Halfdan is concentrating his household men and wider affinity around his capital – a ready militia to hand when the need arose. And it would.

Despite the overwhelming nature of Athelstan's victory at Brunanburh in 937, his apparent achievement in nation building was initially short-lived. In fact, it seemed to die with him. When the king, still a relatively young man aged only 40, died in October 939, Olaf Guthfrithson, bested at Brunanburh, saw another chance and made a bid for the throne of York. He seems to have met little or no opposition and was soon teamed up with his cousin Olaf Sihtricsson (or *Cuardn*) while Guthfrithson's brother Blakari took over Dublin on some form of ad hoc regency basis. The ASC ('E' Version) took a dim view: In this year, 941, 'the Northumbrians were false to their pledges and chose Anlaf [Olaf] from Ireland as their King.'[18] When this Olaf died that year, his cousin immediately filled the vacancy.

Sihtricsson's accession sent out a clear message. Northumbria was a Scandinavian kingdom with settled rights of succession. Athelstan's brother and successor Edmund inevitably saw this as a challenge, a disruption of the legacy the late king had fought so hard to establish. It seems likely that two years of conflict ensued. At the outset, the Northumbrians advanced and gobbled up the crucial 'Five Boroughs': Derby, Leicester, Lincoln, Nottingham and Stamford. Edmund very soon took them back: 'The boroughs five he won, Leicester and Lincoln, Nottingham, Derby and Stamford too. Long had the Danes under the Norsemen been subjected by force to heathen bondage, until finally liberated by the valour of Edward's son, King Edmund, protector of warriors.'[19] The chronicler here is distinguishing between the 'settled' Danes of the East Anglian Danelaw and their more aggressive Norwegian cousins from Northumbria.

The Boroughs may have been in the hands of, or subject to influence by, Norse gentry from York for some time, and the Northumbrians simply reasserted control of this swathe in the immediate aftermath of Athelstan's death. Edmund moved decisively to broadcast the authority of Wessex and in this, he was clearly successful[20]. Charter evidence from after 942 shows Edmund was awarding strategically important landholdings to loyalists. It may well be that his *Reconquista* did not involve any serious fighting, merely a show of overwhelming force[21].

Alternatively, it might have been bloodier, as *ASC* ('D' version) insists: 'In this year [943] Anlaf [Olaf] stormed Tamworth and there was great slaughter on both sides: the Danes had the victory and carried great booty away with them.'[22] Edmund riposted by besieging Olaf and Archbishop Wulfstan* in Leicester and the nimble pair only avoided capture by evacuating fast and under cover of darkness.

It was Archbishop Wulfstan and Oda of Canterbury who, through diplomacy, fixed a demarcation line along Watling Street, thereby ceding control of the Five Boroughs to Northumbria. This was a coup for Olaf and the price, conversion to Christianity, a very modest one. Edmund stood as sponsor for this new convert, but the ceremony, as well as bringing the newly baptised within the orbit of the church, also suggested a degree of vassalage. In

---

* Archbishop Wulfstan is a major figure at this time, seen by some as a mid-tenth century kingmaker in Northumbria. Installed in 931, he held office on and off for twenty years, his story and Eirik's are irretrievably linked. He does seem to have changed sides a lot, but this was possibly the only path to self-preservation. Evidence shows he witnessed many of Athelstan's charters during the first four years of his episcopacy, but his signature is notably absent between 936 and 941. We can assume he was consecrated with Athelstan's approval, but did he then fall out of favour for having sided with the rebel factions at the time of the Brunanburh campaign? Three years prior to 943, he appears quite clearly as advisor to and emissary of Olaf Guthfrithson, negotiating with Wulfhelm of Canterbury when both prelates agreed that the territory between Watling Street and the Northumbrian border should be administered by Olaf.

that same year the King of Wessex sponsored the baptism of another Norse warlord, Rognvald Guthfrithson, who emerges as a form of co-ruler or nominated heir. Rognvald is assumed to have been a surviving brother of the other Olaf[23]. The situation, as Professor Downham notes, is complex and Edmund may well have been actively stoking incipient rivalries between these two Norse leaders; there's a lot to be said for divide and rule.

If so, Edmund was successful and managed to oust both in 944. In a twist that might appear surprising, Archbishop Wulfstan sided with King Edmund. Professor Downham cites the Chronicle of Aethelweard, which names Wulfstan as facilitating these expulsions, declaiming that both Olaf and Rognvald are 'traitors'. This may suggest that the pair had broken their earlier oaths to Edmund, giving him a casus belli, but also forcing Wulfstan to defend the integrity of the agreement he had brokered[24]. Rognvald may well have been a fatal casualty in this process, whereas Olaf, we know, returned to Dublin where he staged a coup of his own, expelling Blakari Guthfrithson.

Edmund's brief but active reign ended abruptly on 26 May 946 when he was killed in what seems to have been a brawl between his steward and a ne'er do well called Liofa. The king had personally intervened to save his servant and was stabbed by the assailant: 'It was widely known how he met his end, that Liofa stabbed him at Pucklechurch... He had ruled six and a half years.'[25] It has been suggested that Edmund was facing growing disaffection and that his death may have been planned assassination rather than a seemingly random crime – losing control in Northumbria might have sparked this resentment. In any event, he was succeeded by his younger brother Eadred.

If anyone in York thought this might herald a respite, they were wrong. Eadred knew exactly how important control of Northumbria was to his rule – its continuing independence a festering sore. He therefore moved rapidly and 'reduced all Northumbria to subjection and Scots gave him oaths and promised to do his will in all things'.[26]

There is an historical tendency to focus the view from Northumbria south towards the giant of Wessex, but Eirik and any king of the north would have to look towards Scotland as well. Northumbria had a long history with its developing northern neighbour. It was the Scots or, at that time, Picts who had brought King Ecgfrith's power surge to an abrupt and fatal halt at Nechtansmere in 685. Scotland ('Alba' in Gaelic, 'Scotia' in Latin so 'Scotland' in English), did not exist for a substantial period afterwards but by Eirik's day was very much a formed and aggressive monarchical nation.

Both the north and west of Scotia were assailed by Norsemen who carved out separate territories in Orkney/Shetland, the Hebrides and Man, an influx of Norse Hibernian *Gall-Gaidill* filtering into the south west to give Galloway its distinctive regional identity. Kings of both Pictland and Dal Riata – the western kingdom nucleated in Argyll – died in battle against Norsemen in 839. Debate as to whether Pictland subsumed Dal Riata or the other way round continues. From the mid-ninth century Kenneth Mac Alpin rose to power and founded a dynasty. The path to a unified kingship was paved with skulls, but when Domnall mac Causautin died at Dunnottar in the year 900, he was recorded as 'King of Alba'. Scotland had arrived.

Northumbria was now no longer the dominant power in north Britain. Slowly, the power of the kings of Scotland began to grow as the influence of Northumbria faded. Kings of York allowed puppet rulers to hold sway at Bamburgh, and as Ivar and Olaf demonstrated so tellingly in 870, could meddle in Scotland, when they reduced the great bastion of Dumbarton – albeit as proxies of the Scottish king.

We've already seen that Athelstan in 934 conducted a major punitive sweep through Scotland by both land and sea. Alex Woolf[*] suggests that the death of the King's half-brother Eadwine, which may or may not have been accidental, had helped to consolidate his position in England. A second death, of Guthfrith who had briefly held sway in Northumbria but had clung on to power in Dublin, freed Athelstan from Norse interference as the dead man's successors, or would-be successors, squabbled amongst themselves.

---

[*] King Mael Coluim mac Domnail (d. 954), anglicised as Malcolm I, was a son of Donald I and of the old Cumbrian line; he acceded to the throne of Scotland at some point before 943 when his cousin King Constantine II abdicated and entered holy orders.

It seems likely that Ealdred of North Northumbria, the old Anglian hub, defeated by Ragnald in 918, also died around the same time. It may have been that this triggered further Scots intervention in the old, shrunken kingdom of Bamburgh. It might be (and this is very unclear) that Ealdred's successor attempted to break off any allegiance to Wessex and received aid in this from the Scots. If so, then it was this impertinence that led Athelstan to decide upon what seems like a disproportionate response. It must surely be that deeper forces were at play. For whatever reason, Scotland was severely chastised and King Constantine humiliated. He would not enjoy that and Brunanburh, in no small part, would be a consequence.

Olaf Guthfrithson, having successfully grabbed the vital Five Boroughs, headed north to attack Lindisfarne and then Tyninghame in East Lothian where, still in 941, he smashed the shrine of St Balthere (Baldred). Quite why he campaigned in the north we cannot say. It seems unlikely this was mere banditry; far more likely, the North Northumbrians had either been slow to recognise his authority or had rejected him altogether and again looked north to Scotland. He was no more pleased that Athelstan had been. When Olaf died suddenly only a few days after vandalising the saint's shrine, this was seen as divine retribution.

We know that Mael Coluim* did launch a major incursion into northern England in 'the vii year of his reign' (950). He penetrated as far south as the Tees and scooped up vast herds of cattle and scores of captives. After Olaf Sihtricsson's expulsion, he may have sought to re-establish himself in Cumbria as a muster point for another crack at Northumbria. We do know that King Edmund riposted by wasting Cumbria and sending punitive expeditions north of the border, which forced Mael Coluim to seek terms. The Wessex kings, like the Norse rulers in York, were aware that the Scots could present both an opportunity and a threat. They could be allies against the southern English but also hawkish predators, ready to seize upon any perceived weakness.

Professor Downham suggests, and this seems entirely likely, that Edmund's death had been a catalyst for further discontent

---

* See Woolf, A., 'From Pictland to Alba 789–1070', *New Edinburgh History of Scotland* (Edinburgh, Edinburgh University Press 2007), chapters four and five.

in the northern Scandinavian realm and that King Mael Coluim might have been stirring the pot. This may also have been the first attempt by Eirik to establish himself at York.

As mentioned earlier, we cannot say that Eirik of York is conclusively proven to be the same person as Eirik Bloodaxe. Professor Downham does cast doubt on this (see chapter ten). I take the view (wholly subjective) that they are one and the same. My reasoning is that the Northumbrians would have been seeking a 'big beast', otherwise they would have opted for another Dublin-based player. That there was a Dublin Eirik we have not previously heard of and who doesn't appear convincingly in any chronicle source must remain a possibility, albeit a remote one. If Archbishop Wulfstan, still wedded to his role as kingmaker, is looking for a suitable candidate, then by conspiring against Olaf and Rognvald he has rather poisoned the well as far as Ireland is concerned.

Eirik can maintain, correctly or (more likely) incorrectly, that he's of Ivar's blood. We have the mystery of where Eirik Bloodaxe has actually been since his expulsion from Norway a decade and more since. He's no longer a young man, probably being into his mid-sixties by now. Alex Woolf has an enticing theory on this (see chapter ten). We can surmise that his raiding career, traditional job description for any Viking nobleman, has furnished him with a substantial war chest. Cash is king as far as kingship is concerned. To maintain his position Eirik would need to pay a substantial armed retinue and his path to the throne in York would be marked by the greasing of many palms.

Eirik would represent the last the last hurrah for an independent north, his dim, weird *Ragnarök* at Stainmore in 954 the final full stop. No northerner would ever be free of southern domination thereafter. This was a pivotal moment in British history where the pattern established in the wake of Rome's ebb was finally and fully eclipsed. The heroic Age of Northumbria, its golden sequel and the thriving, vital Scandinavian kingdom of York, vanished into perpetual vassalage. A fine irony then that we know so little about Eirik. Everything Snorri tells us must be weighed very carefully, the synoptic and chronicle sources are fleeting and often contradictory.

Bloodaxe is the spectre, a dark legend, in no small part conjured by later storytellers. He leaves no trace in York, no Bloodaxe

A Bad Country for old Gods

Pub or Eirik's tea rooms, no street names, no heritage centre. Richard III gets far more press. But Eirik still mattered, and his end was a border stone in the history of these islands.

> Night is falling. Your land and mine goes down into a darkness now; and I, and all the other guardians of her flame are driven from our homes, up out into the wolf's jaw. But the flame still flickers in the fen. You are marked down to cherish that. Cherish the flame, till we can safely wake again.
> David Rudkin:
> *Penda's Fen* (1974)

Eight

'VALHALLA, I AM COMING...'

> Brief words are hard to find,
> shapes to carve and discard:
>
> Bloodaxe, king of York,
> king of Dublin, king of Orkney.
> Take no notice of tears;
> letter the stone to stand
> over laid aside lest
> insufferable happiness impede
> flight to Stainmore, to trace lar, mallet,
> becks, flocks
> and axe knocks.
>
> Basil Bunting, Briggflatts
(Hexham, Bloodaxe Books 2009), p. 16.

Ragnarök – that the world should end in chaos is a recurrent fear. For my generation which lived through the Cold War it was all too real, two vast and opposing power blocs each equipped with the means to cancel life as we know it for millennia – Odin would have definitely understood.

For the Norse this apocalypse is presaged by a series of disasters. First is the death of Baldr, Odin's golden boy by Frigg who has been having bad dreams. Everything – element, human, animal and plant – is made to swear it won't harm the precious baby. Mistletoe is excluded as it couldn't harm anybody.

'Valhalla, I am coming...'

Frigg confides this key detail to an aged crone, the cunning and spiteful Loki in disguise. Baldr seems invincible and the gods, in their happily puerile way, throw all manner of objects at him in council. Loki places a Mistletoe dart in the seemingly harmless grip of Baldr's blind brother Hodr. Loki guides his innocent dupe's hand and down goes Baldr. His wife Nanna dies of grief and she is placed on her husband's funeral ship to be cremated with him.

Loki is caught and made to endure an agonising captivity. Meanwhile on earth, there is climate change, it is perpetual winter, which leads to wars. This rising tide of conflict spills over into the realm of the gods and Armageddon is unleashed. The final battle.

Wolves, serpents, monsters of every kind take part. Loki, freed from his bonds, joins in on the side of the giants. Yggdrasill twists and shudders in the vortex of this deadly hurricane. The wolf Fenrir gobbles up Odin. But one of his surviving sons, Vidarr dismembers the wolf. Thor kills the vast Midgard serpent but its final spew of venom kills the Thunderer himself. Destruction spirals out of control; the world is consumed by fire. The end.

Not quite. Night is followed by a new dawn, another age of man and gods, more temperate than the last. Even the vanished sun has a daughter, the sons of man emerge, the great ash tree it seems, however battered, survives. There is new and vibrant life.

Stainmore. It's bleak. This is May, so spring or what passes for spring, but a cold wind whips down the valley, ricochets off stone to send whetted blades of cold air up. And, on that day nearly 1,100 years ago, no shortage of whetted blades. It was the Romans who threaded a highway through this strategic gap, astride what are now the three county areas of Cumbria, Durham and North Yorkshire. Rey Cross, which may mark the site of Eirik's final battle (see following chapter), is about ten miles (16 kilometres) west of Barnard Castle on what is now the A66, which in this sector hugs the line of the old road. It is an ancient landscape, rugged and uncompromising. It was along this road that Eirik and his army marched towards his final battle, as mist-shrouded as any event in his largely mist-shrouded career.

'And wonder, dread and war / Have lingered in that land / Where loss and love in turn / Have held the upper hand.'[1]

Eric Bloodaxe the Viking: 'I Shall Die Laughing'

Death rune.

At the head of the slow pass, there's a grand view looking westwards. The fertile stretch of Eden Valley gleams below with silhouettes of Lakeland hills beyond. It's more than a watershed, a cultural divide between Northumbrians and Cumbrians, *Westmoringas* as they would have been then. It's also an axis of access and control for either flank. In Eirik's day, it is a main link between York and Dublin. A lot does depend on the direction of travel. There's an assumption Eirik was moving east to west, but I follow Alex Woolf in believing it was likely he was heading west towards York, not away from it. He's not trying to keep possession; he's attempting to regain it.

It's upland and wild, rough moorland stretching north and south, a primeval conduit for ice-flows, designated a Regionally Important Geological/Geomorphological Site – RIGS – and Bowes Moor itself is recognised as an SSI. Stainmore Gap is the high saddle which forms a bottleneck[2] and the present road which climbs slightly higher than the now vanished railway rises to 1,380 feet (420 metres). Roman reminders are plentiful. Rey Cross is abutted by the footprint of an imperial marching camp and the outpost fort at Maiden Castle lies a few miles west towards Brough. Aside from the cross, which is very easily missed, there is nothing to commemorate what was in all probability a major and decisive battle, an event of some significance. Eirik has no grand memorial.

The first written reference to the place does not appear until 990 – *Stanmoir* or stony moor', that's right enough. There's no question the place mattered, early medieval travellers and war bands would still follow the old Roman road, such well-engineered surfaces proved remarkably durable. The pass rising toward its summit, an extended 'V' with high ground swelling north and south, still dominates the route. So, if I'm a leader and I want to stop unwelcome intruders from pushing either east or west, this is where I would fix the block.

'Valhalla, I am coming...'

What did happen? Just about everything I'm reconstructing here is wholly conjectural and any other interpretation is as valid as mine. The sources tend to breed more uncertainty than enlightenment. 'D' version of *ASC* baldly states: '[954] In this year the Northumbrians drove out Eric and Ealdred succeeded to the Northumbrian Kingdom.'[3] Perhaps the best informed and most insightful commentator before the 20th century was W. G. Collingwood. He acknowledges that *ASC* is the best source, even if it is unhelpful here and tends to be south-centric. Florence of Worcester edited the chronicle, but 150 years after Eirik's death in 954. Henry of Huntingdon and William of Malmesbury were writing *c.* 1135 and Roger of Wendover a century after them. Simeon of Durham was born a century after the Battle of Stainmore – he may in fact also be the author of *Libellus* (*c.* 1125). Roger of Hoveden from Yorkshire wrote after Simeon and tried 'to improve' on him[4].

There is a broad consensus that when Edmund succeeded his brother Athelstan, northerners glimpsed a window of opportunity through which they might snatch back their cherished liberty. Olaf Guthfrithson spotted it too and came back at the turn of the year (946). The Northumbrians made him king but as we saw, he died fighting the Scots. Olaf Cuaran succeeded, only to be driven out by Edmund, who chastised Cumbria and exerted a firm grip until his own death on 26 May 946.

Mentioned in the previous chapter but worth restating from the *ASC*: 'Prince Eadred ... reduced all Northumbria to subjection: the Scots gave him oaths and promised to do his will in all things. [948] In this year King Eadred came to Tanshelf [Pontefract] and there Archbishop Wulfstan and all the councillors of Northumbria pledged their allegiance to the king, but within a short while they were false both to their pledges and oaths.'[5] We detect a hint of anti-northern bias here, but we may have to accept that Northumbrians were a tricky bunch at best!

Eadred reacted swiftly to such perfidy, no doubt he was already prepared, after all he had little cause to trust these turbulent northerners: '[948] In this year King Eadred harried all Northumbria, because they had taken Eric for their king: on the raid the famous Minster at Ripon, which St Wilfrid built, was destroyed by fire. Then, when the king was on his way home, the host from out of York overtook the king's rearguard at Castleford, and there was great slaughter.'6 *And there was great slaughter.* Eirik, if indeed this king is Bloodaxe, reacting in character.

He's canny enough to know he does not have sufficient resources to take Eadred on frontally, so he chooses his moment and his ground. He capitalises on an opportunity to ensure the invaders leave with a bloody nose for their troubles. Eadred had burnt Ripon deliberately, a reminder to Wulfstan that the old northern saints like Wilfrid were no longer so potent. They don't retain enough of their provincial, once kingly magic to halt the Wessex dragon. The old days are gone and if the Northumbrians need a reminder, then just smell the ash.

Eirik has countered brilliantly in tactical terms but strategically, he fails. He always does. Eadred isn't ready to accept such a reverse nor call it quits for his earlier desecration: '[948] Then was the king so enraged that he would have invaded that land a second time and completely devastated it, but when the council of the Northumbrians heard of it, they abandoned Eirik and made reparation to King Eadred for their actions.'7

What were the terms of Eirik's engagement? The Northumbrians had repudiated whatever provisions were agreed at Tanshelf and 'taken' Eirik as king. The main player here must be Wulfstan, and we can only speculate about Eirik's exact whereabouts during this time. Was he waiting in the wings or plucked from obscurity? Not the latter. Assuming he is Bloodaxe then he's already well known and has been building up a war chest through raiding. As Wulfstan had earlier broken with Olaf owing to the latter's untrustworthiness, then it stands to reason he has been casting about for another candidate, so his submission at Tanshelf must have been no more than an exercise intended to buy time. Eadred probably wasn't all that surprised.

Having successfully bought time and installed Eirik, the Northumbrians must have known there would be a reaction. Eadred would not simply shrug his shoulders. Wulfstan must have prepared for this and the speed of Eirik's counterattack suggests careful and measured preparation. An onslaught was anticipated and riposted. So why did the council then lose their collective nerve and eject their new-found champion? Here we are again plunged into the realm of speculation. Had Eirik perhaps oversold himself and exaggerated the weight of his own resources which were found wanting? This seems unlikely, he had brought victory but at a cost.

He had not thwarted Eadred's raid, just cut up a part of the southerners' army as they withdrew. Now the old kingdom was exposed to retaliation on a biblical scale. Eadred wouldn't be caught twice, and the Northumbrians had just started a fight they couldn't hope to win. If the king burnt Ripon in vexation, what might he do in anger? This does sound like Eirik Bloodaxe, decisive, even brilliant tactics, but no sense of strategy. Fast yes, savage yes, impressive even, but decisive no.

Wulfstan and his cabal paid up, rejected Eirik and bent their knees, again. Next year, according to the *ASC*, Olaf Cuaran is back! By whose invitation we can't be sure. It may be that Eadred approved or accepted Olaf's return on the basis he was less violent and unpredictable than Eirik. The chroniclers offer no more clues until 952, four years later when: 'King Eadred had Wulfstan imprisoned in the stronghold at *Iudanburh*[8] because he had been frequently accused to the king; in this year too, the King had many put to death in the Borough of Thetford, to avenge the death of Abbot Eadhelm whom they had slain.'[9]

Collingwood is convinced, as am I, that Eirik did enjoy two terms, however brief. Attempts to twist the dating to reduce his tenure to a single span just don't work, nor do they need to. Wulfstan is clearly chief minister, the kingmaker and troublemaker who had pushed his luck just that bit too far, and Eadred had decided he needed to cool his heels for a while. What exactly happened at Thetford, why and by whom the Abbot was murdered, isn't clear. What is clear is that Eadred enacted a harsh reprisal; whether this had anything to do with Wulfstan we can't say. It may have been a wholly unrelated incident.

Simeon expresses the chronology slightly differently. He says that in 948 Eadred overran Northumbria but consequently, the northerners crowned Eirik. He attributes the fight at Castleford and Bloodaxe's expulsion to the year 950. He gives us a terse note for 954 stating baldly that Oswulf was appointed as Earl of Northumbria. earl not king[10]. *Historiae Continuato* clearly asserts that Eirik was 'The last king of that province'. He was installed in flagrant breach of those oaths previously given. This trickery so offended Eadred he threatened to lay waste to the entire region.

This frightened the Northumbrians enough to buckle: 'When their king had been expelled and killed by Macchus, son of Olaf ... the province was given to Earl Oswulf.'[11]

How do we interpret this and attempt to establish a viable chronology? The chronicles give us just a bare summary. Archbishop Wulfstan is evidently the key player. We can assume he dominates the Council, but what are his and their overall objectives? Olaf and Eirik are, to a degree, just the hired help. They may style themselves and may be styled by others as kings but, in modern terms, they're at best CEOs and on notice.

Wulfstan and his northerners were primarily seeking to retain an independent northern state and thereby preserve their own positions and privileges, we needn't get too distracted by local patriotism or any form of altruism. The north had enjoyed, sometimes endured, half a millennium of independence from the south. At its high point in the seventh century its monarchs had been recognised as *Bretwaldas*, high kings. They had absorbed the Norsemen, both successive waves, to create a bond of hybrid vigour. This current threat from the south might also pass. Athelstan had won his epochal victory at Brunanburh, but the union he welded barely outlived him. The bonds of servitude appeared very thin and might yet be shrugged off. With the boon of hindsight, we can see this wasn't going to happen but at the time it must have seemed a very real hope, the Rota Fortunae was still spinning.

Eadred would be wholly aware of this, aware, too, that from a Wessex perspective northern independence was a test of his kingship, one his predecessor Edmund, may have failed, a factor which might have hastened his demise (depending on how much we wish to believe in putative conspiracies). For Wessex, Northumbria was an acid test. For Athelstan's vision of an 'England' to have any validity, Northumbria must toe the line. But we don't know quite what that meant. As yet, it didn't seem to imply assimilation and direct governance. What Eadred was probably seeking was a pliant satrap.

After Eirik's first tenure and expulsion, Eadred seems, for a while at least, willing to accept Olaf as a vassal. We might assume that all the various oaths and undertakings entered into by Wulfstan or Olaf involved a significant nod towards overlordship. This suited everyone. Eadred was recognised as supreme ruler while the northerners continued to enjoy a measure of quasi-independence. Lurking at the back of everyone's mind would be the spectre of direct rule, that such freedom as York retained was held only under licence and that could be revoked; as, finally, it was.

In this process Northerners proved their own worst enemies. Best just to keep heads down and not antagonise Wessex, knowing that the south could, if Eadred so chose, impose direct rule through overwhelming force. That grating reality obviously jarred. Eirik represents the northerners' desire to be totally free. His links to the Dublin dynasty of Ivar were tenuous at best. He had no cause to love the House of Wessex as Athelstan had previously backed Hakon and remained the direct cause of Eirik's exile. Whether, in the confused chronology, there had been some rapprochement and Athelstan had earlier invited Eirik in to assume lordship of Northumbria we cannot say, but it seems unlikely.

Was it Bloodaxe's famous aggression and boldness that convinced Wulfstan? What prior links to the Northumbrian polity did Eirik have? Many questions, few answers. That the Norwegian was fully appraised of events must be a given. He doesn't just spring forth from the sidelines, plucked from near obscurity when called on. His career of piracy has filled his coffers sufficiently to buy information and consolidate influence. He has strong links to Orkney, the Hebrides and even those Norse settlements in Ireland. Money buys warriors, so I dare to assume he travelled with a sizeable war band, an attractive feature for a small state about to defy a much larger and more powerful neighbour.

Again, in this Valley of Unknowing, we can't say just what Wulfstan knew. He, too, would have his sources and was able to fine tune his perception of the state of Eadred's kingship. Wessex was not unstoppable. Those living across England in the mid-tenth century were still very new to any concept of wider nationhood. What we may view as certain today was probably very much less so then. Edmund had become *dégommé* – so might his successor. Eadred for his part reacts with stick and carrot. It's a big stick, he moves unchallenged through Northumbria and burns Ripon. The Northerners appear to have underestimated his grip on power, the extent of his resources and his ability to deploy these to maximum effect.

As I noted earlier, this is no mere act of casual iconoclasm, it's a lesson, blunt, brutal but very much to the point. Wilfrid's Minster is a potent symbol of what Northumbria was, or rather what it had been. Destroying this was a message to the Northumbrians that they were no longer their own men, nor ever would be again. It's a slap in the face for Wulfstan and a clear signal his new Norse king can't do anything about it. But of course, he does. Eirik sallies out as Eadred swaggers back home, flushed by his easy victory, and neatly cuts up his rearguard at Castleford. That's a slap back.

We have no detail whatsoever of the course of the fight, how many warriors were involved or what losses were sustained. But it's a palpable hit, nonetheless. So what? Eirik has won a victory, like Napoleon during the campaign of 1814, time and again he beats the mighty alliance of his collective enemies, but they crush him anyway. A tactical win isn't victory, in fact it just turns out to be yet another provocation. The Northumbrians now have the worst of both worlds. They have seen what damage Eadred can inflict and their own counterattack, however brilliant tactically, only serves to invite even more frightful retribution. Out goes the new CEO. Wulfstan and co grovel, whilst reaching deep into their collective purse.

Then what? The 'E' version of ASC tells us that in 949 'Anlaf Curan came to Northumbria.'[12] It's also the 'E' version which states that three years later 'The Northumbrians drove out King Anlaf and accepted Eric, son of Harald, as their King.'[13] Meanwhile the 'D' version speaks of Wulfstan's incarceration at Bradwell-on-Sea 'because he had been frequently accused to the King'.[14] It's this version which includes the Thetford episode, but without any clear link other than the date. We have no knowledge of whether these events are related. Quite possibly not, the Thetford business looks rather like a local disturbance, though quite what the unfortunate Abbot Eadhelm had done to so outrage the citizens we can't say!

We have to assume that in Northumbria Eadred at least permitted Olaf's reinstatement. Perhaps this was part of the deal brokered after the Castleford debacle. It is possible the king preferred the Dublin Viking as the lesser of two evils. He did need a reliable surrogate to rule the north for him and if Olaf was ready, as he must have been, to bend the knee when necessary, then he could be tolerated. Why then is Wulfstan arrested in 952? It seems clear the Archbishop was a serial intriguer and given his prior falling out with the Dublin cabal, always favoured Eirik. We could even conjecture that it was Eadred's high-handedness in seizing this great prelate which triggered Olaf's ejection and Eirik's return. Eadred knew, however, that Wulfstan was Bloodaxe's most potent supporter.

Eirik then clings on for another two years before his final fall. Why does Eadred tolerate this? Perhaps he doesn't want to have to invade fissiparous Northumbria again or, this time round, he prefers a subtler strategy. Wars are both uncertain and very expensive, they trigger resentment and blood feuds. Perhaps Eadred has concluded he isn't going to win hearts and minds and reduce the north to servitude by breaking heads and burning down churches. He needs a more nuanced, even peripheral approach. This brings us to the question of whether Eirik's second expulsion has the king's hand behind it. On the balance of probabilities and we can't say more, the answer must be yes.

If Eirik, as Wulfstan's preferred candidate, represents a 'free' Northumbria then Olaf is a lesser threat and Eadred has Oswulf, of the ancient line of Bamburgh kings, waiting in the wings. He doesn't aspire to a throne or certainly doesn't appear to, he would be content with a wider earldom. He controls the rump of old Bernicia north of the Tyne and so is well placed to move into York's otherwise empty palace. Olaf gains nothing from Eirik's death and 'treacherous' Macchus his son is quickly killed. All the *ASC* tells us is that Eadred took over the reins of government. Wulfstan is released and presumably is bought off with the bishopric of Dorchester. We nothing more of the great kingmaker until a record of his death two years later.

How Eirik is invited back in, we just don't know, presumably by Wulfstan, and it's this fresh defiance which triggers his arrest. Eirik somehow hangs on for another two years until he's ousted for a final time in 954. By whom? It must surely be the rump of the Northumbrian council, but as far as we can tell, there's no immediate threat of further punitive action from Eadred – of course the threat alone, backed by plentiful silver, might have been enough. Can we assume that Olaf, Macchus and Oswulf are involved? That does seem like a safe bet, given they are the ones in charge of the reception committee when Eirik tries to claw his way back. There is a measure of desperation on all sides. It would have been hard for anyone in the north to have argued that Northumbria's days were anything but numbered. Olaf, Macchus as his son and potential successor, together with Earl Oswulf, all stood to gain.

Whilst we don't know much about Oswulf, he's very well placed to grab whatever prize is left. His earldom is already an essential buffer against the Scots. He comes of an ancient Anglian lineage and therefore should be acceptable to the Council. Perhaps he is canny enough not to covet a kingdom but is content to settle for a much wider fief than he already enjoys. As the Huguenot Henry IV of France remarked at the end of the French Wars of Religion in the sixteenth century – 'Paris is worth a mass.' Fifty per cent of something is better than a hundred per cent of nothing.

We hear of kings, would-be kings, archbishops and perhaps councillors. But we don't hear of the people of York and the wider Northumbrian hinterland. Agriculture and commerce are the kingdom's lifeblood. Palaces are funded by the taxpayers and war is never good for farming or trade (armourers, arrow smiths, fletchers and swordmakers might disagree). Whether the smallholder in a rural riding really cares who is in overall charge so long as his crops are safe is always debatable. To what extent Olaf or Eirik have enjoyed truly popular support throughout the kingdom we cannot know. But it's likely that not everybody, in fact very far from everybody, cares either way.

So much for the Chronicles, what of the synoptic sources? These are more forthcoming but certainly less reliable and more embroidered. *Historia Norwegie*, aside from castigating Gunnhild (she has few fans) has Eirik dying in Spain:

> ... he was appointed earl, commanding the whole of Northumbria, and was most acceptable to all, that is until his villainous wife, Gunnhild, appeared on the scene. As the Northumbrians could not brook her pernicious fury, they straight away flung off the intolerable yoke imposed by this pair. And while Eirik was pursuing a Viking expedition in Spanish territory, he suffered an armed attack and met his end; Gunnhild however returned with her sons to her brother Harald, the Danish King.[15]

Snorri in his *Heimskringla* offers an apparently informed version but again Eirik goes down during an abortive raid:

> [He] sailed thereafter south to England and marauded there as elsewhere. The people fled before him wherever he appeared. As King Eirik was a bold warrior and had a great force, he trusted much to his people that he penetrated far inland in the country, following and plundering the fugitives. King Jaramund [Edmund?] had set a king, who was called Olaf to defend the land and he gathered an innumerable mass of people, with whom he marched against King Eirik. A dreadful battle ensued, in which many Englishmen fell but for one who fell came three in his place out of the country behind and when evening came on, the loss of men turned on the Northmen and many people fell. Towards the end of the day, King Eirik and five kings with him fell. Three of them were Guthorm and his two sons, Ivar and Harek: there fell also, Sigurd and Ragnvald and with them Torfeinar's [Turf Einar] two sons Arnkel and Erland.[16]

What is significant from this account, besides listing the noble casualties, is that Snorri alleges Eirik engaged in regular cruises and that, once hearing King Edmund had appointed Olaf as ruler of Northumbria in his place, he being no friend to the Northmen, Eirik had gathered an army. Some, like Turf Einar's sons, came from Orkney, others from the Hebrides and more from Ireland. This clearly suggests Eirik had a bigger game afoot, this was no mere raid but an invasion, a re-conquest and the notion he marched deep inland would certainly fit with Stainmore as battleground.

We also learn that Eirik's opponent would be Olaf. The date, however, given as 941, does not fit. *Fagrskinna* tells a very similar tale:

> King Eiríkr, when he came to power in Northumbria, considered how extensive his father's lands had been when he ruled over the whole of Norway and many tributary lands, and thought that he himself had little in the way of authority, and for that reason he went on plundering expeditions in the British Isles and raided widely around them. The sons of Jarl Torf-Einarr were Arnkell, Erlendr and Ոorfinnr hausakljúfr [Skull-cleaver]. Ոorfinnr's son Hávarär married King Eiríkr's daughter Ragnhildr.
>
> It happened one summer that King Eiríkr was raiding in the west of Scotland and around Ireland and Wales, and

he continued the expedition until he came south around England and raided there as well as in other places, because King Aäalsteinn had died by then, and his son King Játmundr [Edmund] was ruling England. Eiríkr had such a large army that five kings accompanied him. Because Eiríkr was a very bold and successful warrior, he had such confidence in himself and his forces that he went far inland and went raiding everywhere. Then King Óláfr came against him; he was a tributary king of King Játmundr. They fought, and Eiríkr was overpowered by the land army, and he fell there with all his troop, and with him fell Torf-Einarr's sons Arnkell and Erlendr.[17]

Egil isn't helpful, but his version, succinct and terse as it is, broadly chimes with both *Heimskringla* and *Fagrskinna*: '... Egil received word from Norway that Eirik Bloodaxe had been killed on a Viking raid in Britain, Gunnhild and their sons had gone to Denmark and all the men who had accompanied them had left England.'[18] The notion that Eirik is the loser after an abortive raid doesn't seem to fit with the notion of his being expelled from York; and yet, as explained below, this may not be as far-fetched as it seems.

Back to the chronicles and irritatingly Simeon of Durham has nothing to say on this, nor does Henry of Huntingdon, but Roger of Wendover tells us: 'King Eric was treacherously killed by Earl Macchus* in a certain lonely place which is called Stainmore with his son Haeric and his brother Ragnald, betrayed by earl Oswulf and thereafter King Eadred ruled in these parts.'[19] As both W. G. Collingwood and latterly Michael Woods point out, the similarity of names here to Harek and Ragnvald is striking. Roger's thirteenth-century chronicle may well have relied on an earlier, possibly tenth-century, lost Chronicle of York. Adam of Bremen appears to follow Roger's version[20].

Both W. G Collingwood and more recently Alex Woolf (see chapter ten), favour the idea that Eirik has not sallied eastwards from his capital at York but that all this occurs *after* his expulsion. He is in fact attempting to move to wrest back control of York and

---

* Macchus appears to have been Olaf Cuaran's son – also later killed by the Northumbrians.

his advance is blocked by a powerful enemy force occupying the pass. Eirik, like St Olaf much later at Stiklestad,* tries to bludgeon his way through, trusting to the professionalism of his men to outmatch the greater numbers of his relatively under-equipped and poorly trained foes.

Like Olaf he gets it wrong and the fight degenerates into a battle of attrition in which superior numbers eventually win out. I am of course relying heavily on heroic assumption, but it is possible to reconcile the evidence to this theory. The ASC refers to Eirik being 'expelled'. It says nothing of his death, but that would have to follow any expulsion. There is an implication here that Eirik wasn't defending his throne but trying to win it back.

Where both *Heimskringla* and *Fagrskinna* refer to an extended Viking cruise and Eirik's death whilst raiding, they may be alluding to an historical reality. Eirik has been expelled and takes to his ships along with his queen, family and such *hird*-men as will follow. If he wants his throne back, he'll have to fight for it. Wars are expensive so he will need to re-fill his war chest. He also has relationships with the Norse Jarls of Orkney, which would explain the presence of Turf Einar's sons.

He may be raiding but he's also gathering an army. So, from the Humber he sails up the east coast of Scotland to Orkney, then on to the Hebrides, from there to Ireland and across the Irish Sea to make landfall on the Lancashire coast. He marshals his army for an advance eastwards, leaving Gunnhild and a rearguard to watch their ships. This is Collingwood's and more recently Woolf's theory, which I subscribe to.

What time of year does this happen? Well, if Eirik is expelled let's say early in 954, that would give him time to cruise and recruit during the summer months for a late summer/early autumn campaign. Winter snows would block the pass – sometimes they still do. If he is to get from the west coast to the east, he can't afford to be weatherbound. Speed is of the essence, to use his

---

* Fought on 29 July 1030, this was the final action of King Olaf's attempt to regain power in Norway. The King attempted the Boar's Snout to effect a breakthrough but failed and fell. His much younger half-brother Harald, to be known as *Hardradi*, though wounded, escaped and lived to fight another day. Thirty-six years later, his own saga would end the same way.

army as a surgical scalpel rather than a club. If he moves fast, he will catch his enemies off guard. But the coalition ranged against him has had time to recruit forces of their own, to assemble allies and war bands, call in favours. They would be aware of Eirik's progress and his likely landing ground.

It would be obvious at this juncture which direction his army would take. I say army, one can only guess at the numbers involved. If we allow say thirty men per ship, then 30-odd ships would be needed to convey up to a thousand fighting men. Clearly any numbers of noncombatants, supplies and horses would need additional transport. How many enemy they faced on the day is anybody's guess. It's clear from the synoptic sources, if these are credible, that Olaf and Oswulf commanded many more. A prudent captain facing such a strong war band would look for a minimum superiority in numbers of three to one.

Alea iacta est, Eirik's Rubicon. His scouts will have warned him of the block ahead. Outflanking is out of the question; the ground won't allow. To retreat would be failure, it's probably too late in the season for another attempt and he can't afford to keep his force under arms for very long. Eirik is nothing if not decisive. If he can brush this opposition aside, the road to York is his. Everyone will be looking to him, the grey-haired veteran.

In reality, he doesn't have any choice. Time of day – we've no idea, I'll guess late morning or early afternoon in mid-September, dusk in these northern latitudes perhaps 19.00 hours. Time enough. Unfurl the banners, shake out from column to line, each man stands with his lord. Maybe they're already fully mailed or more likely the armour is stowed on pack animals, heavy links, supple with oil cold to the touch, fitting helmets and tightening chinstraps. Checking weapons and shields, voiding bladders, loud with ribaldry and jest, terror's antidotes.

'They all stood so firmly stiff-minded / the young warriors in the battle, thinking eagerly / who they could soonest conquer / with their swords, the life of fated men / the warriors with their weapons. Slaughter fell upon the earth. / They stood steadfast: Byrhtnoth exhorted them / ordering every warrior to think upon the scrum / who wished for glory in fighting the Danes.' (*Battle of Maldon*, 122-9.)

Whilst the pass is relatively narrow, the contours both north and south aren't overly steep so it would be possible to form a strong

'Valhalla, I am coming...'

shield wall blocking the passage with reserves mustered behind on the reverse (east) slope – a move Wellington would now doubt have thoroughly approved of. Eirik would have been in the dark as to the true numbers of his opponents, perhaps they were counting on his bullish overconfidence, feeding reserves into the fight to shore up their line. Eirik didn't have reserves.

Heimskringla clearly describes a battle of attrition with the allies filling the ranks each time a man fell. In the end it is Eirik's line which cracks. At first, the lines shuffle and sway. Both would adopt the standard shield wall, linden boards not quite overlapping as each man hefted his weapons. In the front line the elite, mail burnished and glinting even in a pallid light, blades honed to razor-edged perfection, glancing across to assess the enemy, looking for faces you know – and you would. The warrior castes confronting each other that day came from a relatively narrow pool. In the shifting sands of cross alliances, today's opponent might have been yesterday's comrade. You may even be related by blood or marriage. Battle fuelled blood feuds.

'Then he swiftly pierced another Viking / so that the mail-shirt burst – that one was wounded in the breast / through the ring-locks, the poisonous point / stood at his heart. The earl was the happier / then he laughed, the mindful man, said thanks to the Measurer / for the day's work which the Lord had given him.' (*Battle of Maldon*: 143-8.)

Above the rim of shields, proud banners of lords and kings, a mass of pennants. Eirik's banner would have been prominent, fitting for a king of York, even one dispossessed for a second time, possibly a black raven on white background but, like so much else, that's wholly conjectural. And whose emblems did he see opposite: Olaf's and Oswulf, Macchus and the other lords now ranged against him, some no doubt former allies. We can be sure Eirik wasn't surprised.

Nor I think was this an ambush in the traditional sense. He may not have expected opposition at this point, but it would appear at some stage. Eirik must have acknowledged that the enemy had chosen their ground well. Battle would not commence at once. A shouting of orders, blare of horns the lines move like a living being, shifting and settling. Possibly there was an attempt at parley. Everybody knew that once the shield walls clashed, it would be a fight to the finish. Neither side really had anywhere else to go. Eirik simply had to break through, the confederates just had to stop him. – *dum spiro, spero*.

Earl Macchus is branded as a traitor whose actions lead to the king's demise. We again have no clue as to what shifting web of alliances has been spun since Eirik first took the throne. In a contemporary context, Northumbria is a 'failed' state. In such circumstances as we saw all too painfully during the terrible civil war in Syria, such conflicts aren't marked by fixed allegiances. The various players cooperate, divide and fight in new coalitions.

Insults and a swig from reassuring flasks as the lines move forward. You don't receive the attack standing, momentum must be soaked up, the push resisted until it runs out of steam. A flurry of missiles skimming overhead, men yelling to drown out their fear. Clash of shields like breakers crashing on the shore, each man's vision reduced to the few feet around him. We can gather this was a long fight, several hours at least.

I'm going to guess that it was Eirik who first advanced to contact. His was more likely a better disciplined and cohesive force, perhaps he even adopted the boar's snout, a wedge to batter through the opposing shield wall. If he did, it didn't work, no more than it would for King Olaf 70 years later. The best Eirik might have achieved was to punch a narrow salient into the line, penetrating but not breaking. This tactic when it failed could in turn be fatal to the aggressor, as the salient was horribly vulnerable.

In such intense combat even fit men tired quickly, water would be needed as dehydration can do for an armoured man as surely as an enemy's point. If we accept the view in the synoptic chronicles, Eirik's forces were able to hold their own for a considerable period and inflict substantial losses. But the confederates could make good their casualties from reserves, Eirik had few or none.

'Then an armoured man came up to the earl – he wished to carry off the rings of the warrior / the armour and the accoutrements and the ornamented blade / Then Byrhtnoth drew out his sword from its sheath / broad and brown-edged and struck him in the byrnie / Too quickly some sail-man hindered him / when he wounded the arm of that earl / The golden-hilted sword fell to the ground – neither could he hold the stern blade / or wield his weapon. Nevertheless, the hoary battle-warrior / spoke a word, emboldening his fighters, ordered them to go forth as good comrades / then he could not stand fast on his feet for long.' (*Battle of Maldon*, 159-71.)

Fear is a contagion. It affects those at the rear, seeing terrors ahead. Men in the front line don't have the leisure and they've nowhere to run anyway. We don't know if Eirik suffered any mass defection or whether, as pressure increased and the line got too thin, his survivors rallied back in a final stand around his and his *jarls*' banners.

Perhaps, like Hardrada over a century later, he died trying to stem the rot. By the end, ravens would feast well as the king's banner dipped for the final time. Now, the business of counting and stripping the dead, cutting the throats of any enemy wounded, victors tending their own. How many men died that day, we cannot say. What final resting place for Eirik Bloodaxe, we do not know, but no great heroic sendoff, food for the crows; 'paths of glory lead but to the grave.'

'Coming home dead, without a head is not very delightful.'[21] Does the old man heft his axe for the final time and mount a last doomed berserker charge into the midst of his foes, or is he just cut down by some flurry of random blows? Who will, round the hall fire that night and many nights to come, boast he ended the life of Eirik Bloodaxe? Did the victors perceive their victim's fame would outlast the generations, still sung by bards a millennium later?

'Loaded with mail of linked lies / what weapon can the king lift to fight / when chance-met enemies employ sly / sword and shoulder-piercing pike / pressed into the mire / trampled and hewn till a knife / in whose hand? – severs tight neck cords / Axe rusts. Spine picked bare by ravens, agile / maggots devour the slack side / and inert brain, never wise / [..] there will be nothing on Stainmore to hide / void, no sable to disguise / what he wore under the lies / king of Orkney, king of Dublin, twice / king of York, where the tide / stopped till long flight / from who knows what smile / scowl, disgust of delight / ended in bale on the fellside.'[22]

Nine

THE GOOD NAME NEVER DIES

> Kine die,
> Kindred die,
> Every man is mortal:
>
> But the good name,
> Never dies,
> Of one who has done well.
>
> *Havamal* ('The Speech of the
> High One' in the Codex Regius)

Today's neo-Nazism is growing more associated with Norse imagery due to the incessant adoption and use of Norse symbols, like various runes or even Thor's hammer. These co-options have reached the point that such symbols, many currently in use by practitioners of the modern-day Asatru religion, have now been officially catalogued as hate symbols by the Anti-Defamation League in its Hate on Display database.

This sort of cultural appropriation is not at all unique to neo-Nazism; in fact, it actually finds its roots in the German völkisch movement of the mid-1800s, before developing through the Weimar era, until it culminates in the widespread use of Old Norse myth and imagery by Hitler's Nazi Party during the Third Reich ...

The closer this association between the Nazis and the Vikings becomes, the more legitimacy these groups' use of traditional Old Norse imagery gains. ... This is a net loss for communities, especially those in northern Europe, that are still deeply tied to their Norse roots, as their cultural symbols and traditions have been radicalized in a way that pushes an extremely dangerous and negative image of the Nordic people ... In what ways were Nordic cultural markers, especially pertaining to Old Norse imagery and mythology, used to influence both the völkisch movement in Germany, as well as the greater Third Reich era as a whole?

The answer is not as simple as one easily identifiable cause or reason; rather, it seems to be due in part to a culmination of various factors leading to the mythification of Nordic peoples based on conjured, elitist racial stereotypes and heightened importance of national myth as a source of pride and power.[1].

At the time of writing, hundreds of thousands of German citizens have taken to the streets to protest at the rise of far-right elements in their polity. The Alt-Right continues to swell, fuelled by xenophobia and racism. To them, Vikings are hallowed forbears. A warrior taking what he wants, despising all weakness – brutal, rapacious, ruthless. Consider the image of Jake Angeli, the 'QAnon Shaman', with his painted face and horned hat, at the US Capitol invasion on 6 January 2021 in Washington, DC.

Populist political movements aren't interested in historical truth. They cherry pick icons and draw on myths, usually to help point fingers at others who fail to live up to some heroic image. Yes, the Vikings were a godsend, clearly still are – ambition, strength, fortitude, honour (or their version of it), supremacy, glorifying war and fetishising weapons.

And let's not pretend it isn't attractive. When Sir Ian McKellen filmed his arresting version of *Richard III* in 1995, he chose a clear Third Reich image for his slyly sneering Richard, and it was disturbingly attractive[2].

Yet the fascists have got it all wrong. Whatever similar characteristics Eirik may show, he's not a Nazi. They're about the corporate power of the state, Eirik is not, he's about Eirik. The Vikings don't really do corporate. They don't much like kings, don't subscribe to pre-packaged ideologies. The Viking is an individual, he is, in fact, the antithesis of the totalitarian model. Men like Eirik will strive to attain ultimate power but they understand this has clearly defined limits. Yes, he wants control, but in the strictly personal, not as expressed in the National Socialist or Communist sense. Kings of Norway frequently, if not invariably, ruled through intimidation and oppression, but that's because they needed to. They demand their subjects nod to their crown but it's not about party politics. There was never a defined ideological base.

As I mentioned in the introduction, I came to the era courtesy of Kirk Douglas and Tony Curtis, and *The Vikings* certainly glorified the Norsemen. It showed them as free spirits, essentially noble and bound by their own virile code. King Aella[3], the Saxon despot, came across as far more the villain. For us, the Viking (in a purely romantic sense) symbolises freedom, the ability to direct life according to your own will, to forge your own destiny without reproach; The entrancing myth has so far outstripped historical reality that it's taken over.

Eirik was the last independent king of York, his two short and extremely unstable stints ended in his death at Stainmore and any serious prospect of an independent or semi-independent northern kingdom died with him. In the flesh but not in the mind. Death provides stamina to legend, and a glorious defeat often counts for more in posterity than victory – think of Roland, Joan of Arc, or Che Guevara. Northern and southern England have always been and remain culturally different, much of this is romantic and regional nonsense, but there is a core of truth.

Eirik's fame rests more on sagas than chronicles and, as we've seen, these are far from reliable sources. His own saga seems to have vanished, and we're forced to rely on others, Egil's in particular. He and Egil were never friends, very far from it and perhaps, in part, that's because they've too much in common. And there's Gunnhild, a very significant player in her own right, a lot of the bad blood (see chapter eleven) with Egil is down to her. Those synoptic histories, Theodoricus[4] and *Historia Norwegie*, offer mitigation for Eirik's failures by pushing the blame onto Gunnhild. Was the great hero in fact just a hen-pecked husband?

Physically, he conforms to the Norse racial stereotype, good looking tall, powerful, brave, a natural fighter and leader of men. He's also recognised as violent, vindictive, short-tempered, and irascible. His successes, whilst frequent, are always short-term,

The Good Name Never Dies

undone by his vices. He tends to typify the Viking freebooter, not unlike Egil himself, who can in the tactical sense be a natural winner but is devoid of any strategic insight and lacking in the essential subtleties for long-term success. Eirik's obscure death at Stainmore does, as it's generally agreed, mark the end of the first Viking Age in England and he follows a pattern of opportunist leaders who are finally no match for the growing power of a centralised English nation state. He and they become anachronisms.

Cnut, leading the charge for a second Viking age, is very different. Every bit as ruthless when he feels the need, he is a consummate politician and diplomat who creates a stable regime in England as part of a northern empire. This creation only endures as long as he does, his successors are short-lived and feeble; but he's a far cry from Ivar the Boneless, or from Eirik, statesman rather than brigand. Harald Hardradi ('Hard Ruler') whose attempt at conquest in 1066, ended in a proper *Ragnarök* at Stamford Bridge, seems to fit better into the earlier mould. Hardradi was the younger half-brother of King, latterly Saint Olaf whose own Little Big Horn was at Stiklestad thirty odd years earlier, another who can claim to be last of the Vikings[5].

'Where now the horse? Where now the men? Where now the benefactor? / Where now the seat at the feast? Where the hall joys? / Alas, bright beaker! Alas, burnished warrior! / Alas, proud prince! How that time has gone, dark under nights' helm, as if it had never been.' (Anon: *The Wanderer*.)

Today, Eirik could be seen as a model for Conan the Barbarian / the Cimmerian. Originally written by American author Robert E. Howard and now a self-sustaining genre, Conan's adventures have been continued by many authors with many publishers across the globe. There's no suggestion that Howard (who committed suicide at the age of thirty), ever specifically used Eirik as an inspiration, but his fictional northland Cimmeria, barren, hard and primeval, does seem to resemble Viking Age Iceland and Conan could be Eirik or Egil's successor. In his short but immensely productive writing career Howard created a whole new paradigm, 'sword & sorcery', which blended elements of fantasy, mythology and the supernatural. He was influenced by both E. A. Poe and H. P. Lovecraft. His writing also coincided with the rise of fascism, and he became tainted with accusations of racial prejudice.

Eric Bloodaxe the Viking: 'I Shall Die Laughing'

The brilliance of Henry Treece's quartet of Viking novels for young people, *Viking's Dawn* (1956), *The Road to Miklagard* (1957), *Viking's Sunset* (1958) and *The Horned Helmet* (1963) has been reworked for an adult audience by Bernard Cornwell in his *Last Kingdom* series Eirik does not feature, as the eponymous hero Uhtred of Bebbanburh (Bamburgh), fights his final battle at Brunanburh in 937, before Eirik arrives on Northern England's shore.

Eirik receives more direct tribute from Basil Bunting in his poem *Briggflatts*, portrayed as a clear if rather obscure northern hero: 'by such rocks / men killed Bloodaxe.' In the hands of a master this earthy, rather brutal approach meshes Eirik into the landscape. Even if his life and certainly death are obscure, his blood still fills the veins of northerners. Eirik did become his own myth, even if his saga is lost, his shade still lingers.

Gunnhild herself becomes the heroine of a fictionalized biography written by Poul Anderson[6]. Whilst this does attempt to stick within a broad historical framework, it features a strong overlay of fantasy. The Queen is indeed a witch who learned her craft from a brace of Finnish wizards and regularly has recourse to the dark arts; she's an accomplished 'shapeshifter'[7]. None of this would have come as much of a surprise to her contemporaries. In his successful run of five Viking Age novels, the *Oathsworn* series, Scottish writer Robert Low includes Eirik as one of his stock characters[8].

Sir Walter Scott has a great deal to answer for. Aside from resurrecting Scottish folklore and fashioning it into history, bringing back the border reivers and parading fat King George in ludicrous tartan pastiche, he was an important contributor to the Romantic movement. This was part of a process that had already been underway for several centuries: 'The Renaissance invented the Middle Ages in order to redefine itself; the Enlightenment perpetuated them in order to admire itself, and the Romantics revived them in order to escape from themselves.'[9] This leads us to the 'noble savage', an ideal of a heroic age unsullied by effete civilisation.

It was fun. Lancelot 'Capability' Brown had shifted formal gardens back to a clever, almost seamless, facsimile of nature. In Northumberland, at Belsay, after *c.* 1810, Sir Charles Monck Middleton created a Tolkienesque quarry garden from a building site, a glorious gothic fantasy of tiny hidden glades, secret glens, with high stone gantries above.

This process continues: 'In fact this fascination with the medieval past has been operative both in the tradition of high and low culture; within the sphere of the popular, the appropriation of the Middle Ages has turned out a most profitable device to sell not only cultural products but also goods as disparate as beer or wooden flooring.'[10] I book my holidays locally through Norsemen Travel, I can go on a Viking River cruise, far more comfortable than any *drakkar*. The upshot is that our image of the Vikings isn't based on history but on subsequent reimagining. Scott and the Romantics were harmless frivolity and still a good read. What came next was not.

During the nineteenth century in Germany, the *Volkisch* movement began to gather momentum. This was a heavy-handed nationalist fervour which rejected Christianity in favour of a more exciting pagan past, Wagnerian and linked to eugenics.* The main thrust was the promotion of the Teutonic race or *Volk* as racially superior to lesser breeds. We can see where this is heading. Hitler was never an innovator, he exerted a parasitic pull on convenient, already extant cultural markers, to cobble together the National Socialist philosophy. He was effectively pushing against an open door, bringing this earlier aberration squarely into the mix.

> Although the link between Old Norse imagery and eugenics might not seem particularly clear, it is evident that the *völkisch* idolization of all traits that were considered Nordic is merely another step toward embodying the Viking idealism that was widely facilitated during this time. The idea was to replicate the desirable traits and aspects of the mythic heroes in the very same Norse mythology the völkisch movement and Nazi Party both utilized as a means for political programming and control at this time. This brand of idealism would come to be known as 'Nordicism.' In general terms, Nordicism is commonly

---

* Largely the invention of Sir Francis Galton, eugenics was branded as a 'scientific' concept, aimed at improving the human race, essentially racial stereotyping, it was adopted as a tool by the Nazis and wholly discredited though even such illuminati as Sir Flinders Petrie had earlier subscribed to the concept.

defined as being the celebration of the so-called 'Nordic race.' However, one particular point to note is that Nordicism also views the Nordic race as one endangered and superior racial group, which was used largely to give accreditation and esteem to the idea that the Nordic race is something to be protected.[11]

Spirituality thus meshed neatly with nationalism to generate a toxic brew rooted in a dark romanticization of a largely mythic past. No Viking would have had a clue what his alleged descendants were ranting about. This fixation does make it very easy to focus hostility against the *other* – 'us or them', for us or against us.

> This dynamic of race-based conflict leans largely into the idea of *Herrenrasse*, a concept which suggests the Nordic people are supposedly descended from the Proto-Aryans and are thus considered to be racially 'pure'. This origin story places mythical levels of value on Nordic peoples and their genetics, and thus the stereotypical Nordic imagery of what people should look like – heavily influenced by the tall, strong, blonde Vikings of medieval times – was often circulated to exemplify who was Aryan, and who was not. A 1933 scientific journal entry in *Scientific American* describes the Nordic Aryans of Europe as 'having long, high heads, tall bodies, blue or grey eyes and light-coloured hair'.
>
> This sort of concrete prescription of what Nordic Aryans would look like allows for easily identifiable traits to be distributed as a clear idea of what the 'master race' should look like; there is no room for interpretation in the Nordic ideal for appearance.[12]

We hear much about cultural appropriation at the present time, but the Nazis were dab hands at this and *The Poetic Edda* was hijacked quite early on by the *Volkisch* movement as a literary canon for a re-imagined German past. The collection, which does indeed form a foundation for much of Norse mythology and thereby cultural identity, was made to dovetail into the fantasy tapestry of this new Teutonic heritage.

Snorri Sturluson probably wouldn't have thought much of Adolf Hitler and his gang of seriously un-Teutonic henchmen.

A joke-shop fire sale of cranks, losers and misfits, none of whom came close, in physical terms, to any semblance of the ideal they so fervently preached. Nonetheless, historical mud sticks and to understand, insofar as we're able, our Norse heroes we have to peel away these levels of cloying fustian and get back to the clay. It isn't easy because so much of subsequent film and literature portrayal has fallen wholly or at least in part into the trap.

How then do we achieve this, to see Eirik Bloodaxe as the real man he was, not as a romantic noble savage or as Nazi stormtrooper? The synoptic sources don't really help us here and the skaldic tradition must be treated with some circumspection. Eirik has come down to us as an exemplar of what it meant to be a Viking, even if he had never encountered the term.

To put ourselves into the mind of as tenth-century Norseman is impossible. One of the very best attempts I have encountered is Low's *Oathsworn* series. He picks up the timbre of the sagas and gives them a modern rendering, not a full makeover, an adjustment, so we can understand. Eirik's story is a millennium old, but he has more in common with Homer than he has with us. His time is so culturally and socially remote, we possess no real markers to guide us and never will. This branch of history requires an enormous leap of imagination, back beyond the Nazis and Romantics, away from the censorious pens of monkish chroniclers to an era when the worlds of gods and men co-existed and collided.

These meshed in 2022 in Robert Egger's film *The Northman* with Alexander Skarsgard as the revenge-fixated hero after Danish actor Claes Bang as a suitably unpleasant villain. Taken loosely from Saxo Grammaticus,* this is a visually arresting attempt to bring the sagas to the big screen and in a way we'll understand. The swords matter.

Odin was real to Eirik and embracing Christ didn't really affect that. Christianity was then a thin veneer grafted onto pagan hardwood, which had itself endured for millennia and placed mortals in the world of both mythos and nature. We must always remember that none of the chronicle sources is Norse. We don't

---

* *The Legend of Amleth* is said to be the basis for the story of Hamlet. Saxo himself (c. 1150–1220) was a Danish historian and theologian, clerk to the Bishop of Lund and an advisor to King Valdemar I of Denmark.

read what the Vikings ever had to say about themselves, we hear from others who encountered them. Given the bloody and bruising nature of so many of those encounters we can grasp how a note of censure might creep in.

Our Norse ancestors were closer to life than we are, they had no insulation. Death was commonplace, famine and disease were always lurking in the wings. For months in the year, they lived in near total darkness. They would instinctively expose any infant showing sign of disability to the elements. They would see this not as cruelty but inevitability, even a kindness. Survival was hard and uncertain enough, even for the fittest. A man would be lucky to make it into what we would call middle age, women not much older. Egil reaching his mid-eighties is almost as fantastical as a magic sword.

People lived with their genealogies, they knew who they were and where they belonged. The barrows of their ancestors ringed them like a shield. Their lives, daily, were infinitely more insecure than ours but their grounding was far more concrete, their lineage was cultural and social armour. It stood them in rather better stead than we can perhaps appreciate.

There were much fewer people and very few urban centres. Distances were often vast, travel both uncertain and dangerous, yet the Norse, through their genius for shipbuilding conquered the waves, crossed seas and oceans. They navigated river systems, portaged their vessels between them and discovered new lands, Faroes, Iceland, Greenland and Vinland, the eastern coast of today's America and Canada. They traded across the globe, carved out footholds in England, Scotland, Ireland and what is now France. Eirik flits across the historical record like a mailed wraith, yet he and his fellow Vikings left an indelible footprint, a magnetism that draws us today

In the small plaza just before the entrance to Reykjavik's impressively brutalist Hallgrimskirkja Cathedral, stands a large bronze effigy of Leif Eriksson. This monument was America's gift to Iceland in 1930 to mark a millennium of democracy (the first Althing having been convened in 930). Leif is tall, broad and lantern jawed. He predates Kirk Douglas, but the look is very similar. This is from the US, not Germany, but the suggestion of a superior race is contoured in Leif's biceps and natural self-confidence. In fact, the historical Leif was a rather stocky, salty and portly fellow, nowhere near as glamorous. But then who wants to see that kind of reality, certainly not the thousands of tourists who stare admiringly.

Eirik has no statue, the best he gets is Rey (or Rere) Cross just north of the A66 at Stainmore[13]. It would not have held happy memories for Eirik who probably died wondering how he managed, after such a long and seriously eventful life, to end up in such a nowhere place.

Not much of the original cross survives, just the hub of the socket and a sliver of shaft. For a while, after 1990, it was housed in the Bowes Museum before being returned to site – not its original location, that was atop a tiny hillock on the south side of the road. Back in Speed's day (1611), elements of carving were apparently still visible, traces of which, W. G. Collingwood asserts, could just be discerned in the late nineteenth century. The name is derived from Old Norse *hreyrr*, meaning a cairn or boundary stone. It's generally described as an Anglo-Norse 10th-century cross. No evidence of any associated burials has ever been found. A broad consensus seems to favour the idea it was a boundary marker between Cumbria and Northumbria.

Not all agree, the Reverend William Slater Calverley[14] suggested that the deployment of such markers to delineate boundaries was post-Conquest and that their initial function was as tombstones. It was Calverley who linked Rey Cross to the fight at Stainmore. Now this sounds a lot like wishful thinking, but even a sage as eminent as Collingwood refused to dismiss the idea out of hand. As he rather condescendingly notes, 'A romancer might be justified in fancying that the Rey Cross was carved and set up by Northumbrian admirers of the once mighty and long famous last King of York.'[15] Who knows? But for Eirik, this is as good as it gets.*

Eirik Bloodaxe, the real man, emerges as a throwback to an earlier, even more brutal age: 'Yet in the end, he stands as an example of a failed hero; one who having no one to tell a story, faded into the mists of time, leaving only his name behind.'[16]

---

* Eirik does seemingly have another memorial, a stone cross located at Gard in Haugesund in his native Norway. It is said this was erected by his sons in their father's honour, although this is certainly open to question, (see chapter eleven).

I don't think he would have agreed. Nor do I. Eirik is an important link in the emergence of hereditary kingship in Norway. He was his father's son and successor, albeit unsuccessful in hanging on to his throne and he went on to fly the final standard for an independent Norse state in the North of England. His death at Stainmore in 954 is a seminal point in English history because thereafter there *is* an England. The idea wasn't new, Athelstan had pulled it off before and after Brunanburh, but that effort briefly foundered under his successors. The situation engineered by Ivar the Boneless and his immediate successors as leaders of the Viking Great Army ran into a brick wall against Alfred but sustained their status until the time of his grandson. Eirik was the Northumbrians' final Great North Hope, yet they still turned their backs on him.

Realpolitik always trumps the Noble Savage. Yet Eirik wasn't noble in any Utopian sense, he was a serious player in a complex and sophisticated game. And as for savagery, his court at York would rank as exceedingly cosmopolitan, the hub of a widespread, diverse and very extensive trading network, a bustling and industrious if un-fragrant industrial nexus and also a significant political and cultural centre.

> He dreamed. He lay like a rib of earth buried under centuries of waste and dissolution. Black night hung over him and filled every cranny of the spaces within him, and the silence seemed as final as death. But sometimes it was broken. Sometimes it was as if he had slept and now lay still with his eyes closed, listening to the roaring of the sea as it broke and boiled beyond him. He seemed to hear the sound of rain on grass and there were voices, of men and birds and beasts. But thunder was the loudest of all. At times he seemed to feel the hollow tread of animals, and the tiny tremors of the ground sent shivers through his bones, and the minute movement of insects and the feet of birds made echoes in his skull. He could not see. All he saw were pictures of the mind, images of burning, of a boat and of his son.[17]

Eirik is a wraith, an old legend worn thin by telling, denied that immortality guaranteed by the sagas, his end too fogged to be glorious. Despite all that, he is to many, the epitome of the Viking Age. As epitaphs go, there are worse.

Ten

WILL THE REAL EIRIK BLOODAXE...

Ragnar Lodbrok is survived by his four sons: Ivar, Halfdan, Ubba and Sigurd Snake-in-the-Eye. Of these, the cunning and resourceful Ivar is the natural leader. He commands two of his brothers and their war bands on a cruise into the Mediterranean. They attack the territories of what will become the Emirate of Granada, Almeria and several other coastal towns. Pushing inland, they are confronted by large local forces and battle ensues. This time the Vikings come off worse and are forced to retreat to their ships. It takes all of Ivar's considerable skills and charisma to prevent the withdrawal turning into a rout.

Even when they escape out to sea, they are pursued by swift Moorish galleys, but Ivar's superior seamanship and tactics turn the tables, and they destroy the enemy vessels. Despite their earlier hammering, Ivar leads the survivors on a surprise raid on Malaga where they manage to penetrate the fortified palace of the local ruler and make good their losses with his treasure. His wives and catamites are all left dead in their wake.

On Ivar's eventual return, the brothers learn of their father's death in England and vow revenge. No mere raid this time but a planned campaign of conquest. Northumbria is about to experience the Viking scourge notched up another level.

Eric Bloodaxe the Viking: 'I Shall Die Laughing'

Year 866

And Ivar
Who ruled at Jorvik,
Cut an Eagle
On the back of Aella

Were Ivar and Eirik of York related? It's a good question. What we really know of Eirik, as we have seen, is fragmentary at best and fraught with uncertainties. This life of Eirik is constructed from a whole raft of broad context and some serious leaps of faith. We can accept that he existed – his legend didn't grow through happenstance or literary fiction. He's surer than King Arthur or Robin Hood, but not necessarily by any great margin. The key question is whether Eirik, son of Harald Fairhair and brother of Hakon the Good, is the same man as Eirik of York. Not everyone thinks so and it's simply not possible to give a definitive answer.

One of the earliest debaters is the eminent Victorian antiquary William Gershom Collingwood, who argues forcibly that these are indeed one and the same. It is worth re-capping here: the Icelandic sagas, Egil's in particular, tell us that Eirik was obliged to flee Norway when his half-brother Hakon the Good, sponsored by his adopted father Athelstan of England, meddled in Norway to put his protégé on the throne. Even Eirik could not withstand such odds and besides, the Norse had apparently had quite enough of his heavy-handed oppression. Snorri echoes this with his account in *Heimskringla*.

Yet not long after, Athelstan is happy to entrust the governance of Northumbria to the renegade, poacher turned gamekeeper perhaps. Eirik meanwhile supports his uncertain finances by frequent raiding. When Eadred becomes King of Wessex, his animus towards northerners means Eirik has to resume large-scale raiding as a way of life, until his luck runs out against Eadred's satrap Olaf in a final 'dim, weird battle in the west' – Stainmore.

Collingwood points out this simply doesn't stand up as the Olaf in question has to be the same Dublin Viking who held sway – if rather precariously – under both Edmund and Eadred[1]. We can probably all agree that Snorri, writing 250 years after these events, exercises a fair measure of poetic licence, but the level of detail he

Will the Real Eirik Bloodaxe...

imparts persuades that some of what he says is correct, if simply out of sequence and marred by distortion. How much credibility to grant will always be subjective, though Alex Woolf argues very eruditely that the Icelandic sources may not be that far off the mark after all.

Collingwood[2] goes on to consider Adam of Bremen's seemingly odd assertion that Harold Bluetooth,* King of Denmark, sent his son Hring to Northumbria, and it was this Danish prince who was 'betrayed and killed by the Northumbrians'. In which case Eirik is a son of King Harold of Denmark, not of Harald Fairhair from Norway. Skene and others discount this, saying that surely this Hring was the same as the Hring who dies at Brunanburh and that Eirik was indeed a son of Harald Fairhair. Collingwood points towards *The Annals of Clonmacnoise*[3] which claim a king of Denmark's son lay amongst the many confederate dead. So, it does seem possible that a Danish prince did indeed come into northern England, but not that he ever ruled there. This tale may in fact be an echo from an earlier legend of a Sigurd Hring who features as a fictitious conqueror of the north. There are other contenders whom Collingwood dismisses out of hand[4].

As for *ASC* and medieval chroniclers, *viz* Florence of Worcester, Henry of Huntingdon, William of Malmesbury, Roger of Wendover and Symeon of Durham, none refers to Eirik during Athelstan's lifetime. Edmund came to his late brother's throne aged only 18 and Olaf Guthfrithson saw a chance to retake York. The Scots did for him soon after and Olaf Cuaran slid into the vacancy. Edmund soon showed who was top dog, driving out this Olaf, attacking Cumbria and keeping a firm hold until his untimely death in 946. His successor Eadred obliges the northerners to demonstrate obeisance and ensures the king of Scotland does the same, but then the record gets confused, (as we saw in chapter seven).

It's worth reconsidering the chronology: in 947, Archbishop Wulfstan and the Northumbrian Witan swear an oath to Eadred. They soon overlooked that to set Eirik up as king. Eadred marches

---

* Harald Bluetooth, King of Denmark (*c.* 911–*c.* 985, ruled from 958 was a son of Gorm the Old who consolidated royal authority throughout Denmark and is credited with introducing Christianity. He was succeeded by his son Svein Forkbeard, father of Cnut.

north, blitzes Northumbria and burns Ripon in reprisal. As he withdraws, ruins smouldering behind, Eirik ambushes and cuts up his rearguard at Castleford. Eadred swung back to take revenge and the Northumbrians, bowing to his overwhelming might, expel Eirik. Next year, Olaf Cuaran is back, presumably with Eadred's blessing or at least consent. Yet in 952, Eadred imprisons Wulfstan and attacks Thetford (the two incidents are not necessarily related), but the people nonetheless drive out Olaf and accept Eirik for his second and final tenure. Cryptically, *ASC* states that in 954 Eirik is again overreached and Eadred rules Northumbria directly until his death the following year.

Symeon of Durham broadly agrees but tells us nothing of Eirik's second rule, merely observing that in 954 Earl Osulf was appointed to 'govern' (rather than rule) Northumbria, presumably, though this is unstated, by King Eadred himself[5]. The *Historiae Continuatio* adds more flesh, referring to Eirik's expulsion in 954 and death at the hands of Earl Maccus, described as 'son of Olaf'. Roger of Hoveden goes further, alleging the Northumbrians, prior to their full and final submission to Eadred, also killed Amancus [Maccus?] son of Anlaf and that Oswulf (of Bamburgh) was appointed as 'governor' – a mere satrap – no more kings[6].

William of Malmesbury offers some startling addenda, averring that Eadred, after his accession in 946, nearly annihilated the Northumbrians – now clearly he didn't, but his subsequent ravaging was no mild rebuke. The Northumbrians knew all about ravaging. Roger of Wendover lays the blame for Eirik's demise at the door of Earl Oswulf, even if the deed was accomplished on the battlefield by Earl Maccus. Eirik's son Henry and brother Ragnald (Harek and Rognvald as named by Snorri?) also perished[7].

As we saw, Collingwood takes the view that Eirik was approaching Stainmore along the old Roman road travelling south west to north east, leading an army of Norsemen, probably mustered in and recruited from Lancashire and seeking to crush fissiparous remnants under his rival Olaf, the opposition centred in Yorkshire. Olaf was allied to Oswulf of Bamburgh with a contingent of Cumbrians making common cause.

It seems, as Collingwood suggests, Eirik had underestimated the strength of the opposition and was finally overwhelmed. This ties in with the idea of a protracted and hard-fought contest, finally and only decided by superior numbers. Maccus, the chroniclers seem to agree, was both a son of Olaf and nemesis of Eirik. As he appears to have been killed himself immediately afterwards, we could assume that Oswulf and the Northumbrians took care of that detail. Olaf apparently returned to Ireland and disappears from view. It sort of fits together, even if we're walking on historical quicksand.

We can further infer that these chronicle accounts, while they say nothing of Eirik's origins, broadly concur with Snorri's and the skaldic versions, except we know Snorri is wide of the mark in some key respects. Where he gets it seriously wrong is to view Eirik's expulsion from Norway and his arrival in England as following one upon the other. He tells us Athelstan invited him, but that appears patently absurd (though Alex Woolf thinks otherwise, see below), given that it was the king who had just sponsored Eirik's successor Hakon the Good in his successful takeover of Norway.

Egil's account of his meeting with his old enemy Eirik at the latter's court in York is thrilling, it's high adventure at its most dramatic, but can't be relied upon as history as again, the chronology doesn't fit. Collingwood takes the view that this was probably a failure by an early compiler of the text and that the incident may well have occurred but at a rather later date, when Eirik was in fact ruling. This would be at least a decade after a literal interpretation of the saga would suggest.

Next, we return to *The Life of St Cathroe* and a possibility the saint attended Eirik at his court in York. Indeed, there is a suggestion, rather vague, that Cathroe was related to Queen Gunnhild. Whilst it may, at first glance, seem unlikely, the idea should not be dismissed out of hand. The saint was very far from being a commoner and Norse/Hibernian marriages and liaisons were commonplace. Collingwood concludes that as the visit was supposed to have been timed during king Edmund of Wessex's reign, then if the saint did journey to York, it's more likely Olaf who would be in the high chair[8]. Woolf has a persuasive counterargument.

Eirik later receives some unexpected validation from an unlikely source – Edward I of England – 'Longshanks'. The Norse King of York was cited as part evidence that the kings of England had always exercised a form of lordship over their Scottish contemporaries. The suggestion here, though it seems unlikely, is that Eadred regarded Eirik as bona fide ruler over the Northumbrians. This rather suggests subsequent tampering, as we've no evidence to back this up. Indeed, Collingwood points out that the King of Wessex never recognised Eirik as anything other than an obstacle to his own power[9], an enemy and an inconvenience.

As a rule, *The Annals of Ulster* aren't too interested in battles in England but an entry which corresponds to the year 952, referring to a fight between Norsemen and an army of Scots, Cumbrians and English might be highly relevant. Collingwood thinks this fight could be Eirik's last stand. As we know, he sees Stainmore as the culmination of a campaign begun by Eirik when he lands a force on the north-west coast at Ravenglass or Ellenborough, before moving eastwards, assaulting Westmorland as he advances. An allied force of Northumbrians under Oswulf, Norse/Gaels led by Olaf with disaffected locals from what is now Cumbria, combine to block his progress at the crucial bottleneck.

It was a big fight, not some petty skirmish. Survivors scramble back to their ships where Collingwood suggests Gunnhild is waiting, and they escape by sea. He cites local traditions which, though imprecise, mention a great battle. Such traditions, however vague, should never be dismissed out of hand. Collingwood refers to Stainmore as 'one of the most decisive battles of English history'.[10] It brought to an end the ancient Kingdom of Northumbria, which had endured, despite many vicissitudes, for over four hundred years since Ida's day, 'ane end to an auld song' indeed.

Can we then accept that Eirik ruled during two short periods in Northumbria? I think we can – but is this Eirik also the son of Harald Fairhair, is he Bloodaxe? That's more complex. The English chroniclers simply don't tell us. We can't point to any of them pointing at Norway. Eirik is clearly Norse but is he the dispossessed half-brother of Hakon the Good? Compelling as this may seem, and it does indeed seem more than just tempting, we can't produce a single chronicle source that tells us so. Egil indeed tells us so. Snorri does too, but we must be wary of believing them just because we want to. If I can borrow from redoubtable Colonel Burne and his great theory of Inherent Military Probability ('IMP'), then it does get persuasive, even though modern academic thinking isn't too keen on the Colonel's reasoning.

It seems unlikely that there are two Eiriks who operate in the same milieu at the same time. If we accept that Eirik, the son of Harald Fairhair and briefly King of Norway, is expelled by his half-brother, who is in turn backed by his sponsor Athelstan, what then happens to him if he's not the same Eirik as later rules from York? This Eirik isn't the type to quietly disappear. The Northumbrians, needy as they were, pressured as they were, are going to need somebody with significant presence if they ever hope to see off the Wessex threat. Eirik Bloodaxe has a reputation as a great Viking of royal blood, probably, almost certainly with a healthy bank balance from his raiding activities, who already has a well-armed following. Eadred knows exactly who he is and ought to be wary. He fits the job description.

In 1995 Professor Sawyer* published a short article in *Northern History* in which he argued, convincingly, that the sources for the reign of the West Saxon king Eadred did not satisfactorily support the established view that the Norwegian king Eirik ruled over Northumbria twice, from 947 to 948 and from 952 to 954. The strength of his argument lay in his demonstration that the various annal entries in manuscripts 'D' and 'E' of *ASC*, in Roger of Wendover's *Flores Historiarum* and in the *Historia Regum* attributed to Simeon of Durham for the period between 937 and the accession of Edgar were unreliable in detail, between them frequently recording the same event under different years. His revised chronology for the kingship of Northumbria in the reign of Eadred would be: Eadred 946-47, Olaf Sihtricsson 947-50, Eirik 950-52.[11]

Alex Woolf, senior lecturer at the University of St Andrews, supports the contention, as do I, that Eirik did rule twice in Northumbria. He also cautions against over-reliance on skaldic sources: 'Although a surprising amount of accurate information does seem to be contained in some of the sagas there are also many errors and anachronisms, and it is unwise to utilize material from

---

* Peter Sawyer (1928–2018) was a noted expert in Viking history and very influential – he was the historian who espoused a stance that the Vikings were more 'traders than raiders'.

these late sources which cannot be supported by more reliable informants.'[12]

He does cite the *Life of St Cathroe* as being a valuable resource, dating the saint's visit to England as taking place *c.* 941:

> In Alba, according to the *Life,* Cathroe is accompanied by Constantine mac Aedh (*c.* 900–43), and in Strathclyde by his own kinsman, Dyfnwal (post 937–ante 971), who takes him to Loidam Civitatem, 'on the boundary of the Northmen and the Cumbrians' whence one Gunderic conducts him to 'Erich' at York, whose wife is said to be a kinswoman of the saint, and thence to King Edmund (939–46) in England.[13]

Woolf finds this peruasive and again, I concur. Earlier scholars, including Sawyer and Alfred Smyth,* had been rather dismissive, finding this reference to 'Erich' (Eirik?) anachronistic.

Woolf does suggest that the alleged kinship between St Cathroe and Gunnhild seems like a significant stumbling block, but he theorises that as Egil doesn't mention Gunnhild by name, Eirik might well have had an additional consort in York who may have shared a bloodline with the saint. This is pure conjecture. Alex Woolf takes a further leap, suggesting we can accept 934 as the year of Hakon's invasion, that being an extension of Athelstan's Scottish campaign that certainly took him as far north as Caithness.

> On the English side we are faced, to some extent, with an argumentum ab silentio. After the Battle of Brunanburh … no events are recorded in any of the manuscripts of the *Anglo-Saxon Chronicle* or the *Historia Regum*, or by Roger of Wendover, until the death of Athelstan on 27 October 939. It is perhaps possible to explain the absence for annals covering this period in the various recensions of the *Anglo-Saxon Chronicle* with the suggestion that a late insertion of the Brunanburh poem, under 937, a relatively substantial

---

* Alfred P. Smyth (1942–2016) was an Irish-born academic historian and medievalist. From 2002 he was appointed Dean of Arts and Humanities at Canterbury Christ Church University.

piece of text, overlay existing entries for the next two years. Most of the annals that then record the King's death then go straight on to recount Olaf Guthfrithsson's capture of York and invasion of Mercia.

Given the lateness of the season, however, and the time it would have taken for news of Athelstan's death to reach Olaf and, subsequently, for him to raise an army and cross to Northumbria, it is unlikely that these are really events of 939. More than likely here, as elsewhere in the Chronicle, a contemporary event is accompanied by a narrative of its ultimate consequences, and Olaf will have crossed to Britain in the spring of 940. It was certainly in 940 that Olaf and Edmund came to terms and recognized one another's 'spheres of influence'. This, then, creates a 'window of opportunity' for Erik's meeting with Cathroe between late October 939 and spring 940.[14]

This is brilliantly argued but again, in purely factual terms, is no more than well-constructed hypothesis.

Woolf goes on to highlight that the chronicle sources – once the dust has settled on the field of Brunanburh – are remarkably vague as to what happens in the immediate aftermath. Olaf is on the run and the king's enemies are prostrate before him. What next? We hear little of the remaining two years of life left to Athelstan. Crucially, as Woolf ponders, did the king, despite the stunning weight of his victory, decide that the North was still too alienated for direct rule? He did give that significant land grant of ground in Amounderness to the Church at York, suggestive of Palatine rights[15]:

> ... imposing a Scandinavian sub-regulus, albeit a Christian with a Christian wife, coming from a different dynasty from the descendants of Ivar, might well be a worthwhile compromise to make. Erik's Christian credentials, as witnessed by his appearance in the *Liber Vitae* of Durham also smack, in this early period, of an otherwise unattested submission to a Christian overlord. It may also be relevant to note that despite the existence of thirty-seven royal diplomas surviving from the period between 936 and 941 Wulfstan, Archbishop

of York, appears in the witness list of none of them, in contrast to his appearance on fourteen out of eighteen in the period 931-35 and forty-four out of seventy-six between 942 and 950. The absence of such a powerful churchman from Athelstan's court in these years suggests, perhaps, that Northumbria was not quite as securely in the King's hands as it had been prior to Brunanburh.[16]

Alex Woolf's conclusion is that by interpreting of all the tenth-century sources and interfering with none, it's possible to construct a viable chronology that broadly ties us into that offered by the sagas. He therefore dates Eirik's initial tenure within Athelstan's life and reign, so that sagas aren't in fact glaringly wrong. Olaf chases Eirik out during the very early period of Athelstan's successor, his brother Edmund's reign. This is highly persuasive. Woolf concludes that it would be useful to re-evaluate the numismatic evidence. Traditionally, surviving coinage has supported the generally accepted view of Eirik's dual tenure. If these were looked at again in the light of a possible alternative timeline, then they may prove more informative.

Professor Clare Downham has examined the entire problem in detail[17], (see appendix four), writing some three years before Alex Woolf. She identifies two schools of thought beginning in the nineteenth century concerning the identity of Eirik's father: Sharon Turner, J. M. Lappenburg, Charles Plummer and James Todd all favour Harald Bluetooth, while Charles Haliday, Joseph Stevenson and of course W. G. Collingwood prefer Harald Fairhair. The 'E' Text of ASC refers to him as a son of Harald, without specifying which Harald! Henry of Huntingdon repeats this but there's no compelling evidence from this side of the North Sea which unequivocally links Eirik of York to Eirik Bloodaxe – 'they provide no proof that he can be identified with Eirik Bloodaxe.'[18] It's impossible to disagree.

She is not persuaded by Adam of Bremen, who tosses Prince Hring of Denmark's cap into the ring. She cannot see any link between the names Hring and Eirik, despite some efforts by scholars to shoehorn one into the other. I agree. Adam's chronology doesn't work and his assertion Hring conquered all of England is plain daft. However, when it comes to the Scandinavian sources

Will the Real Eirik Bloodaxe...

Professor Downham thinks there is a very real possibility that tales of Eirik Bloodaxe from Norway became conflated with stories of Eirik of York, two different characters who legend melded into one. That possibility cannot be discounted.

Theodoric the Monk, writing his *Historia de Antiquitate Regum Norwagiensium* 1177–1188, tells us that Eirik was the son of Harald Fairhair and that he succeeded his father, ruling for three years until he was driven out due to not only his cruelty but that of Gunnhild his wife – beginnings of the Queen's enduring bad press. The exiles sail to England where they are well received but Eirik dies shortly afterwards. No mention of any kingship in York[19]. A slightly later account, the *Agrip* (1188–1200), establishes the link. The author states Athelstan granted Eirik the Kingdom of Northumbria, but he soon loses this as well – blame Gunnhild again. Forced back to piracy, Eirik finally comes fatally unstuck while raiding Spain[20].

Historia Norwegiae follows *Agrip* and has Eirik dying in Iberia. Obviously, none of the English sources mention Eirik dying in Spain, and this may be a confusion between 'Stan' (Stainmore) and 'Spain'. Professor Downham is not convinced – Stainmore doesn't crop up in any of the Scandinavian sources.

Chronology is the very devil. It is generally agreed that Harald Fairhair rules for a very long span and that this ended with his death in (say) 930. Eirik then has a tenure of between one to three years before his expulsion – this would chime with Alex Woolf's theory that Hakon's successful expedition occurs around the same time as Athelstan is conducting his massive *chevauchée* in Scotland. And here we have the gap, one we cannot fill. Various sources have Eirik in Denmark and/or the Orkneys. If we accept Woolf's version it makes more sense and I'm happy to allow Eirik an interim career of brigandage. This was family business for Vikings and an essential tool to building up a decent war chest. But we must always be ultra-cautious not to allow narrative convenience to harden into accepted fact.

Professor Downham, rightly, warns against too much reliance on the skaldic sources. However much we might want these to give us a concrete historical footing, they don't. There are a lot of Haralds and Eiriks in Norwegian history and lore, confusion compounded over time.

An obvious solution as Professor Downham explains is that Eirik Bloodaxe and Eirik of York are two different individuals:

> It is ... possible that oral memories from Northumbria regarding Eirik of York were re-contextualised to fit with legends of the Norwegian Eirik Bloodaxe. This could be because Eirik of Norway was more famous than Eirik of York at the time when the sagas were written. The fame of the former may be due to the importance of the sons of Eirik Bloodaxe who ruled Norway, and because of the greater fame of his father Harald Fairhair.[21]

Such syntheses occur throughout history and the fame of an individual attracts an accretion of legendary stories, but fame is a magnet and the tales stick. As a modern example, in 1944, General Eisenhower, Allied Supreme Commander, was virtually imprisoned in his HQ by his own security detachment during the height of the crucial Ardennes battle because intelligence sources indicated German commando ace Otto Skorzeny was on an assassination mission, leading a horde of fanatical diehards 'werewolves'. The origin of these fears was of course 'Scarface' himself. He never left Germany but his fearsome (and entirely justified) reputation as a miracle worker of Special Forces 'Black' Ops, was enough to spread panic. And it did.

Professor Downham also asks why these two figures came to be regarded as one and the same by the end of the twelfth century, if this did not reflect an historical reality. It may be because key players Harald Fairhair and Athelstan became titans in the development of their respective national identities. Harald unites Norway, Athelstan gives birth to 'England' in the political sense.

In the case of Harald, he is credited with having exercised influence not just over the petty rulers of Norway but of spreading his legendary cloak over Orkney, the Hebrides, Iceland, Man and even as far as Normandy. Some of this happened, but not all of it, and the association is derived from the king's perceived role as founding father. It's ironic that Harald features as a key player in Icelandic identity, given that many early settlers went there to escape his ruthless hegemony and heavy-handed tactics. He is seen as both a founding father and a motive for the flight of refugees!

During her narrative Professor Downham looks at each of Finehair's list of imperial achievements with a critical eye and, like previous scholars, comes across some gaping lacunae. Egil alleges that most of these near and farther flung Norse settlements were peopled by refugees fleeing from Harald's tyranny. In this the big man of the saga may just have been articulating a commonly held traditional belief which served to bind and distinguish those of Norse origin from their indigenous neighbours and gave them a sense of shared history that was probably wildly exaggerated. Many did quit Norway to be free of the king's shackles but many more, probably the significant majority, had arrived in an earlier steady but unrelated trickle.

Harald's fame provided a springboard about his son's real or supposed activities in England, which appealed to chronicler and poet alike. Professor Downham cites the apparent impossibility or extreme unlikelihood that Eirik received a grant from Athelstan, and this has been a significant stumbling block. But if we accept Alex Woolf's interpretation, then the pieces can still be made to fit. I would also suggest that it could have suited Athelstan, having installed or helped to install his protégé in Norway, to have had Hakon's dangerous half-brother, hitherto at large, tied to him. Athelstan would be playing a clever game by neutralising any residual threat to a friendly regime in Norway.

As the historical and political legacies of Harald Fairhair and Athelstan grew in importance during the medieval period, so showing a clear fusion of Norse and English heritage in Northumbria perhaps took on a less nuanced aspect and tying these two great founding figures through the son of one and important vassal of the other gained momentum[22].

If Eirik of York isn't also Eirik Bloodaxe, then who is he?

Let's return to Ivar the Boneless (d. 873). His Norse-Hibernian dynasty is known in Gaelic as the *Uí Ímair*. It is they who provided six kings who rule in Northumbria during the tenth century[23]. Professor Downham notes that there would have to have been very persuasive reasons for admitting a Scandinavian contender with no apparent ties into this lineage. She comments that Eirik Bloodaxe would have had only 'minimal' resources but I would argue that Eirik's sideline in piracy, in which he was well versed, like King Olaf and Harald Hardradi after him, would likely fill his war chest, so I assume Eirik Bloodaxe wouldn't have come to the table empty-handed, and he was the son of far-famed Harald Fairhair.

Nonetheless, is it possible that Eirik of York was in fact of the *Ui Imair* line? Professor Downham certainly thinks so. She postulates that the struggle for control of York between 947 and 954 was a family dispute. There are clear precedents and Eirik seems to be in the ascendancy when Olaf is distracted by a situation in Ireland. After an internecine struggle Olaf holds sway in Dublin from 952 until his abdication in 980 when he must have been elderly. The *ASC* firmly tells us that in 952 the Northumbrians drove Olaf out and opted for Eirik. Is this a case of Olaf's relative simply taking advantage of his distraction across the Irish Sea?[24]

It is also possible to interpret the numismatic evidence from Eirik's rule as supporting a link to the *Ui Imair*, though of course Eirik, be he Norse-Hibernian or just Norse, would have wished for PR and propaganda purposes to have stressed his links to the established line, declaiming his legitimacy in the face of southern encroachment[25].

St Cathroe as we will recall is said to have been related by marriage to Eirik of York's queen, which likely, if not conclusively, excludes Gunnhild and suggests a consort with blood-ties to high status lineage from Scotland and/or Strathclyde. This assertion is deemed reliable, *The Life* having been written down not long after the saint's death. If so then this could be another pointer towards Dublin.

Stainmore and Eirik's last stand there can be interpreted in several ways. Woolf, as we've seen, takes the view that Eirik is heading east along this ancient strategic umbilical to recover ground, but Clare Downham postulates he's retreating westwards to regain territory traditionally under strong Norse-Irish influence. He could be attacking or he could be withdrawing, but one thing is sure, Stainmore lies on a direct route between York and Dublin.

We've already looked at Earl Maccus who gets credit for finally killing Eirik. The name is Norse-Gael mix and, of course, we know Maccus is said to be Olaf's son. But whose son is this Eirik of York? The *Ui Imair* can field a trio of Haralds from about the right eras, but none is known to have had a son called Eirik but absence of evidence is not necessarily evidence of absence, and the Irish Chronicles tend towards the unhelpful[26]. Efforts to uncover any Eirik who might fit the bill from that side of the water appear to founder. A 'Lairaic' who is raiding Ireland in the early 950s might just possibly be a corruption, but it's very thin[27]. Linkages are singularly sparse all round.

Nonetheless, Professor Downham identifies a contender. Harald Sihtricsson held sway in Limerick, dying in 940. He had sons we know, but not their names. It is *possible* that Eirik of York was a son of this Harald. These sons were certainly very active during the right timeframe, one had power on the Isle of Man and another in the Hebrides, regions in which the power of the *Ui Imair* persisted for several more generations. Now if Harald did have a son called Eirik then he would have a viable claim to the throne in York from his uncle Olaf and grandfather Sihtric. Professor Downham cites possible validation of this through the coin evidence[28].

Professor Downham's contention that Eirik of York may have come from the established Norse-Hibernian dynasty based at Dublin is persuasive and would iron out a few of the anomalies in the skaldic, synoptic and chronicle accounts. Yet we cannot identify any Eirik who fits the bill or the chronology. Looking at Alex Woolf's interpretation, it's possible to juggle the timeline sufficiently to squeeze out a viable show, if only just.

We cannot plot the course of Eirik's life with any real certainty and we cannot categorically say that Eirik who ruled in Norway was the same man who once or twice ruled in York. My own view is that he is one and the same and the son of Harald Fairhair met his violent end at Stainmore in 954. But that's the thing about legends, they're more attractive than history in some ways, as you can fill in the blanks as you choose.

That's probably why real legends never die; as T. E. Lawrence, a legend and a man, observed:

> All men dream, but not equally. Those who dream by night in the dusty recesses of their minds, wake in the day to find that it was vanity: but the dreamers of the day are dangerous men, for they may act on their dreams with open eyes, to make them possible.

Eleven

MOTHER OF KINGS

Njal's Saga[1] tells us of Hrut, half-brother of Hoskuld, both Icelanders from the Rangarvellir region. Now Hrut owned a fine cargo ship which made port, captained by his uncle Ozur who informed the hero that his brother Eyvind had died and Hrut stood to inherit his estate in Norway, but only if others didn't grab it before he could fix his claim. Hrut had agreed marriage terms (a union he'd have cause to regret), so first had to speak to his future father-in-law to string to lengthen his engagement. The property at stake was substantial, so all agreed that inheritance should come first. Hrut loaded fresh cargo onto his vessel and set sail for Norway.

Harald Greycloak (Gunnhild's eldest surviving son by Eirik) was then ruling. For her part Gunnhild was intrigued to hear of the Icelanders' arrival, she was well aware of the inheritance Hrut was after and that another litigant named Soti had taken possession. She sends her servant to bring Ozur and Hrut to her, promising friendship and hospitality. Not only that, but she also promises to intercede in Hrut's claim. Ozur counsels his nephew to fall in with the dowager queen's wishes, a powerful ally but a deadly enemy. Her hospitality was an offer Hrut couldn't refuse.

Prior to their meeting, Gunnhild left a message for Hrut that he should seek an audience with King Harald and undertake to serve him as a household warrior. The king is impressed by the forthright and formidable Icelander who wastes no time in stating that whilst he wishes to join Harald's household, he needs to attend to family business first. Gunhild speaks up to put in a good word and the king, while inclined to accede, advises Hrut he has, as a matter of protocol, to wait for a couple of weeks, naturally as his mother's honoured guest.

Gunnhild proved hospitable, her hall built in stone and adorned with fine tapestries. She took Hrut as her lover. We learn later in the saga that Hrut is extremely well endowed. Gunnhild is also labelled as a Messalina by the skalds. In due course, King Harald admits the Icelander into his personal elite, but Hrut had still to settle with this Soti who had jumped his claim. Gunnhild furnished him with two longships and her own household paladin, the wonderfully named Ulf the Unwashed. Harald offered more ships and the flotilla sailed for Denmark, where Soti was said to be lurking.

Things didn't go quite according to plan as Hrut's squadron became involved in a sea fight with a local pirate called Atli. A fierce battle ensued in which Hrut dealt with Atli, but not before Ulf the Unwashed had gone down to a well-aimed spear. Soti slipped past unnoticed but foolishly made landfall on the Norwegian coast, where he was recognised by one of Gunnhild's tenants. Soti let slip that he was about to make a run for it to England, but Gunnhild acted swiftly, sending her son Gudrod to dispose of Soti. When Hrut returned after a profitable cruise, he wisely handed over a third of his loot to the king. He was naturally delighted to hear that his inheritance, thanks to Gunnhild's ruthless efficiency, was now safe and he, very prudently, rewarded her with half!

His mission accomplished, Hrut now began to feel homesick and petitioned King Harald to be allowed to return to Iceland. His wish granted, he took leave of his regal lover; 'she put her arms around his neck and kissed him and spoke, 'If I have as much power over you as I think I have, then I cast this spell. You will not have sexual pleasure with the woman you plan to marry in Iceland, though you'll be able to have your will with other women.'[2] You don't cross a witch and inevitably Hrut's marriage goes horribly wrong on account of this curse.

If we assume that Queen Gunnhild (c. 910–980) is a real person and indeed 'The Mother of Kings' then we are obliged to take a very sceptical view of the sagas. It's been suggested that the

Icelanders held an enduring grudge against the issue of Harald Fairhair – legend insisted that many settlers came there to avoid his tyranny. This may or may not be true, but the mud stuck.

She becomes famous (or notorious), on account of her skills in magic and witchcraft, her desire for power and innate cruelty and her sexual insatiability (inevitable) but also highly regarded for her beauty and generosity. She is portrayed as a serial conspirator:

> Gunnhild had two brothers called Eyvind Braggart and Alf Askmann, sons of Ozur Snout. They were big powerful men and great fighters and held in very high regard by King Eirik and Gunnhild, although they were not popular with most people... Gunnhild said to her brothers, 'I want you to take advantage of the crowd here and kill one of Skallagrim' s sons, or preferably both.'[3]

Evil consequences followed and her vendetta with Egil (no stranger to feuding) runs like a toxic thread through his saga.

So much for skaldic attack. In historical reality, she was most likely a daughter of Gorm the Old King of Denmark, brother of Harold Bluetooth and aunt to Sweyn Forkbeard, so great-aunt to Knut. Her marriage with Eirik, Harald Fairhair's son and preferred heir, was a sensible dynastic union, but the saga-writers found this a bit bland for such a villainess and crafted a more Tolkienesque past.

Gunnhild is cast as the daughter of a wealthy *hersir* from Halogaland in Northern Norway, a territory that abuts Finnmark (Finland). Here in a land of darkness and even darker magic, Gunnhild, like Morganna, is thoroughly schooled in the black arts by Finnish necromancers. She proves a very apt pupil, soon outstripping her mentors. For Icelanders, the fact their old enemies had the benefit of diabolical forces makes the gall of exile easier to swallow. Much of Eirik's heavy-handedness and outright cruelty is blamed on his evil shrew of a wife. This is probably a total fabrication.

Viking Queens and noblewomen tended not to be shrinking violets (think of legendary Lagertha, Queen Thyra, formidable Aud the Deep-Minded and terrifying Freydis Eiriksdottir) and we can safely assume Gunnhild was a strong-minded, self-willed and very clever woman. If we accept she came from Danish royalty then she would have been educated and groomed for a queenly throne, trained in the arts of statecraft rather than wizardry. In short, she was born to rule. And sovereignty wasn't a game for the faint-hearted.

We do know her marriage to Eirik produced several children: Gamle, Guthorm, Ragnald, Erling, Godrod and Rognvald Eiriksson, Sigurd Sleva, Ragnhild Eiriksdottir, and last but by no means least Harald, called Greycloak,* who would become King of Norway.

Eirik's death and her subsequent flight were not the end of Gunnhild's story – her sons would indeed be kings, as the author of *Fagrskinna* tells us: 'Then Gunnhildr left England with her sons and went to Denmark and received asylum there with [King] Haraldr Gormsson. He fostered Eiríkr's son Haraldr and set him on his knee, and he remained in the court, but Gamli and Guäbormr went raiding first in the Baltic and then in Norway, and caused as much trouble as they could in King Hákon's kingdom.' At this time Denmark and Norway were at war and for the Danish king, Gunnhild and her sons were allies and auxiliaries.

So, with Danish backing, Hakon the Good now faced a very real threat from his half-brother's sons:

> In the twentieth year [of King Hakon's reign] the sons of Eiríkr Bloodaxe, Gamli, Haraldr and Sigurär, came north from Denmark with an army, and raided wherever they went in Norway. Then King Hákon was based with his troops in the southern part of Norämœrr at a place called Freiäarey, and Hákon was taken unawares when Gamli and the others with their army put into Féeyjarsund by Féey, in the vicinity of Freiäarberg. People tried to mediate between them, but the sons of Eiríkr were not offering any alternative to a fight.⁴

---

* Harald gained his sobriquet 'Greycloak or Grey-hide' after meeting the crew of an Icelandic cargo vessel carrying a consignment of *vararfeldir*, a type of imitation fur made from sheep's wool. These Icelanders were having trouble selling their wares, so when the king asked them if they would make a present to him of one of the hides, grey in colour, the traders didn't hesitate, and Harald immediately donned it as a cloak. This created an instant market and before long the Icelanders had offloaded their entire cargo.

Blood kin against blood kin:

> King Hákon also did not allow himself to hesitate once he knew that his kinsmen were set on it. There was an old man called Egill, who had been King Haraldr hárfagri's standard-bearer in his youth, but he was now infirm. He had said that he wanted it to be his lot to die in a full-blown battle. There was such a disparity in the size of the armies that there were six men against each one of Hákon's. Then Egill asked the king to give him one standard for each ship, and a man for each standard, and there were ten standards there. But the sons of Eiríkr, when they saw that Hákon's force was much smaller, went ashore to draw up by Freiäarberg and so advance against Hákon.[5]
>
> A great battle took place there. And when the attack had begun, Egill went with ten men, and each had a standard in his hands, and they advanced along the slope which was up on a headland above where they were fighting, so that the standards could be seen from where the fighting was, but not those who went with them or carried them. Then the Danes saw where the standards were moving and believed that the main body of the army must be there and were afraid that it would get between them and the ships. Because of this, flight broke out in the army of Eiríkr's sons, and they themselves and their troops fled, and when they reached the height opposite Freiäarberg they saw, looking back out onto Rastarkálfr, that there were no troops with the standards.[6]
>
> Then Gamli had his standard raised up and his trumpet sounded. Their troops gathered and drew up in battle array, but the Danes and the levied men were fleeing for the ships. Then King Hákon advanced against them with all his troops; the battle began again, and many fell on both sides, and it soon began to go against Gamli's side; their troop was divided, and Gamli and all the brothers fled on along the cliff, but some got up onto the cliff and were killed there, and others jumped down over the cliffs and died there. And when Gamli and his men got to the shore he was seriously wounded by King Hákon and dived into the sea to escape and drowned. Haraldr and Siguräř, Gamli's brothers, reached the ships by

swimming, but Hákon killed three shiploads of their troop there on the beach, and they piled them up on the ships; the slain were laid in those ships and burial mounds were raised up over them. A high memorial stone also stands in the place where Egill fell.[7]

Hakon succeeded in seeing off this challenge but the sons of Gunnhild weren't done yet:

Then it happened on one occasion that Gunnhildr's sons sailed northwards from Denmark, passing far out to sea, and only came close enough to the coast for people to learn of their journey, and so they also learned where King Hákon was being feasted. They had ships well furnished with troops and weapons, and with them was a great Viking who was called Eyvindr skreyja ['Braggart', Gunnhild's disreputable brother]. King Hákon was being feasted, when they came, at Fitjar on Storä, and this news was kept hidden from him and all his men right up till the time when the ships were sailing from the south and were only a short distance from the island.

Then King Hákon was presiding at the tables. Now a rumour spread among the courtiers that ships had been seen sailing, and some of them who had the sharpest eyes went outside, and each said to the other that they must be hostile forces, and they told each other to tell the king. But there was no one who would do so but Eyvindr Finnson, who was called *skáldaspillir*. He went in before the king and said: 'Fast goes the fleeting time, lord; but your feasting lasts long.' The king answered, 'Skald, what is passing now on the wide ways?' Eyvindr replied in verse, crises called for wit as well as action.[8]

Then the king answered, 'Eyvindr, you are a fine warrior and a wise man; you would not tell news of war unless it was true.' Then everyone said that it was true that ships were sailing and were not far from the island. At once the tables were taken up and the king went out to see the host. And when he had seen it, he called his advisors to him and asked what should be done then: 'Here there are many ships sailing from the south, and we have a small though fine force, and

Eric Bloodaxe the Viking: 'I Shall Die Laughing'

I do not want to lead my best friends into danger. Indeed, I would wish to flee, if wise men did not consider it a great disgrace or folly.'

Now they answered each other that each would rather fall across the other than flee before the Danes. Then the king said, 'Well spoken! Let each take his weapons, and it will make no difference how many Danes there are for each Norwegian.' After that the king took up his shield and put on his coat of mail and girded himself with Kvernbítr and set a gilded helmet on his head. After that he took his shield and halberd and drew up his troops and treated his retainers and the guests at the feast all the same way, as Eyvindr says in the poem he composed after Hákon's fall, and he composed it in imitation of the one which Gunnhildr had had composed about Eiríkr, in which Óäinn invited him home to Valhalla and he tells in the poem of many events from the battle.[9]

From such things it can be seen how fearless the king was, since he considered his fortunes in this way. Gunnhildr's sons now went ashore and drew up their troops, and their army was much the larger. That day the weather was hot with sun, so King Hákon threw off his mail coat and set his helmet in place and urged his men into the advance laughing, and so cheered his troop with his glad demeanour.

Hakon might be 'The Good' but he had not ruled Norway for two decades without being a formidable warrior. He was also Harald's son and Eirik's half-brother, battle fury was as much in his blood as theirs:

After that the battle began and was very fierce. When the storm of missiles was over, King Hákon drew his sword and stood in front under the standard and hewed on either side. He never missed, and the sword cut as if it did miss, Eyvindr skreyja began to press forward so strongly in the battle that he was a challenge to the courage of the Norwegians, and he attacked most fiercely where Hákon's standard was, and said: 'Where is the king of the Norwegians? Why does he hide himself, and dare not come forward and show himself? Who can tell me where he is?'

> Then King Hákon answered, 'Keep straight on if you want to find the king of the Norwegians.' Then King Hákon threw his shield aside and grasped the hilt of his sword with both hands and ran forward from under the standards. Then said Þórálfr Skólmsson: 'Lord, let me go against Eyvindr.' The king replied, 'I am the one he wanted to find, and so he shall meet me first.' But when the king got to where Eyvindr was he was striking on both sides, and then the king struck with Kvernbítr, holding it in both hands, into Eyvindr's head, splitting the helmet and the head down to the shoulders. On one side of King Hákon Þórálfr sterki [the Strong] Skólmsson stood and killed many men with his sword, which was called Fetbreiär [Broad-tracks], and which the king had given him.[10]

Though Hakon won the day again and Gunnhild's surviving sons took to their ships, the king had sustained a wound in the fighting which refused to heal, and it became obvious to him he was not long for this world. He had ruled for 26 years and would be the ninth of Fairhair's sons to die by the sword. Having put his affairs in order, the king died and was buried according to the old rites, with full honours. It appears he may have already provided for the succession to go to Eirik's oldest surviving son Greycloak, who acceded as Harald II. He would find the throne of Norway as dangerous as his forbears.

Inevitably there was bad feeling and incipient blood feuds between the new king's household men and Hakon's survivors, but this was settled by skalds duelling with wit, not swords. The wheel seemed to have come full circle. Harald clearly had more sense than his father. 'Gamle is avenged by Harald / Great is they deed, thou champion bold / The rumour of it came to me / in distant lands beyond the sea / how Harald give King Hakon's blood / to Odin's ravens for their food.'[11]

With her son triumphant and now enthroned, Gunnhild returned in splendour to Norway (c. 961) as revered elder stateswoman and *konungamooir* – 'Mother of Kings'. Her wilderness years were finally over, and she could again taste the power she and Eirik had so briefly savoured a generation before. She is probably in her fifties by now and not ready for retirement, as *Heimskringla* confirms: 'Gunnhild ... mixed herself much in the affairs of the country.'[12] At the outset of Harald Greycloak's reign, there was some tricky diplomacy afoot. The new king, clearly circumspect, didn't wish to alienate powerful jarls who had hitherto enjoyed significant power in their various regions. Harald and his surviving brothers had evidently learned from their father's mistakes. That didn't rule out brute force when the need arose.

Gunnhild, even if she's not sitting on the throne, appears still to be very much the power behind it, and her sons consult regularly with her on matters of policy, especially the feared independence of the Trondheim men, led by Earl Sigurd. Gunnhild, true to her Machiavellian image, conspires with Sigurd's disaffected brother Grjotgard. Sigurd, lulled into a false sense of security by friendly overtures, is betrayed by his treacherous sibling and his hall burnt down around him. Outraged, his subjects rallied to his surviving heir Hakon, destined to be a formidable figure in his own right. War followed and Gunnhild's plotting did her sons no good as they could not subdue Hakon. At length, after three years of bitter civil strife, a truce was brokered and Earl Hakon confirmed in all his dead father's titles. Oddly, he and Gunnhild became close[13]. This was a truce, a ceasefire, not a resolution.

Peace did not endure and after a short interlude Harald, his brothers and Earl Hakon were back at each other's throats. The earl found time to deal with his deceitful uncle before seeking temporary refuge in Denmark, which allowed King Harald an opportunity to exert his will over the separatist Trondheim folk. Things in general were bad in Norway, a series of failed harvests was blamed on the king and his siblings, shortages said to be significantly exacerbated by their boundless greed.

Gunnhild was concerned over the issue of King Trygve, one of the sub-kings murdered by her sons. His widow Astrid gave birth to a son while in hiding – the future hero Olaf Tryggvason. The Queen-Mother sent a squadron of trusted henchmen to pursue a deadly game of hide and seek. Despite her thugs' best efforts both mother and child escaped.

After fifteen years on the throne King Harald Greycloak fell in battle like his father and most of his siblings. Earl Hakon, allied to the Danish king, led a triumphal entry into the Trondelag. History now began to repeat itself for the surviving sons of Bloodaxe. In 969, the queen with her surviving brood now reduced to two, took ship for Orkney – an echo of the past. Jarl Thorfinn would surely not have been pleased with the arrival of his guests, who may have demonstrated a rather too proprietorial attitude. Whatever relationship the surviving sons of Eirik Bloodaxe may have had with Thorfinn, his dominion nevertheless provided, as ever, a handy base for harassing raids. He was undoubtedly glad that Norway's loss did not become his misfortune.

By now an ageing Gunnhild was probably played out, anxious for a quiet life. Perhaps unsurprisingly, this was not her lot. She appears to have returned to Denmark in 977 when she would have been in her late sixties. For reasons we don't understand, King Harald gives orders for her to be ritually drowned in a bog*[14] and with this watery footnote the life of Queen Gunnhild, Mother of kings, comes to an end. Eirik's saga ends with the death of his consort.

Like her husband, Gunnhild fades into legend but legends never die: 'Lady, Queen of Night / Queen of Day / Always you do hunt / Searching for prey / Lurking in the forest, deep in time / With claws of silver / You do rake the chests of hunters / Making lines of pain.'[15]

---

* In 1835 a bog burial – that of the so-called Haraldskaer Woman – was unearthed in Jutland. This was immediately believed to be Gunnhild's mortal remains and King Frederick VI of Denmark commissioned an elaborate tomb. It was an attractive interpretation but proved entirely unfounded. Subsequent scientific examination by radio carbon dating in 1977 proved that the remains were very much older than Gunnhild, dated to around 490 BC.

NOTES

A note on sources
1. Abbot Cathroe (*c.* 900–971) was roughly a contemporary of Eirik's, abbot of St. Felix Monastery in Metz, a monk there wrote a hagiography of the saint shortly after his death – numerous miracles of healing had been ascribed to Cathroe during his lifetime; see Dunville, D. N., 'St. Cathroe of Metz and the hagiography of exoticism' in J. Cassidy, M. Herbert and P. O'Brien (editors) *Studies in Irish Hagiography; Saints and Scholars* (Dublin, Four Winds Press 2001), pp. 172–178.
2. William Gershom Collingwood (1854–1932), latterly professor of fine art at University College, Reading, was a noted watercolourist and art historian as well as being a celebrated antiquarian. See: Collingwood, W. G., 'The Battle of Stainmore in Legend and History' in *Transactions of the Cumberland and Westmoreland Antiquarian Archaeological Society*, Series 2 no. 2 (1902), pp. 231–241.
3. Clare Downham is professor at the Medieval History Institute of Irish Studies at the University of Liverpool, see: Downham, C., 'Eric Bloodaxe Axed – the Mystery of the Last Viking King of York' in *Viking and Medieval Scandinavia* 14, pp. 51–77.
4. *Arinbjarnarkviða* is a skaldic poem attributed to Egil and forms a lament for his friend and comrade Arinbjorn, who certainly helps Egil out of a few scrapes, always of his own making. It is preserved in a fourteenth-century Icelandic source, the *Modruvalla*, but not all these verses appear in other texts, so a further potential ambiguity arises.

5. Snorri writes up his dynastic history *Ynglinga Saga* sometime towards the end of the first quarter of the thirteenth century, the first instalment of his *Heimskringla,* but bases his work on the earlier ninth-century *Ynglingatal.*
6. The Lordship of the Isles was a real fiefdom, though doesn't really feature fully until the time of Somerled (d. 1164) but the notion of an inchoate semi-independent Lordship over the Inner and Outer Hebrides is entirely credible.
7. Constantine of Scotland had bent his knee to King Athelstan even before Brunanburh and the Wessex line held titular dominion over their northern neighbour thereafter. This would mature after 1296 into 'The Great Cause', a fight for Scottish independence, also known as 'The Three Hundred Year War'.
8. Johann Martin Lappenburg (1794–1854) was a German historian and diplomat. See: Lappenburg, L. M., (transl. B. Thorpe), *A History of England under the Anglo-Saxon Kings* (in two volumes, Hamburg 1834–1837).
9. Adam von Bremen was a German cleric and scholar who lived during the second half of the 11th century (his exact dates aren't clear). He was admitted to the Church in Bremen around the same time as the Battle of Hastings and then worked as director of the Cathedral school. See: Adam of Bremen, *Gesta Hammaburgensis Ecclesiae Pontificum*, 'Deeds of the Bishops of Hamburg' (1073–1076).

Introduction
1. Jones, G., *A History of the Vikings* (London, BCA 1973).
2. For the year 793, both Parker and Peterborough versions of the Anglo-Saxon Chronicle give the Old English name for Lindisfarne as *Lindisfarena*. In the 9th-century *Historia Brittonum*, the archipelago appears under its earlier Old Welsh name *Medcaut*. Philologist Andrew Breeze, following up on an idea from Richard Coates, postulates the name ultimately derived from the Latin *Medicata* ('Healing'), owing perhaps to the island's reputation for medicinal herbs. The soubriquet 'Holy Island' was in use by the 11th century when it appears in Latin as '*Insula Sacra*'. The reference is, as we'd expect, to resident Saints Aidan and Cuthbert.
3. London, Catnip Publishing 2007 edition.

4. Honeycombe, op., cit.
5. https://victorianpersistence.files.wordpress.com/2012/03/on-heroes-hero-worship-and-the-heroic-in-history-1841-t-carlyle1.pdf, accessed 15 December 2023.
6. See Williams, T., *Viking Britain* (London, William Collins 2017), p. xvii. The offending review appeared in *The Guardian* 4 March 2014, written by I. Jones.
7. Tolkien. J. R. R., *The Battle of Maldon* (ed. P. Grybauskas, London, Harper Collins 2023), pp. 28–29.

One: Streamers of Fire

1. Larrington, C., *The Norse Myths* (London, Thames & Hudson 2023), p. 27.
2. *HN*, p. 53.
3. Shown from September 2013.
4. Douglas Adams: *The Long Dark Tea-Time of the Soul* (1988). Actually, this is the Midland Grand Hotel, which Dirk Gently likens to the vast Gothic interior of Valhalla!
5. Snorri Sturluson (1179–1241) was a leading Icelandic statesman with a fatal penchant for meddling in external affairs, which finally led to his assassination, but it was he who collected much of what we now possess of Norse sagas and mythology.
6. *Prose Edda*, p. 6.
7. See, Curry, A., 'Slaughter at the bridge: uncovering a colossal Bronze Age battle' in *Science Magazine*, 24 March 2016. Thanks to Bev Palin for finding this.
8. William Paton Ker, as quoted by J. R. R. Tolkien in his celebrated *Beowulf* lecture of 1936.
9. MacLennan, W. J., & W. I. Sellers, 'Ageing through the Ages', *Edinburgh Proceedings of the Royal College of Surgeons*, 1999 29:71–75.
10. Aud was the daughter of a Norse-Hebridean, the wonderfully named Ketil Flatnose who was married to Olaf of Dublin (see chapter five). She as a Christian divorced her pagan spouse and finally emigrated to Iceland, where her grandson Erik the Red would become one of the most famous (and notorious) of Vikings.
11. Freydis Eiriksdottir features in the sagas as one of those who journeyed to Vinland, the Americas. Judging from her alleged adventures, Iceland's loss was Vinland's misfortune. Leif, her

brother, was apparently appalled by his sister's numerous murders. In one encounter with native Americans, she defiantly bares her bosom, which is enough to send them running!

12. Olaf was probably born in the 960s and died at the finale of his epic last battle in September 1000. He was possibly a great grandson of Harald Fairhair.
13. Carlyle, T., *On Heroes, Hero-worship and the Heroic in History* (London 1841)
14. After C. S. Lewis.
15. See Loyn, L., *The Vikings in Britain* (Hoboken NJ, Wiley-Blackwell 1995), pp. 55–56.
16. *Beowulf*, translated by Seamus Heaney (London, Faber and Faber 1999), lines 75–82, p. 5.
17. See Todd J. H., (transl.), *Wars of the Gaedhil with the Gaill* (London, Longmans 1867), pp. 51–52.

Two: Tangle-Hair

1. *Historia Norwegie*, p. 70.
2. *Fagrskinna*, p. 41. This gave Harald a tangible link to Ragnar Lodbrok!
3. *Heimskringla*, p. 43.
4. Ibid., p. 44.
5. Ibid., pp. 42–43.
6. *Egil's Saga*, p. 5.
7. *Fagrskinna*, p. 49.
8. *Egil's Saga*, p. 5.
9. *Heimskringla*, p. 45.
10. Ibid., p.p., 48–49.
11. Price, N., *The Children of Ash & Elm – a History of the Vikings* (London, Penguin 2020), pp. 201–2.
12. Rognvald is credited by *Historia Norwegie* as being the first Norse settler or conqueror to reach Orkney. Prior to the Vikings, the islands had been inhabited by primitive peoples, 'pygmies' who, though immensely industrious otherwise, apparently lost all their vigour at midday and took refuge in their underground shelters. Rognvald 'totally destroyed these people' and appropriated their dwellings. Now whether this is an admission of genocide is debatable. *Historia Norwegie*, p. 65.
13. *Egil's Saga*, p. 7.

14. Ibid.
15. Ibid., p. 15.
16. *Fagrskinna*, p. 61.
17. Rognvald's son Einar Rognvaldsson, or Torf-Einar (d. c. 910) became Jarl of Orkney in turn and sired a long line of jarls, it appears that two of his sons stood and died beneath Eirik's banner at Stainmore. These genealogies are confused and heavily reliant on skaldic sources of dubious provenance. Another son appears to have been called Hrolf – according to *Historia Norwegie* the very Rolf (or Rollo), who would become Duke of Normandy and the first of a royal dynasty. *Historia Norwegie* goes on to provide an account of Rollo's successes in Normandy including his digging concealed pits to confound Frankish cavalry – a most successful tactic. See *Historia Norwegie*, p. 67 et seq.
18. *Historia Norwegie*, p. 69.
19. *Egil's Saga*, p. 9.
20. *Heimskringla*, p. 45.
21. Ibid., p. 50.
22. Gwyn Jones, op. cit., p. 93.
23. *Egil's Saga*, p. 20.
24. *Historia Norwegie* credits Harald with having sired 16 sons with Eirik as the oldest with his brother Hakon ('the Good') next in line. The rest were Olav, Bjorn, Sigurd the Giant, Gunnrod, Gudrod, Halvdan Hafott, Ragnvald (apparently reared by a sorceress), Oystein, Jorund, Sigtrygg, Yngvar, Tryggve, Ring and Rolf. (*Historia Norwegie*, p. 81.)
25. *Egil's Saga*, p. 113.
26. Ibid., p. 121.
27. See Gwyn Jones, op. cit., p 89.

Three: Sword Song

1. *Egil's Saga*, p. 64.
2. Originally called Tunsberg and located 102 kilometres south-southwest of Oslo, latterly a major whaling port.
3. *Egil's Saga*, p.p. 113 – 114.
4. ASC 'A' Version (The Parker Chronicle), p. 112.
5. It is generally agreed that the fight Egil refers to as Vin Heath is in fact Brunanburh. Egil gives us additional detail, other

sources omit but, as ever, his reliability is open to question, and he's never shy of inflating his own role.
6. *Egil's Saga*, p. 96. Despite such Homeric hutzpah or perhaps because of it, Thorolf does not survive the battle.
7. Cornwell, B., *Death of Kings* (London, Harper Collins 2011), p. 162.
8. https://oldenglishpoetry.camden.rutgers.edu/battle-of-maldon/, accessed 15.11.2023.
9. ASC 'E' Version (The Laud Chronicle), p. 199.
10. Hadley D. M., & J. D. Richards, *The Viking Great Army and the Making of England* (London, Thames & Hudson 2021), p. 148.
11. Page, R.I., *Chronicles of the Vikings* (Toronto, Toronto University Press 1995), p. 109.
12. *Heimskringla*, p. 276.
13. The bearskin caps still worn by ceremonial guards are a survival.
14. Low, R., *The Whale Road* (London, Harper Collins 2007), p. 137.
15. Griffith, P., *The Viking Art of War* (London, Greenhill 1995), pp. 105–127.
16. A thirteenth-century Swedish fragment from Vastergotland.
17. A set of twelve rules laid down to regulate the conduct of boxing matches, first published in 1867.
18. *Egil's Saga*, p.p. 139–141.
19. Happily, this fight ended with first blood.
20. Pattern welding is the name given to a process whereby bars of iron and steel are forge-welded together, twisted, heated, hammered and manipulated to produce a very distinctive and lovely wave to the surface, they can also take a very sharp edge – not to be confused, as this technique often is, with Damascus steel.
21. The site is located in farmland near Ringerike. This initial discovery led to the excavation of a grave where more artefacts were unearthed.

Four: Wood-wreathed Ships

1. Onund's exploits are set down in the anonymous early fourteenth-century Icelandic epic, *The Saga of Grettir the Strong* (transl. G. H. Hight, London 1914, Penguin Classics edition 2003).

2. Found in a burial mound by Oseberg Farm, near Tonsberg, Vestfold, excavated 1904–1905.
3. Unearthed close to Sandar, Sandefjord, Vestfold in 1880.
4. For more detail on ship construction see Williams, G., *The Viking Ship* (London, British Museum Press 2014).
5. *The Saga of Olaf Tryggvason* by Oddr Snorasson (transl. T. M. Andersson (London, Cornell University Press 2023).
6. *Orkneyinga Saga*, p. 26.
7. Ibid., p. 65.
8. See Rixson D., *The Highland Galley* (Edinburgh, Birlinn 1998).
9. *Orkneyinga Saga*, p. 67.
10. Ibid., p. 122.
11. Ibid.
12. See https://www.britannica.com/biography/Sverrir-Sigurdsson, accessed 6 December 2023.
13. *Beowulf* (200–211).
14. Henry Wadsworth Longfellow; 'The Saga of King Olaf' (1902).

Five: Northanhymbre

1. Fiona Macleod; *Washer of the Ford*.
2. Welsh triads and genealogies.
3. Higham, N. J., *the Kingdom of Northumbria 35 1100* (Gloucs., Alan Sutton 1993), p. 82.
4. This battle isn't mentioned by Bede, nor is it in in the *ASC*.
5. *ASC*, 'A' version p. 16.
6. Magnus Maximus also features in the Welsh sources as Prince Macsen; Ammianus Marcellinus, *The Later Roman Empire* (London, Penguin 1986), p. 417. For a full assessment, see *Magnus Maximus, The Neglected Roman Emperor and his British Legacy* by Maxell Craven (Stroud: Amberley Books 2023).
7. Possibly born towards the end of the fifth century, Thornton, David E. 'Urien Rheged' in *Oxford Dictionary of National Biography* (online edition; Oxford University Press doi:10.1093/ref:odnb/28016); his memory survives in a rather strange retail centre outside Penrith; not sure he'd feel in any way flattered.
8. Our principal source is Nennius, a Welsh scholar, his work first compiled in the ninth century; see *Historia Brittonum* (England, independently published 2022), p. 42.

9. Supposedly at Battleshield Haugh, north-west of Alwinton in Northumberland.
10. Aneirin is a sixth-century poet of the Welsh school and his *Gododdin* is part of that oral tradition; the first written version didn't appear until some 250 years after the events it describes; see Clarke, G., *The Goddodin – Lament for the Fallen* (London, Faber & Faber 2021).
11. Bede, Book I; chapter 34, p. 61.
12. Ibid.
13. Ibid., Book II; chapter 2, p. 71.
14. Ibid, Book II; chapter 12, p. 93.
15. Ibid, Book II; chapter 9, p. 83.
16. See, Heaney, S., *Beowulf* (London, Faber 1999). I was in the 2015 ITV series filmed in Weardale, though not many would be brave enough to admit that – it was pretty dire.
17. Bede, Book II; chapter 16, p. 100.
18. From Mainz, preserved in Vatican Library, see Williams, op. cit., pp. 181–182.
19. Bede, Book II; chapter 20, p. 106.
20. Ibid, Book II; chapter 1, p. 108.
21. Ibid, Book III, chapter 1, p. 109.
22. Bede, Book III; Chapter 2, p. 110.
23. Ibid, Book III; Chapter 8, p. 123.
24. Probably somewhere near Leeds; Bede, Book III; Chapter 24, p. 151.
25. Bede, Book III; Chapter 3, p. 112.
26. Ibid, Book IV; Chapter 25, p. 113.
27. *ASC* 'D' version, p. 39.
28. *Vita Sancta Wilfrithi* – Eddi was Wilfrid's chanter and latterly biographer. (Cambridge, Cambridge University Press 1985).
29. Bede, Book IV; Chapter 23, p. 223.
30. Pevsner N. & E. Williamson, 'Durham' in *Buildings of England* (London, Penguin 1985), pp. 340–341.
31. *ASC* 'D' version, p. 55.
32. Ibid
33. Johnson, A., 'Battle of Athelstaneford' in *Battlefields Trust Magazine*, volume 24, issue 3, Winter 2020, pp. 10–13.
34. Bede, Book IV; Chapter 23, p. 225.
35. Tolkien, *op. cit.*, p. 15.

Six: 'Never Greater Slaughter'
1. *Fagrskinna*, p.p. 54–55.
2. Ibid., p. 55.
3. *Egil's Saga*, p. 61.
4. Ibid., p. 62.
5. Ibid., p. 84.
6. Ibid., p. 119.
7. *Fagrskinna*, p. 55.
8. Ibid. p. 56.
9. *Heimskringla*, p. 75.
10. *Orkneyinga Saga*, p. 29.
11. Ibid., p. 30.
12. Ibid., p. 32.
13. Ibid., p. 33.
14. Ibid.
15. Jorvik Viking Centre is to be found on York's Coppergate, YOI 9WT.
16. William of Malmesbury, *The Deeds of the Bishops of England*, transl. D. G. Preest (London, Boydell Press 2002), p. 139.
17. ASC 'A' Version, p. 68.
18. Simeon of Durham, *Historical Works*, (editor J. Stevenson, Franklin Classics 2018), p. 470.
19. Roberta F., 'Viking Atrocity and Skaldic Verse – the Rite of the Blood Eagle' in *English Historical Review*, Oxford Journals XCIX, 1984, pp. 332–343. Alex Harvey in *Forgotten Vikings* points out that 'All the sources that mention the "blood eagle" were written after Scandinavia was converted to Christianity, half-remembering (or imagining) a bloody heathen past. The phrase is a hybrid of the most vilified heathen tropes, misunderstood and then dialled up to shock Christian audiences. Contemporary mentions of eagles and scavenging birds in skaldic verses are employed as alliterative kennings; being given a "blood eagle" was to be killed and left for bird food. An "eagle of blood" might just mean a raven.'
20. See Hadley, D. M., & J. D. Richards, *The Viking Great Army and the Making of England* (London, Thames & Hudson 2021).
21. ASC 'A' Version, p. 70.
22. ASC 'D' Version, p. 75.
23. Ibid.

24. Higham, op. cit., p.p. 179–180.
25. ASC 'A' Version, p. 84.
26. Ibid.
27. Ibid., p. 86.
28. Ibid., p. 87.
29. Higham, op. cit., pp. 188–89.
30. https://celt.ucc.ie/published/T100001A/, accessed 1 4 2024.
31. Higham, op. cit., p. 184. The huge Cuerdale hoard, found in 1840, is comprised of some 1,300 pieces of hacksilver, plus ingots, much of which is of Irish origin.
32. Ibid., p. 188, evidence comes from local government and land structures, and by place names.
33. Ibid., pp. 188–189; there is coin evidence from Lincoln, showing motifs identical to those coming out of York at this point.
34. Ibid., p. 189.
35. ASC 'D' Version, p. 107.
36. Woolf, A., *From Pictland to Alba 789–1070* (Edinburgh, Edinburgh University Press 2007), pp. 158–165.
37. Poem, *The Battle of Brunanburh* in ASC 'A' Version, p. 106.

Seven: A Bad Country for old Gods

1. *Egil's Saga*, p. 122.
2. Ibid.
3. Ibid.
4. Ibid., p. 124.
5. Ibid.
6. Ibid., p. 125.
7. Ibid.
8. Ibid., p. 132.
9. Ibid., p. 133.
10. Clifford's Tower (of timber construction at this date), was the scene of a pogrom and mass murder and suicide of the city's Jewish community in 1190.
11. Hall, R., *Viking Age York* (London, Batsford 1994), p. 31.
12. Ibid., p. 33.
13. Ibid., p. 34
14. We have no evidence for this prior to the twelfth century, so we cannot prove that this is so; gate comes from old Norse *gata* = street; see Hall op. cit., p. 35.

15. Ibid., p. 37.
16. Ibid., p. 39.
17. Ibid., p. 42.
18. ASC 'D' Version, p. 111, this probably refers to Olaf Sihtricsson, not Olaf Guthfrithson.
19. Ibid.
20. Downham, C., *Viking Kings of Britain and Ireland – the Dynasty of Ívarr to AD 1014* (Edinburgh, Dunedin Academic Press 2007), pp. 108–109.
21. Downham, op. cit., p. 109.
22. ASC 'D' Version, p. 111.
23. Downham, op. cit., p. 111.
24. Ibid., pp. 111–112.
25. ASC 'A' Version, p. 112
26. Ibid.

Eight: 'Valhalla, I am coming...'
1. Armitage, S., *Sir Gawain and the Green Knight* (London, Faber & Faber 2007), p. 5.
2. OS grid ref. NY8314.
3. ASC 'D' Version, p. 113.
4. Collingwood op. cit., p. 318.
5. ASC 'D' Version, p. 112.
6. Ibid.
7. Ibid.
8. Identified with Bradwell-on-Sea, see Woods, M., *In Search of the Dark Ages* (London BBC 1981), p. 172.
9. ASC 'D' Version, p. 112.
10. Collingwood, op. cit., p. 319.
11. Ibid., p. 321.
12. ASC 'E' version p. 113.
13. Ibid.
14. Ibid., 'D' version, p. 112.
15. *Historia Norwegiae*, p. 83.
16. *Heimskringla*, p. 26.
17. *Fagrskinna*, p. 66.
18. *Egil's Saga* p. 145.
19. Roger of Wendover p.p. 402 – 403.
20. Woods, op. cit., p. 174.

21. Tolkien, J. R. R., ed. P. Grybauskas, *The Battle of Maldon* (London, Harper Collins 2023), p. vii.
22. *Briggflatts*, p. 21 – Eirik was never King of Dublin.

Nine: The Good Name Never Dies

1. Nighswander, L., 'No Nazis in Valhalla: Understanding the Use (and Misuse) of Nordic Cultural Markers in Third Reich Era Germany' (*International ResearchScape Journal*: Vol. 7, Article 6, 2020), pp. 2–3.
2. The gear is superbly well displayed on the upper level of the Richard III Centre in Leicester, and it is compelling.
3. Played in the movie by Frank Thring.
4. Theodoric the Monk relied heavily on Icelandic sources, possibly including the *Oldest Saga of St Olaf* and Snorrason's *Óláfs saga Tryggvasonar*.
5. Certainly, according to his most recent biographer the late Desmond Seward, see *The Greatest Viking* (Edinburgh, Birlinn 2022).
6. *Mother of Kings* (New York, Tor Publishing 2001).
7. Shapeshifting is an ancient and established form of totemism and shamanism found in several cultures. Using dark arts, the practitioner can take on the form of another creature, such as the werewolf or vampire. It was generally considered anti-social behaviour if, at times, very handy. (See glossary.)
8. Starting with *The Whale Road* (London, Harper Collins 2007).
9. Calderon M .J. G., *Romancing the Dark Ages – The Viking Hero in Sentimental Narrative* (University of Seville): file:///C:/Users/John/Downloads/Dialnet-RomancingTheDarkAgesThe VikingHeroInSentimentalNarr-2592835%20(3).pdf, accessed 8 January 2024.
10. Ibid.
11. Nighswander, op. cit., p. 4.
12. Ibid., pp. 6–7.
13. Grid ref. NY 89991230, see 'Rey Cross' in *Corpus of Anglo-Saxon Stone Sculpture. Volume VI: Yorkshire North Riding (Except Ryedale)*, ed. James Lang. pp. 283–84.
14. Calverley (1847–1898) was one of those curious Victorian clerics who became avid amateur antiquarians. He made wonderfully accurate drawings of many ancient stone carvings found in

Cumbrian churches and churchyards and his legacy is the beautifully executed full-size copy of the famous Gosforth Cross.
15. W. G. Collingwood, *King Eirik of York*, op. cit., p. 327; *The Battle of Stainmore*, op. cit., p. p. 240–41.
16. Ann Williams, 'Thorkell the Tall and the Bubble Reputation: The Vicissitudes of Fame' in R. Lavelle and S. Roffey (eds.) *The Danes in Wessex: The Scandinavian Impact on Southern England, c. 800–c.1000'* (Oxford, Oxbow Books, 2016), p.144.
17. Honeycombe, op. cit., p 5.

Ten: Will the Real Eirik Bloodaxe...
1. Collingwood, W. G., 'King Eirik of York' in *Saga Book of the Viking Club*, Vol II January 1897–December 1900 (London, privately printed), pp. 313–327.
2. Ibid., p. 315.
3. *The Annals of Clonmacnoise* are a seventeenth-century compilation of earlier now lost sources, covering Irish tradition from prehistory to the dawn of the fifteenth century.
4. Collingwood, op. cit., p. 317.
5. Ibid., p. 319.
6. Ibid., p. 321.
7. Ibid., p. 322.
8. Ibid., p. 325.
9. Ibid.
10. Ibid., p. 326.
11. Woolf, A., *Erik Bloodaxe Revisited* (Edinburgh, University of Edinburgh) https://www.academia.edu/313144/Erik_Bloodaxe_Revisited, accessed 9.4.24, p. 189.
12. Ibid.
13. Ibid., p. 190.
14. Ibid., p. 191.
15. Ibid.
16. Ibid., pp. 191–192.
17. Downham, C., 'Eric Bloodaxe – Axed? The Mystery of the last Scandinavian king of York' (*Mediaeval Scandinavia* 2004), 14: 51-77.
18. Ibid., p. 54.
19. Ibid., p. 56.
20. Ibid.

21. Ibid., p. 63.
22. Ibid., p. 70.
23. Ibid.
24. Ibid., p. 72.
25. Regarding coin evidence two issues have been identified. The first imitates the coins of Olaf Sihtricsson, his predecessor, although this may just represent an element of administrative continuity. Eirik's second issue harks back to Olaf's father Sihtric. On the reverse of each is stamped a sword emblem which is interpreted as invoking Ragnald's 're-conquest' of 919 and a strong link to the *Ui Imair*, as the sword emblem could be 'The Sword of Carlus' – part of their royal insignia. Such symbols were very important, subject to close kingly control and an obvious means of proclaiming legitimacy (see Downham, op. cit., p. 72).
26. Downham, op. cit., p. 74.
27. Ibid., p. 75.
28. Ibid., p. 76.

Eleven: Mother of Kings

1. *Njal's Saga*, pp. 6–9.
2. Ibid., p. 13.
3. *Egil's Saga*, p. 86.
4. *Fagrskinna*, p. 66.
5. Ibid.
6. Ibid., p. 67.
7. Ibid., pp. 67–68.
8. Ibid., 69.
9. Ibid., p. 70.
10. Ibid., pp. 74–75.
11. From the poet Glum Geirason, *Heimskringla*, p. 101.
12. Ibid.
13. Ibid., p. 107.
14. *Jomsviking Saga* ch. 8.
15. Jerome Brooke, *Queen of Darkness* (2008)

GLOSSARY

Aesir – The large, dysfunctional family of Norse Gods including Thor, Odin Loki et al.

Asgard – Home of the gods.

Battle – division of an army, traditionally deployed in three battles.

Berserker – possibly apocryphal but these were warriors who psyched themselves up to go 'bare-sark' into battle (i.e. without mail shirts). Hallucinogens may have had a part to play. If these men existed, they were possibly criminals and others who could be expended for the psychological effect they might exert over an untrained enemy.

Birka – the principal trading entrepot for the Baltic region, one of the first centres to adopt Christianity. Heading for decline in Eirik's day.

Bonder (Bondi) – a tenant or freehold farmer or craftsman, a free man, often of wealth and status, the Norse middle classes, eligible to bear arms and speak at a Thing or Assembly.

Bretland – Wales.

Burh – a fortified town or settlement, encircled by timber and earth ramparts.

Coif – A mail hood.

Compensation – can be *wir-geld* or blood money, a system of monetary compensation. The courts could order a cash settlement as a free standing decision or as an alternative to lesser outlawry. If the offended was fully outlawed he couldn't buy his way out. If he was outlawed the transgressor was wholly expelled from society, he became a non-person.

Danelaw – those parts of England, east and north-east where Scandinavian law applied, as opposed to Anglo-Saxon England where Anglo-Saxon law prevailed.

Drakkar (Longship) – the largest warship, typically crewed by 60 or more crew, Olaf Trygvasson's famous flagship, *The Long Serpent*, was a famous example.

Drapa – Norse poetry, in essence an eight-line verse, each in two half-lines which contains two stressed syllables. Each line-pair was linked by alliteration and three of the four half-lines per couplet would carry the same sound at the start of a stressed syllable. The art lay in extemporisation, keeping to the agreed form. Over time and in translation some effect is inevitably lost.

Dreng – comrade in arms, sometimes interchangeable with Bonder.

Ealdorman – roughly equivalent to the Norse jarl, an important regional figure very possibly related to the king, responsible for mustering local levies; the term 'earl' comes into use in the 10th century, first in Northumbria.

Einherjar – graduates of Valhalla where the Valkyries perform regular waitress service, and where these illuminati make ready for the final battle.

Fyrd – Saxon levies, either 'select' men with some basic kit and experience or a wider, general muster of all able-bodied males.

Gardariki – Russia.

Geld – monies paid by treaty or as a tribute.

Godi – essentially a wise man, not a priest as such but one who might through learning and experience have an insight into the minds of the gods. Someone to be listened to.

Hauberk – mail shirt.

Hedeby – another busy entrepot, located at the base of Jutland peninsula, then Danish (now German, blame Bismarck).

Hel – Queen of the Underworld, one of tricky Loki's brood.

Herred – a parcel of land, assessed for military obligation, very roughly equivalent to the English 'Hundred'.

Hersir – an ad hoc military rank who commanded a company of perhaps a hundred men and who would owe allegiance to his local jarl.

Hide – a parcel of land, not fixed in measurement but regarded as sufficient to support a single family.

High-Reeve (*heahgerefa*) – a crown official responsible for the administration of an estate, it applies particularly in Northumbria. A reeve was generally an administrator charged with collections, taxes and tolls in an urban centre. In the Danelaw a *hold* had the same role as a high reeve.

Hird – the king's bodyguard, elite household followers.

Holmgang (duel) – literally going to as island, as the contest might take place on a small islet or on a piece of ground marked out as an arena. Each combatant was allowed up to three shields for the fight. In later later duels first blood might be enough to end the fight and the wounded man had lost, he would have to then buy off his victorious opponent.

Holmgard – Novgorod.

Host (*here*) – a body of men but not necessarily a large unit, the Norse regarded a platoon of 36 men, the standard ship's crew, as a 'host'.

Howe – burial mound.

Hundred – a district within a county area – nominally of a hundred hides.

Jarl – equates to an earl, though his status wasn't fixed, one who achieved dominance in a region. A Rig-Jarl could be a petty king, such supremacies were never willingly surrendered.

Jorvik – Viking York, formerly Roman Eboracum and Saxon Eoforwic.

Glossary

Knarr – workhorse of the seas, fat-bellied all-purpose primarily cargo vessel.

Lamellar – a style of harness comprised of iron strips laced together, lighter than mail, more favoured in the east.

Leidang – ship levy.

Lendman – a rank within the king's household, a senior officer within his *hird*, second in status only to a jarl. The Lendman was the king's man though and less susceptible to local interest, so could be the royal watchdog in any given region to curb fissiparous tendencies – he was allowed up to 40 warriors in his own affinity.

Loki – trickster and general bad boy of the gods but more fun than the rest.

Maille, (or mail/chain mail) – a flexible design of body armour made from small (6mm) steel rings drawn from wire and then riveted together, in use from the third century BC until the Renaissance.

Midgard – the world of men, roughly half-way up the tree of life.

Midgard Serpent – a monster so vast it encircles the world and bites its own tail.

Miklagard – Byzantium/Constantinople, largest city on earth.

Mjollnir – Thor's great hammer and general problem-solving toolkit.

Narvesund – Straits of Gibraltar.

Nidaros – The original name for Trondheim, the seat of Norwegian kingship.

Odin – the All Father, senior and progenitor of the gods, who sacrificed an eye for all the world's wisdom.

Ragnarök (or Ragna Rokk) – twilight of the gods – doom of all powers, that final cataclysm when the world is ripped apart but then reborn. It's said that Norse culture is unique in that they knew their version of the world was time-limited and that their ancient belief system would one day give way to something new.

Runes – the Norsemen's pictographic written language, symbols used for stating factual information, known as 'futhark' – the first six letters spell futhark. Originally the runic alphabet contained 24 letters, but this subsequently shrank to 16.

Rus – Norse immigrants who settled and fostered the creation and growth of Kiev and Novgorod, the word may be Finnish in origin. Quite quickly, the Norse newcomers mingled bloodlines with indigenous Slavs and formed a distinct racial entity.

Saga – an epic tale of gods and men.

Scatt – tax, no more popular then than now. Saxon equivalent is *gyld*.

Seax – can be long or short, all-purpose, single-edged fighting and general utility knife.

Sheriff – royal official responsible for the government of a county area.

Shield-Burg – a defensive formation akin to the Roman testudo, a ridge of raised and overlapping shields to counter missiles.

Shield-Maiden – a Norse Amazon, a trained female fighter, probably far less common than TV would like to have us believe; women were too valuable as breeding stock to be consumed as cannon fodder.

Shield Wall – the standard military formation of the Viking era, a packed linear formation of locking shields, or shields that had the potential to lock for contact, then open up for combat.

Shieling – an upland summer pasture, *saeter* in Norwegian.

Skiphired – a muster of fighters for amphibious operations.

Strake – hull board on a Viking ship.

Strandhogg – coastal raiding for resupply, effectively living off the land – other peoples' land.

Swine Wedge (or *Svinfylkja*) – an arrow-headed assault formation, intended to drive a wedge into and through an enemy shield wall.

Thing – a public meeting and assembly where freemen could air their views and cast a vote.

Thor – Odin's son and the gods' enforcer.

Glossary

Valkyrie – one of a group of female deities who guide the souls of the freshly slain to the Halls of Valhalla, but they can also decide upon who lives or dies, choosing their favourites.

Varangian Guard – elite personal guard and household troops of the Byzantine emperor.

Viking – this is not a racial or genetic name and there are various interpretations. One of these is that the term derives from *vik*, meaning a creek, inlet, small bay or possibly from the regional name *Vikin* – so one who hails from that district. The word is open to numerous other putative derivations and appears to have entered the English language no earlier than the eighteenth century, the time of a romantic 'Viking' revival. During the last century this was expanded to cover those who came from the settlements such as Iceland, or the Faroes, taking on the heroic connotation it retains today.

Vinland – the eastern seaboard of North America.

Wapentake – a Scandinavian measure of land, roughly equivalent to the Anglo-Saxon hundred.

War arrow/token – a symbolic item passed around localised communities, summoning warriors to service.

Wyrd – fate, personal destiny.

Yggdrasill – The Tree of Life.

Appendix 1

EGIL'S DRAPA, THE *EIRIKSMAL* AND *HRAFNSMAL*

Egil's Drapa

West over Water I fared,
-Of the war-god's heart;
My course was set.
I launched my oaken craft
At the breaking of ice,
Loaded my cargo of praise
Aboard my ship aft.

The warrior welcomed me,
To him my paise is due.
I carry Odin's mead
To England's meadows, the leader
   I laud, sing surely his praise;
I ask to be heard,
An ode I can devise.

Consider, lord – well it will
   befit –
How I recite
If my poem is heard.
Most men have learned

Of the king's battle deeds
And the war-god saw
Corpses strewn on the field.

The clash of swords roared
On the edge of shields, battle
   grew around the king,
Fierce he ventured forth,
The blood-river raced,
The din was heard then
Of metal showered in battle,
The most in that land.

The web of spears
Did not stray from their course
Above the king's
Bright row of shields.
The shore groaned,
Pounded by the flood
Of blood, resounded
Under the banners' march.

Egil's Drapa, The Eiriksmal and Hrafnsmal

In the mud men lay
When spears rained down.
Eirik that day
Won great renown.

Still will I tell
If you pay me heed,
More I have heard
Of those famous deeds.
Wounds grew the more
When the king stepped in,
Swords smashed
On the shields' black rims.

Swords clashed, battle-sun
And whetstone's saddle;
The wound-digger bit
With its venomous point.
I heard they were felled,
Odin's forest of oaks,
By scabbard icicles
In the play of iron.

Blades made play
And swords bore down.
Eirik that day
Won great renown.

Ravens flocked
To the reddened sword,
Spears plucked lives
And gory shafts sped.
The scourge of Scots
Fed the wolves that trolls ride,
Loki's daughter Hel,
Trod the eagle's food.

Battle-cranes swooped
Over heaps of dead,
Wound-birds did not want
For blood to gulp,
The wolf gobbled flesh,
The raven daubed
The prow of its beak
In waves of red.

The troll's wolfish steed
Met a match for its greed.
Eirik fed flesh
To the wolf afresh.

The battle-maiden keeps
The swordsman awake
When the ship's wall
Of shields breaks.
Shafts sang
And points stung,
Flaxen strings shot
Arrows from bows.

Flying spears bit,
The peace was rent;
Wolves took heart
At the taut elm bow.
The war-wise king fended
A deadly blow,
The yew-bow twanged
In the battle's fray.

Like bees, arrows flew
From his drawn bow of yew,
Eirik fed flesh
To the wolf afresh.

Yet more I desire
That men realise
His generous nature;
I urge on my praise.

Eric Bloodaxe the Viking: 'I Shall Die Laughing'

He throws gold river-flame
But holds his lands
In his horn-gripping hand,
He is worthy of praise.

By the fistful he gives
The fire of his arm.
Never sparing rings' lives
He gives riches no rest,
Hands gold out like sand
From the hawk's coast.
Fleets take cheer
From the grindings of dwarfs.

The maker of war sheds beds
    for spears
From his gold-laden arm,
He spreads brooches afar.
I speak from the heart;
Everywhere he is grand,

Eirik's feats were heard
On the east-lying shore.

King, bear in mind
How my ode is wrought,
I take delight
In the hearing I gained.
Through my lips I stirred
From the depths of my heart
Odin's sea of verse
About the craftsman of war.

I bore the king's praise
Into the silent void,
My words I tailor
To the company.
From the seat of my laughter
I lauded the warrior
And it came to pass
That most understood.

The Eiriksmal

ÓTHIN [Odin]:
What dreams be these, now? Methought that ere daybreak
I got Valholl ready to make room for warriors;
I waked the einherjar, asked them to rise up,
to put straw on benches, and to rinse the beer-jugs;
and the Valkyries, to deal wine out as though a warrior drew nigh.
"Lords from man-home are to be looked for,
high-born and hardy, which my heart gladdens.
'What thunders, Bragi, as though thousands stirred,
or whelming hosts?'
BRAGI:
'Crack all boards of the benchess though Baldr were coming
back to Óthin's beerhall.'
ÓTHIN:
'Of witless words shalt beware, wise Bragi,
for full well thou wotst:

'tis Eric this heralds, who to us is wending,
the earl, into Óthin's hall.
'Sigmund and Sinfiotli, leave your seats, ye heroes,
and go forth to greet the king!
Bid him enter in, if Eric it be:
him I have hopes to see.'
SIGMUND:
'Why of Eric, rather than of another?'
ÓTHIN:
'Because in many a liege-land this lord hath warred
and borne a bloody sword.'
SIGMUND
'Why, then, didst rob him of victory, since valiant thou thought
   him?'
ÓTHIN:
'No one knoweth—
looks the grey wolf (grimly) toward the gods' dwellings.'
SIGMUND:
'Hail to thee, Eric, here thou art welcome!
wise war-lord, in hall.
This fain would I know: who be following thee
of athelings, from the edge-fight?'
ERIC:
'Kings five there are, them all I shall name thee:
am I the sixth myself.'

Lee M. Hollander: *Norse Poems*

Hrafnsmal

1 Hearken, ye ring-bearers, while of Harold I tell you,
the mightily wealthy, and his manful war-deeds;
words I overheard a maiden high-minded speaking,
golden-haired, white-armed, with a glossy-beaked raven.
2 Wise thought her the Valkyrie; we were welcome never
men to the bright-eyed one, her who birds' speech knew well.
Greeted the light-lashed maiden, the lily-throated woman,
the Hymir's-skull-cleaver as on cliff he was perching.
3 'How is it, ye ravens— whence are ye come now
with beaks all gory, at break of morning?

Eric Bloodaxe the Viking: 'I Shall Die Laughing'

Carrion-reek ye carry, and your claws are bloody.
Were ye near, at night-time, where ye knew of corpses?'
4 Shook himself the dun-hued one, and dried his beak,
the eagle's oath-brother, and of answer bethought him:
'Harold we follow, Halfdan's first-born,
I the young Yngling, since out of egg we crept.
5 'That king thou knowest, him who at Kvinnar dwelleth,
the hoard-warder of North men, who has hollow warships
with reddish ribs and with reddened war-shields,
with tarred oar-blades and with tents foam-besprinkled.
6 'Fain outside would he drink the ale at Yuletide,
the fight-loving folk-warder, and Frey's game play there.
Even half-grown, he hated the hearth fire cozy,
the warm women's room, and the wadded down-mittens.
7 "Hearken how the high-born one in the Hafrs-firth fought there,
the keen-eyed king's son, against Kiotvi the wealthy:
came the fleet from the eastward, eager for fighting,
with gaping figureheads and graven ship-prows.
8 'They were laden with franklins and linden shields gleaming,
with Westland spear shafts and with Welsh broadswords.
The berserkers bellowed as the battle opened,
the wolf-coats shrieked loud and shook their weapons.
9 'Their strength would they try, but he taught them to flee,
the lord of the East-men who at Útstein dwelleth.
The steeds-of-Nokkvi he steered out when started the battle.
Then boomed the bucklers ere a blow felled Haklang.
10 'The thick-necked atheling behind the isle took shelter:
he grew loath, against Lúfa to hold the land of his fathers.
Then hid under benches, and let their buttocks stick up,
they who were wounded, but thrust their heads keel ward.
11 'Their shoulders shielded the shifty heroes —
were they showered with slung-shot—with the shingles-of-Glad
   home.
Home from Hafrs-firth hastened they eastward,
fled by way of Iathar, of ale-cups thinking.
12 'On the gravel lay the fallen, given to the one-eyed
husband of Fulla; were we fain of such doings.
13 'Of more and other things shall the maids of Ragnhild,
the haughty women-folk, now have to gabble

than of the heath-dwellers which Harold not ever
feasted on the fallen, as their friends had done oft.
14 The high-born liege-lord took the lady from Denmark—
broke with his Rogaland sweethearts and their sisters from Hordaland,
with those from Heithmork and Halogaland eke.'

THE VALKYRIE

15 'Whether is open-handed he-who-hastens-the-battle,
to those who fend faithfully foemen from his homeland?'

THE RAVEN

16 'With much goods are gladdened the gallant warriors,
who in the hall of Harold while the time with chess-play:
with much wealth he rewards them, and with well-forged broadswords,
with gold from Hun land and with girls from the East folks.

17 'Most happy are they when there is hope for battle,
all ready to rouse them and to row strongly,
so as to snap the thongs and to sunder the tholepins,
to churn the brine briskly at the beck of their liege-lord.'

THE VALKYRIE

18 'Of the skalds' lot would I ask thee, since thou skill of that boastest:
how the bards fare there thou full well knowest—
they who are in Harold's hall.'

THE RAVEN

19 'Is seen from their raiment and their red-gold finger-rings
that a kind king they have.
Red fur-cloaks own they, most fairly bordered,
swords wound with silver, and sarks ring-woven,
gilded baldricks and graven helmets,
heavy gold bracelets which Harold bestowed on them.'

THE VALKYRIE

20 'Of the berserkers' lot would I ask thee, thou who batten'st on corpses:
how fare the fighters who rush forth to battle,
and stout-hearted stand 'gainst the foe?'

THE RAVEN

21 'Wolf-coats are they called, the warriors unfleeing,
who bear bloody shields in battle;

the darts redden where they dash into battle
and shoulder to shoulder stand.
'Tis men tried and true only, who can targes shatter,
whom the wise warlord wants in battle.'
THE VALKYRIE
22 'Of Andath and all his ilk, too, have I asked thee but little:
how fare the fiddlers, how fare the jugglers
in the halls of Harold?'
THE RAVEN
23 'His earless dog does your Andath fondle;
the churl with his fool-tricks makes the folk-warder chuckle.
Yet be there others who about the fire bowls of hot wine bear;
their flapping fools'-caps they tuck fast in their belts—
fellows you're free to kick.'

Appendix 2

GENEALOGY OF THE KINGS OF BERNICIA AND DEIRA (AFTER NENNIUS)

Bernicia

Woden begat Beldeg, who begat Beornec, who begat Gethbrond, who begat Aluson, who begat Ingwi, who begat Edilbrith, who begat Esa, who begat Eoppa who begat Ida. But Ida had twelve sons, Adda, Belric, Theodric, Ethelric, Theodhere, Osmer and one queen, Bearnoch, Ealric. Ethelric begat Ethelfrid: the same is Aethelred *Fleasaur* ['The destroyer']. For he also had seven sons, Eanfrid, Oswald, Oswin, Oswy, Oswudu, Oslac, Offa. Oswy begat Alfrid, Elfwin, and Egfrid [Ecfrith] Egfrid is he who made war against his cousin king of the Picts, and he fell therein with all the strength of his army, and the Picts with their king gained the victory; and the Saxons never again reduced the Picts so as to exact tribute from them.

Deira

Woden begat Beldeg, who begat Sibald, who begat Zegulf, who begat Soemil, who first separated [Deira] from [Bernicia], Soemil begat Siguerthing, who begat Giulgis, who begat Ulfrea, who begat Iffi, Edwin, Osfrid and Eanfrid. There were two sons of Edwin, who fell in with him in battle at [Hatfield], and the kingdom was never renewed in his family, because not one of his race escaped from that war; but all were slain with him by the army of [Cadwallon], king of the Guendota. Oswy begat Egfrid, the same is Ailguin, who begat Oslach, who begat Althun, who begat Adlsing, who begat Echun, who begat Oslaph. Ida begat Eadric, who begat Ecgulf, who begat Leodwald, who begat Eata, the same is Glinmaur, who begat Eadbert and Egbert, who was the first bishop of their nation.

Appendix 3

KINGS OF NORTHUMBRIA 685–867

685–705; Aldfrith, half-brother of Ecgfrith

705–15; Osred, killed in battle against the Picts

716–718; Coenred

718–729; Osric

729–737; Ceolwulf (brother of Coenred) and to whom Bede dedicated his Ecclesiastical History in 731. He himself was 'forcibly tonsured' a year later but clawed back power for another five-year period until he finally abdicated.

737–758; Eadberht (Ceolwulf's cousin), finally abdicates.

758–759; Oswulf (Eadberht's son), assassinated.

759–765; Aethelwald Moll; dethroned.

765–774; Alhred (Oswulf's son in law), exiled.

774–779; Ethelred, son of Aethelwald, succeeded as a minor and driven into exile.

779–788; Aelfwald, a relation of Oswulf, also assassinated.

788–789; Osred II, son of Alhred, exiled.

789–796; Ethelred reinstated, eventually assassinated.

796; Osbald, lasted less than a month then exiled.

796–806; Eardwulf, avoided assassination, expelled and reinstated by continental allies in 808.

806–808, Aelfwald II, reigned just long enough to die in his bed.

808–811/812; second reign of Eardwulf – deposed for second and last time.

811–840; Eanred, died.

840–844; Ethelred II, son of Eanred – deposed.

844; Raedwulf, killed by Viking raiders.

844–848; Etheldred II, next attempt, assassinated.

848–866; Osberht, exiled.

866–867; Aelle (putatively Osberht's brother), killed alongside him in Battle of York against Ivar.

Appendix 4

ERIC BLOODAXE – AXED? THE MYSTERY OF THE LAST SCANDINAVIAN KING OF YORK BY PROFESSOR CLARE DOWNHAM

The identity of Eiríkr of York was a matter for debate among historians of the nineteenth century. Mediaeval English sources were rather vague on this issue, although they did report that he was a son of someone called Haraldr. This enabled two rival theories of Eiríkr's identity to be developed. One view – espoused by Sharon Turner, J.M. Lappenberg, Charles Plummer and James Todd – was that Eiríkr was the same person as Hringr son of Haraldr Blátönn (Harald Bluetooth) of Denmark. The other opinion - advanced by Charles Haliday, Joseph Stevenson, and W.G. Collingwood – was that Eiríkr of York was in fact Eiríkr Blóðøx (Eric Bloodaxe), erstwhile King of Norway and a son of Harald Hárfagri (Harold Finehair). Collingwood persuasively argued this view in 1902 and since then Eiríkr of York has been regarded as synonymous with Eiríkr Blóðøx.

Collingwood's case was developed within the context of Late Victorian methods of analysing saga as historical evidence. There is also a certain imaginative appeal, in the epithet 'Bloodaxe' and in the portrayal of this figure in saga, which has encouraged the acceptance of this identification, It is however striking that the earliest source used to identify Eiríkr of York with Eiríkr Blóðøx belongs to the end of the twelfth century. As this seems rather late, and as the evidence itself may be challenged, I propose to review the sources for Eiríkr's identity, guided by more recent developments in source criticism. For the purpose of this paper, I shall adopt the guise of Devil's advocate and suggest the existence of another possible identity for Eiríkr of York, which has never yet been considered. I hope that this will provoke further debate either to disprove or to support this theory, and to promote further analysis of the evidence from England, Germany, Scandinavia and Ireland on this issue.

In making a case against the identification of Eiríkr of York with Eiríkr Blóðøx, I shall first discuss the English evidence for Eiríkr's reign. This includes chronicles whose authors drew on tenth-century annals, namely 'The Anglo-Saxon Chronicle', *Historia regum Anglorum* (Part 1, section 6), and Roger of Wendover's *Flores historiarum* (although in the last of these the tenth-century evidence is much supplemented). There are also twelfth-century historians who referred to Eiríkr, including Henry of Huntingdon, John of Worcester, William of Malmesbury, and Roger of Howden.

None of these identified Eiríkr of York as Eiríkr Blóðøx or mentioned that Eiríkr of York had been King of Norway. Nor do later sources from England acknowledge this connexion. For example, when in the late thirteenth century the spin-doctors of Edward I were recasting history to make a case for his claim to rule Scotland, Eiríkr was cited as an example of a Scottish king who had been installed by a royal English overlord. The absence from English sources of any mention of Eiríkr's previous rule over Norway is perhaps surprising if it had been historical.

The most reliable clue to Eiríkr's identification in English sources is that he was a son of Haraldr. This is stated in the E-text of 'The Anglo-Saxon Chronicle' and repeated by Henry of Huntingdon. The early thirteenth-century author Roger of Wendover supplied further details of family-connexions. He stated that Eiríkr died with his son Henry *(filio suo Henrico)* and with his brother Reginald *(frater Reginaldo)*. It is possible that these details are a later invention incorporated into the text and are not historically accurate.

Here it is enough to note that they do not match Scandinavian accounts of Eiríkr Blóðøx: he was said to have had six sons whose names are listed in Norwegian sources, but none of these names is equivalent to the name Henry. However, Collingwood attempted to identify these names, Henry with that of Hárekr son of

Guthormr and Reginald with an unidentified King Røgnvaldr who are listed among the dead in the final battle of Eiríkr Blóðøx in the thirteenth-century saga-compendium known as *Heimskringla*. This is a rather tenuous similarity which could be coincidental. Even if it is not coincidental, we must note that Alan Binns, Axel Seeberg, and others have suggested that the author of *Heimskringla* drew these names from an English source. This could therefore be a late addition to the legend of Eiríkr Blóðøx in *Heimskringla*, influenced by English accounts of the Northumbrian king. These reports in *Heimskringla* and Roger's *Flores historiarum* seem too imprecise and too doubtful to show that Eiríkr Blóðøx was Eiríkr of York.

A king called Eiríkr is recorded in the Anglo-Norman *Liber uitae* of Durham as *rex Danorum*. In some Scandinavian sources Eiríkr Blóðøx is presented as a convert to Christianity, and this has been regarded as a reference to the same king, although it is possible that Eiríkr of York was Christian, Lesley Abrams has recently identified the king in the *Liber uitae* as Eric Eiegod, who ruled Denmark from 1095 to 1103. This is because his wife, *Botild regina*, is mentioned alongside him. It seems therefore that English sources provide little guidance concerning the identification of Eiríkr of York. They provide no proof that he can be identified with Eiríkr Blóðøx.

Evidence from Germany has been used to support the idea that Eiríkr was the son of Haraldr Blátönn, king of Denmark, rather than a Norwegian king. The earliest surviving record for this idea is *Gesta Hammaburgensis ecclesiae pontificum* written by Adam of Bremen. This was originally composed around 1075, although some notes appear to have been added soon after. Adam reported that Haraldr Blátönn 'sent his son Hringr to England with an army. When the latter had subjugated the whole island, he was in the end betrayed and killed by the Northumbrians' ('Hring filium cum exercitu misit in Angliam, qui subacta insula tandem proditus et occisus est a Nordhumbris'). We know that Adam used Danish informants as a source when writing his *Gesta*, including the Danish king, Svein Estrithsen. Thus we may have evidence of a Danish witness in this passage which eulogises the deeds of Haraldr Blátönn and his successors of the Danish royal line. Adam's record of Hringr was quoted in later collections of Icelandic literature, namely *Flateyjarbók* and *Fornmannasögur*.

There are several reasons to doubt that this record of Hringr is an accurate reference to Eiríkr of York. First, the name, Hringr, is manifestly not Eiríkr. John Green and Charles Plummer resorted to calling Eiríkr of York 'Eric Hiring', but there is no evidence that the names should be connected. The second problem is with Adam's chronology, according to Adam, this event happened when Hákon the Great was ruling Norway (c. 971/995), which is too late to fit Eiríkr's career in Northumbria. Furthermore, he asserted that Hringr subjugated all Britain, which is manifestly not true. Even if this is an exaggerated account of the seizure of Northumbria, it does not fit with other sources. Adam of Bremen was perhaps relying on oral witnesses who gave an inaccurate account exalting the deeds of Haraldr Blátönn and his family.

The account appears to be very unreliable, although it was written barely a century after the events were said to have happened. It is possible that the story of Hringr may have developed from the name of Culén Hringr, king of Alba, who died in 971. This fits the timeframe and the geographical context suggested by Adam. However, no one is arguing that Culén was a son of Haraldr Blátönn. It is possible that Adam's story developed from a desire to glorify the royal line of Denmark, and it is possible that a similar motive comes into play in the saga-portrayals of Eiríkr Blóðøx.

Scandinavian histories and sagas dating from the end of the twelfth century assert a connection between the Northumbrian Eiríkr and Eiríkr Blóðøx. It is clear from these sources that several different stories circulated regarding the fate of Eiríkr Blóðøx once he left Norway (these may be compared with the survival-legends of other mediaeval kings). It is my hypothesis that, in the Scandinavian sources, legends concerning Eiríkr Blóðøx became influenced by, and were combined with, the legends of Eiríkr of York. This may simply be the result of confusion of sources describing two kings of the same name. Alternatively, such a conflation could have been motivated by a narrative desire to fill the gap in the story of Eiríkr Blóðøx once he had left Scandinavia. The association of Eiríkr of York with Eiríkr Blóðøx also fits with the legends evolving around the *persona* of Haraldr Hárfagri (father of Eiríkr Blóðøx) and the royal line of Norway at this time.

The Scandinavian evidence is best discussed in two parts. I shall treat the prose texts separately from the skaldic poems embedded in them. This is because scholars have often assigned the poems a separate genesis from and earlier date than the surrounding prose. For the purposes of historical analysis the prose may therefore sometimes cloud rather than clarify the poems' interpretation. The Norwegian Latin *Historia de antiquitate regum Norwegiensium* of Theodoric the Monk appears to be the earliest source linking Eiríkr Blóðøx with England.

This text was composed between 1177 and 1188. Theodoric stated that his account was based on the oral testimony of Icelanders. He made the apology that, although the Icelanders were well versed in historical lore, such oral evidence is weaker than written testimony. In his *Historia,* Theodoric reported that Eiríkr, whom he called *fratrum interfector* ('brother-killer'), succeeded Haraldr Hárfagri on the Norwegian throne. His brother drove him out after three years on account of his cruelty and particularly that of his wife Gunnhildr. Eiríkr then sailed to England where the king received him honourably and he died immediately afterwards. No reference is found to Eiríkr having ruled Northumbria.

The link between Eiríkr Blóðøx and York is first attested in the slightly later history known as *Ágrip*. This has been dated between 1188 and 1200. According to *Ágrip*, when Eiríkr fled Norway and came to England he was granted the earldom of Northumbria by King Æthelstan (927-39). However, Eiríkr soon lost hold of Northumbria (again this is blamed on Gunnhildr). Eiríkr finally resorted to a pirate's life and died while fighting in Spain. The origins of the other 'synoptic' history of Norway, *Historia Norwegiae*, are open to question. It appears to be a later text than *Historia de antiquitate* and *Ágrip* (although its exact date is disputed). *Historia Norwegiae* agrees with *Ágrip* that Eiríkr died in Spain. However, *Historia Norwegiae* also states that Eiríkr was baptised in Northumbria.

These accounts diverge in detail. They also contradict English sources about Eiríkr of York, the reports – given in *Historia regum Anglorum*, Part II, and by Roger of Wendover – or Eiríkr's violent death in England, do not match any of the three Norwegian 'synoptic' histories mentioned above. Theodoric implied that Eiríkr died peacefully in England, while *Ágrip* and *Historia Norwegiae* record his death in Spain. Finnur Jónsson suggested that there was confusion in the Norwegian sources which turned *Stan* from Stainmore, where Eiríkr died according to Roger of Wendover, to *Span*, Spain. I do not find this convincing. Moreover, none of the

Scandinavian accounts names Stainmore. In the Life of St Cathroe, written at Metz in the late tenth century, Eiríkr had (not later than 946) a wife who was a member of the royal dynasty of Alba. According to the Scandinavian accounts, Gunnhildr, who is named as wife of Eiríkr Blóðøx throughout his time in England, was of Danish or Norwegian descent. It seems that records of the details of Eiríkr's life diverge between Insular and Scandinavian sources.

Another difficulty in reconciling Scandinavian and Insular evidence resides in their chronology of events. Scandinavian sources relate that Eiríkr Blóðøx was king of Norway after Haraldr Hárfagri. Haraldr is said to have begun his reign in 858 or 863, and he is reported to have held power for as long as seventy or seventy-three years. On this basis Haraldr completed his reign between 928 and 936. Most recently Jesse Byock has supported the conventional date, around 930, for the end of Haraldr's reign. Eiríkr Blóðøx then ruled for a period of one to three years independently of his father. This leaves a significant gap in time before Eiríkr is first recorded in Northumbria in the written sources. This gap is not satisfactorily filled in the Scandinavian accounts.

Theodoric's *Historia*, *Ágrip* and *Historia Norwegiae* all state that Eiríkr went directly to England. There are, however, two reports in *Ágrip*: one says he went to Denmark first. In *Heimskringla* and *Egil's saga* we read that Eiríkr Blóðøx stopped at Orkney first, but this seems to have been for a short amount of time before he went raiding in North Britain and England. This conflicts with the *Orkneyinga saga* which states that Eiríkr came to Orkney after he had been expelled from Northumbria. The Scandinavian chronology does not seem to fit with Insular sources and the evidence is somewhat contradictory.

Two Scandinavian sources, *Ágrip* and *Historia Norwegiae*, link Eiríkr to Kind Æthelstan, an unlikely relationship in terms of the English historical record. The idea may be due to the fame of the brother of Eiríkr Blóðøx, Hákon inn góði, who was said to have been fostered by Æthelstan (I shall discuss this in more detail below). Details of the life of Eiríkr Blóðøx and his chronology in Scandinavian sources do not therefore match up with English accounts of Eiríkr of York. We might permit the Scandinavian sources some margin of error on the assumption that they depend on oral tradition, but their very imprecision calls other features of the story into doubt. Furthermore, their factual correctness may be called into question.

The saga-accounts of Eiríkr which postdate the synoptic histories, including *Egil's saga, Heimskingla,* and *Orkneyinga saga,* provide further elaboration of the story of Eiríkr Blóðøx. Some of his information appears to have originated in an earlier written version, but the accounts are contradictory in nature, as Margaret Cormack has recently pointed out. It is necessary to employ a sceptical approach to this information. Ideally, the Icelandic evidence should be analysed on a case-by-case basis and compared with other available evidence.

More investigation is therefore necessary of the Scandinavian sources for the reign of Eiríkr Blóðøx. In terms of their reliability concerning the association of Eiríkr Blóðøx with Eiríkr of York, there are difficulties in trusting the accurate transmission of information over time (from the tenth century when the events happened to the late twelfth and thirteenth centuries when they were committed to writing) and distance (how deeds in Northumbria were reported in Iceland). It is also necessary to analyse this evidence (as all historical sources) for potential bias, or misrepresentation of the past to suit contemporary political agenda or literary predilection. On all three counts, I suggest that there is potential for error in the saga-accounts of Eiríkr.

It seems that Icelandic lore knew of a Northumbrian ruler Eiríkr: he was perhaps mistakenly associated with Eiríkr blóðøx, as the Icelandic sources show some uncertainty to that king's fate once he left Norway. Eiríkr blóðøx according to some accounts died in England, while according to others he died in Spain. The reign of Eiríkr of York was also mistakenly associated with the time of Æthelstan, sagas, based on oral accounts over a century after Adam of Bremen was writing, cannot be accepted as historical evidence without question. A case of mistaken identity is possible. The frequency with which the names Haraldr and Eiríkr were used in Scandinavian ruling families makes it plausible that there were two (or more) rulers with the same name active in western Europe at much the same date.

The next type of Scandinavian evidence, though closely related, is skaldic poetry. Some of this has been thought to have been composed in the tenth century and to have survived in the oral culture of the skalds, who passed down their learning from generation to generation. These poems were brought into writing in the thirteenth century. The skaldic poems connected with Eiríkr blóðøx or Eiríkr of York are mainly preserved in *Egil's saga, Heimskringla*, and *Fagrskinna*. It should be said at the outset that – once isolated from the untrustworthy prose surroundings – none of these skaldic poems explicitly identifies Eiríkr blóðøx or Eiríkr of York.

There are various opinions as to the historic validity of skaldic verse: this is a complex issue. Russell Poole has stated that it is 'mostly authentic', but at the other extreme Sigrún Daviðsdottir has argued that there is 'no reason [...] to put much faith in the historical value of the court poetry'. Most scholars have been willing to admit some failings in the skaldic corpus as a historical witness, while recognising it as a valuable resource. Attention has been drawn to frequent divergence in the record of the same poem in different manuscripts, unreliable authorial attribution, deliberate archaisms in poetic language which inhibit linguistic dating, and the observed plasticity of poetry composed in oral cultures, when studied over time.

Specific criticisms have been made concerning the poems in *Egil's saga*, which is the main repository of verses relating to Eiríkr of York and Eiríkr blóðøx. The saga-writer asserted that they were tenth-century compositions of the poet Egill Skalla-grimsson. Russell Poole has demonstrated that verses (relating to the slaying of Ljotr) in S65 of the saga must be dated later than the tenth century on stylistic and linguistic grounds. Another verse, in S73, bears signs of alteration when compared with independent and datable record elsewhere. It therefore seems likely that the verses in *Egil's saga* had diverse origins. They may have been gathered together (and some perhaps even composed) by the saga-writer to fit within the structure of his prose creation.

A general approach to verses in *Egil's saga* has been to regard loose stanzas as less authentic but to deem the longer poems – *Arinbjarnarkviða, Höfuðlausn*, and *Sonnatorrek* – a distinct group composed by one author, even if that author cannot be identified as Egill. Two of these poems are particularly relevant to this study, *Arinbjarnarkviða* and *Höfuðlausn*. These too have been criticised. Carolyne Larrington has suggested that the tenses of verbal forms in *Arinbjarnarkviða* may have been altered. More fundamentally, a tenth-century date for the composition of *Höfuðlausn* has been doubted on linguistic and stylistic grounds. It is thus debated how reliable these poems are regarding tenth-century political history where specific details (names, relationships, and royal deeds) are essential. These details may have fallen victim to elaboration, alteration, or 'improvement' over such a long span of time.

Despite the reservations expressed by various commentators, skaldic poetry is generally still deemed a significant source for early Scandinavian political history, albeit one where each example needs to be judged on its own merits. In relation to Eiríkr of York and Eiríkr Blóðøx, there are four relevant poems in *Egil's saga*. Poems which are linked to these characters by prose context alone I have not included. An isolated stanza in S59 refers to a warlike son of Eiríkr blóðøx found in *Heimskringla*. Another loose stanza in S60 refers to a king of Haraldr's line ruling in England. This is rather ambiguous: which Haraldr is not clear, and no Eiríkr is named. No reliable clue as to the stanza's date of composition has yet been found.

Most poetic information about Eiríkr in *Egil's saga* is found in *Höfuðlausn* (S61) and *Arinbjarnarkviða* (S80). These clearly relate to Eiríkr, king of York, with no apparent reference to Eiríkr blóðøx. *Höfuðlausn* is a eulogy of Eiríkr. According to the prose, the poem was composed under duress, a statement which negates the poem's praise-content to fit the bad image of Eiríkr in the saga as a savage ruler with a sorceress for a wife. Alfred Smyth and John Hines have suggested that the saga may not present an accurate account of the circumstances in which *Höfuðlausn* was composed. This poem describes Eiríkr as a scourge of the Scots, whose fame travelled to the eastern shore (presumably Norway).

The other lengthy poem, *Arinbjarnarkviða* is said to have been recited by Egill for a friend. It begins with an account of Egill's escapades in England, and Eiríkr is named as a member of the Yngling line. From this royal lineage were descended the kings of Norway. This genealogical statement has been used to support the identification of Eiríkr of York with Eiríkr Blóðøx. However, it was not only kings of Norway who claimed descent from the Yngling dynasty. Certainly, by the early eleventh century, Uí Ímair of Ireland claimed such a link, which we see in 'The Fragmentary Annals of Ireland'. Members of this Hiberno-Scandinavian dynasty had ruled in Northumbria before Eiríkr. The skaldic poems in *Egil's saga* do not therefore conflict with the theory that Eiríkr of York and Eiríkr blóðøx were separate individuals who were confused in Scandinavian literature from the end of the twelfth century.

There are other skaldic poems relating to Eiríkr blóðøx and Eiríkr of York, which are not found in *Egil's saga*. There are stanzas in *Heimskringla* which refer obliquely to Eiríkr blóðøx, through the deeds of his sons. A fragmentary poem attributed to Glúmr Geirason in praise of a certain Eiríkr also survives, but it provides little help to the historian. Finally, there is *Eiríksmál* whose language indicates a Northumbrian origin. It is likely to refer to Eiríkr of York. The author of this lay is anonymous, and the text seems (frustratingly) to be incomplete. It survives only in *Fagrskinna*, whose prose asserts that Gunnhildr had the poem composed soon after the death of her husband, Eiríkr blóðøx, during her stay on the Orkney Islands.

The historicity of this statement is uncertain. The poem tells of Eiríkr's welcome into Valhalla, following his death in battle with five kings. These kings are not named. This may be because the poem is incomplete or it may be, as Axel Seeberg has suggested, that they were not historical kings but were rather mentioned as a literary embellishment intended to raise the profile of Eiríkr. *Eiríksmál* merely provides a witness that Eiríkr died in battle and that those who wished to commemorate him felt comfortable using overtly pagan imagery, whether or not Eiríkr himself was a Christian. This does not contradict the argument advanced so far in this paper that Eiríkr blóðøx and Eiríkr of York are separate individuals.

The conclusion of this discussion is that we have no identification of Eiríkr of York with Eiríkr blóðøx from a date earlier than the end of the twelfth century. What was written at that time seems to come from oral tradition, which over such a span (250 years) is likely to have been subject to embellishment or invented. There is also conflict between accounts of the life of Eiríkr blóðøx in Scandinavian sources and the evidence concerning Eiríkr of York in Insular sources. Nevertheless, the small body of skaldic poetry which clearly relates to Eiríkr of York does not conflict with Insular records. One possible solution to these problems is to suggest that Eiríkr of York and Eiríkr blóðøx were separate individuals who were confused in later Scandinavian accounts.

This would not be the only case of confused identities in mediaeval Icelandic saga. Alistair Campbell noted in a lecture published in 1971 'that prose may be wrong in its attribution of the verse to particular persons or events', and he went on to cite some examples. Matthew Townend has more recently discussed the conscious or accidental re-contextualisation of memories of Scandinavian kings of York into a setting which was more meaningful to Icelandic saga-writers. The two cases which he presented were Óláfr Guðrøðsson and Sigtryggr Caech, who belonged to the dynasty of Ívarr (Uí Ímair) whose members ruled Dublin and York intermittently in the tenth century. In developing his argument Townend drew on the work of earlier scholars. Campbell had argued that Óláfr Guðrøðsson, leader of the Scandinavian troops at *Brunanburh*, was reinvented as Óláfr the Red, king of Scotland, by later saga-writers.

Campbell suggested that this was because at the time when the sagas were written 'the likeliest nation to invade England were the Scots'. It is therefore possible that oral memories from Northumbria regarding Eiríkr of York were re-contextualised to fit with legends of the Norwegian Eiríkr blóðøx. This could be because Eiríkr of Norway was more famous than Eiríkr of York at the time when the sagas were written. The fame of the former may be due to the importance of the sins of Eiríkr blóðøx, who ruled Norway, and the greater fame of his father, Haraldr Hárfagri.

However, one may ask why Eiríkr of York and Eiríkr son of Haraldr Hárfagri were regarded as synonymous at the end of the twelfth century if that was not a historical reality in the tenth century. Other features of the Scandinavian literary record raise such questions, notably the association claimed between Eiríkr blóðøx and Æthelstan. I suggest that the answer to these questions may lie in the legendary significance which Haraldr Hárfagri and Æthelstan had after their deaths. During the Middle Ages both were perceived as founding figures of national unity, to the extent that in legend they became emblematic of their peoples' identities. I suggest that this status was influential in the way in which both kings became involved in the story of Eiríkr of York.

I shall deal first with Haraldr hárfagri and his alleged paternity of Eiríkr of York. This should be assessed in the context of Haraldr's links to Scandinavian settlements across Northwest Europe, and it is worth taking some time to discuss this issue. Haraldr, his sons, and his associate Røgnvaldr, jarll of Møre, were linked to stories of Scandinavian settlement in Iceland, the Scottish

Isles and Mann, Ireland, and Normandy. Some of these stories have been regarded as mythical rather than historical. They relate to Haraldr's significance as founding figure of a unified Norwegian kingdom and progenitor of the Norwegian royal line.

Haraldr is a major figure in mediaeval Icelandic literature and its ideology of nationhood: Iceland was settled as a consequence of the tyranny of Haraldr Hárfagri, which caused many to leave Norway and start a new life in Iceland. Some commentators have doubted the story. Most recently, Jesse Byock has suggested that Haraldr may have had some influence in the settlement of Iceland, but that his role has probably been exaggerated. Haraldr seems eventually to symbolise the Norwegian cultural origins of the Icelanders, and he also represented the royal oppression from which the first settlers sought liberty. Both issues (origins, and freedom from royal rule) were a matter of cultural pride and identity among mediaeval Icelanders. Furthermore, it is through the medium of Icelandic sources that we gain more information concerning Haraldr's alleged involvement in other Scandinavian colonies.

Peter Swayer has argued that Haraldr Hárfagri's association with Scandinavian settlements in the Scottish Isles and Mann was influenced by his status in Icelandic legend. Sawyer has stated that 'It is not surprising that the Icelanders were ready to believe that Haraldr extended his power to the British Isles for it enabled them to reconcile a conviction that their ancestors had fled to Iceland from the tyranny of Haraldr with the knowledge that many of them came to Iceland not from Norway, but from the British Isles.' Sawyer has also suggested that the saga-accounts of Haraldr harrying the Northern Isles and Hebrides may have been inspired by the expeditions of Magnús berfœttr (Magnus Barelegs) to the same region in 1098 and 1102. These later events may have affected Scandinavians' interpretations of their past.

The story of Haraldr's involvement in the Scottish Isles is most fully expressed in SS8-9 of *Orkneyinga saga*, where we read that Haraldr plundered the Northern Isles, the Hebrides and Mann as punishment for the piracy of their Scandinavian inhabitants. The Northern Isles were then granted to Røgnvaldr, jarll of Møre. However, Røgnvaldr's position was usurped by Hálfdann son of Haraldr Hárfagri who established himself as a king in Orkney. Hálfdann was slain by Røgnvaldr's son Einarr. This provoked Haraldr Hárfagri to undertake another expedition to the west, but eventually Einarr and Haraldr came to terms. Peter Sawyer has presented a strong case for rejecting this narrative as legend derivative of a range of Insular source-material, In S9 of *Orkneyinga saga*, we read that Eiríkr blóðøx visited Orkney after being exiled from York and that his daughter Ragnhildr married Arnfinnr, son of Jarll Þórfinnr. Ragnhildr is portrayed very much like a fickle sovereignty-goddess of the sort found in Irish legends. She disposes of husbands, but only the men who marry her attain the earldom. I suggest that these details in SS8-9 of the *Orkneyinga saga* are unreliable as a historical source.

Haraldr Hárfagri was deemed to have been a founder-figure in the Scandinavian colonies in Ireland too. This assertion is found in the thirteenth-century Welsh text *Historia Gruffudd vab Kenan*. We read that Haraldr built the city of Dublin, along with many other strongholds, and that his progeny still ruled there. This legend may have been derived from 'the oral accounts of twelfth-century Dubliners aware of their distant Norse heritage' or it may bear the stamp of Icelandic influence. Any notion that Haraldr Hárfagri ruled any part of Ireland has been entirely rejected on the basis of analysis of Irish records.

A conflicting and equally spurious account is found in the *Topographia Hiberniae* of Gerald of Wales (1146-1223). He asserted that three brothers Amelauus, Sitaracus and Yuorus (Óláfr, Sigtryggr, and Ívarr) founded the three Viking-towns of Dublin, Waterford and Limerick. This 'three-brothers' motif may be seen elsewhere in literature concerning Scandinavian kings. Thus we can see that by the twelfth century there was a lively interest in legends concerning Scandinavian rulers in Britain and Ireland. This may have influenced stories of Eiríkr blóðøx, which were evolving at the time.

Historia Gruffudd vab Kenan also provides evidence to supplement that of 'The Fragmentary Annals of Ireland', indicating that the kings of Uí Ímair perceived themselves as descendants of the Norwegian royal line of the Ynglings. This takes the form of a genealogy of Gruffudd, king of Gwynedd. Gruffudd was related to the royalty of Dublin. One of his ancestors was Óláfr Cuarán, who ruled York from 949 to 952. According to the *Historia*, Óláfr was a great-grandson of Haraldr Hárfagri. Eiríkr blóðøx is therefore not the only mediaeval link made between the rulers of Northumbria and the Norwegian royal family.

The other point of interest regarding the *Historia* is Judith Jesch's suggestion that the inclusion of Haraldr Hárfagri was influenced by the fame of his alleged descendant Haraldr hardráði. This leads me to suggest that later events, notably the reign of Haraldr hardráði over Norway, which was followed by his very brief success in holding Northumbria, could provide a model for the story of Eiríkr blóðøx. Following Sawyer's argument regarding the influence of Magnus berfœttr on the legend of Haraldr Hárfagri in the Scottish Isles, we could suppose that Scandinavian legends about Northumbria were inspired by later historical examples of interaction.

Two conflicting accounts which link Haraldr Hárfagri with Normandy are preserved in mediaeval literature. In *Historia Gruffudd vab Kenan*, Rollo, the ancestor of the Norman ducal line (and consequently of the Anglo-Norman kings), is presented as a brother of Haraldr Hárfagri, however, in *Heinskringla*, Rollo, or Göngu-Hrólfr) is portrayed as a son of Røgnvaldr, jarll of Møre, the same who is said to have received Orkney from Haraldr. Another version of events is presented in *Laxdaela saga*. Here we read that Göngu-Hrólfr was a son of Oxna-Þórir, 'a hersir of good family' in Norway. However, as Normandy is not mentioned in *Laxdaela saga*, it may be that another Göngu-Hrólfr is intended. The account given in *Heimskringla* of Rollo's paternal origins was accepted by David Douglas in 1942, and he has been followed by subsequent scholars in the field of Norman history.

Douglas accepted the saga-evidence because he thought the other main source of early Norman history, *De Moribus et actis primorum Normanniae ducum*, unreliable. This was written by Dudo of Saint-Quentin between 996 and 1020. It is significantly earlier than either *Historia Gruffudd* or *Heinskringla*. Dudo asserted that Rollo had noble Danish origins. This view is not substantiated by other mediaeval texts. It may reasonably be doubted, for *De moribus* is a fantastically imaginative composition. Eric Christiansen has recently, and I think correctly, pointed out that the Scandinavian sagas and the genealogical claims of *Historia Gruffudd vab Kenan* are also superb texts but dubious sources for Rollo's pedigree. These texts should not be regarded as more reliable evidence than Dudo. They reiterate the same pattern noted so far, of Haraldr Hárfagri or his associates being given a legendary role in the history of Scandinavian colonies.

Eric Bloodaxe – Axed?

The Northumbrian link to Haraldr Hárfagri should perhaps be considered in this context. The literary links made between Norway's most famous king and the Scandinavian colonies of Britain, Ireland and Normandy could all be historically inaccurate. The exaggerated nature of this link may be seen in *Egil's saga*, S4, where we read that Jämtland and Hälsingland, the Hebrides, Ireland, Normandy, the Northern Isles and Caithness were all settled by Norwegians in flight from Haraldr Hárfagri.

These stories served to reinforce a sense of Scandinavian identity and common origins, which distinguished the inhabitants of the colonies from their neighbours. This sense of Scandinavian identity persisting in the colonial settlements abroad is evidenced in the material culture and literature of these areas in the twelfth and thirteenth centuries. The development of the legends of Haraldr Hárfagri was also much to the taste of Norwegian and Icelandic historians and saga-writers. Their perceptions of the role of Haraldr Hárfagri in their own cultural and political identity may also have influenced the development of the legends. For this reason, Scandinavian historians and saga-writers may have been keen to develop stories about the son of Haraldr Hárfagri in England.

One further matter to pursue in relation to Eirík blóðøx is his alleged association with Æthelstan, first king of England. In *Egil's saga* we read that Æthelstan granted Northumbria to Eiríkr blóðøx on condition that he protected the land from the Scots and Irish. In *Historia Norwegiae* and *Heinskringla* this grant is recorded as having the proviso that he would accept baptism. The idea that Eiríkr blóðøx ruled Northumbria with Æthelstan's consent is at variance with the contemporaneous English chronicle-record. A similar legend appears in the story of Rollo as narrated by Dudo of Saint-Quentin. According to this account, Rollo was exiled from Denmark; he fled to England. Following a peace-agreement, Æthelstan offered him the opportunity to settle in England if he would defend the land from aggressors and agree to baptism. This agreement, as David Douglas showed, is chronologically implausible. Rollo had already settled in Normandy before Æthelstan came to power. We have two similar stories which do not match the historical record.

Neither story challenges the supremacy of Æthelstan in England, but this 'most Christian king' is shown as holding the Scandinavian exile in high esteem. In each case, positive reference is made by the

English king to the deeds and repute of the exile's family, and this is said to be a cause of his generosity. These accounts therefore shed a flattering light on the leading families of Norway and Normandy by reference to Æthelstan. Elsewhere, Æthelstan is said to have cultivated links with Norway during his reign. According to William of Malmesbury, Haraldr Hárfagri sent a fine ship to the king, which had a golden beak and purple sails. It is uncertain what is to be made of this, as William was the narrator of many tall stories.

There is also a claim in Scandinavian literature that Eiríkr's brother and enemy Hákon was fostered at Æthelstan's court. The earliest evidence for this seems to be a poem attributed to the skald Sighvatr Þórðarson, which may have been composed in the 1030s. As the two kings appear to have been contemporaries, a link is possible. It may be in consequence of such contact that Æthelstan features in the Scandinavian pseudohistory of Eiríkr blóðøx and Rollo. Æthelstan also loomed large in historical record and legend as the king who had created the kingdom of England. It may have seemed appropriate to saga-writers to link this prestigious English king with Norwegian royalty.

It may be argued that in the twelfth century, when the legends of Eiríkr blóðøx were first written up, the political cults of Haraldr Hárfagri and Æthelstan had developed alongside growing awareness of national identity in Norway and England. I suggest that this had a direct bearing on the literary image of Eiríkr of York, particularly as Northumbria displayed a fusion of identities which were English and Scandinavian in origin. In sum, I hope to have shown that the identification of Eiríkr of York as Eiríkr blóðøx may be doubted. The evidence that they were identical is late and contradicts what is known from tenth-century sources. I therefore wish to explore whether an alternative identity for Eiríkr of York can be suggested.

The evidence from Insular sources may be used to suggest that Eiríkr was a member of the Hiberno-Scandinavian dynasty known in Irish as Uí Ímair. These sources bear testimony to Uí Ímair as providing the main opposition to English rule in Northumbria. At least six kings of Uí Ímair ruled at York in the course of the tenth century. Their names are underlined in the genealogical chart below. There would probably have had to be strong reasons for preferring an outsider on the Northumbrian scene (a king

Eric Bloodaxe – Axed?

exiled from Norway with minimal resources) over the rights of an established royal dynasty which also dominated the major sea-ports of Ireland. If an alternative identity were to be proposed for Eiríkr of York, a candidate from Uí Ímair would therefore seem a likely alternative.

As I have already shown, the skaldic poetry relating to Eiríkr of York (which can be separated from that which relates to Eiríkr blóðøx) provides no contradiction of the idea that Eiríkr hailed from Ireland. The interchange of the kingship of York between Eiríkr and Óláfr from 947 to 954 could therefore be seen as a struggle between two claimants of Uí Ímair rather than between a Norwegian and a Hiberno-Scandinavian faction.

A similar situation prevailed in Dublin in the 940s, when royal power alternated between Óláfr (945-47, 948-49) and his rival Blákari Guðrøðsson (940-45, 947-48). It is also interesting to discover from the Irish chronicles that Eiríkr took power over York at times when Óláfr was distracted by affairs in Dublin. In 947/48, Óláfr was battling against Blákari Guðrøðsson, and in 952 Óláfr may have been struggling to secure Dublin, which had lost its king Guðrøðr Sigtryggsson late in 951 (the heir apparent, Ívarr, had also died in 950). Óláfr ruled at Dublin from 952 until his abdication in 980. Version E of 'The Anglo-Saxon Chronicle' indicates that Eiríkr instigated a coup against Óláfr in 952, 'Norðhymbre fordrifan Anlaf cyning. 7 underfengon Yric Haroldes sunu' ('the Northumbrians drove out Óláfr and submitted to Eiríkr Haraldsson'). The timing

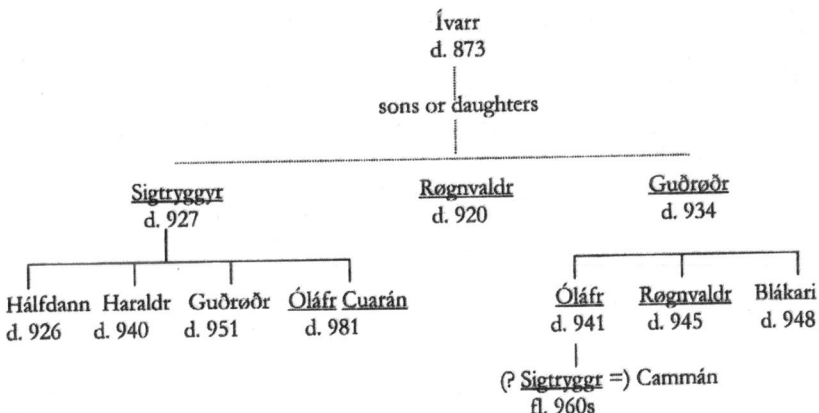

Genealogical chart of tenth-century Scandinavian kings of York.

of Eiríkr's accession to the throne of York may indicate that he was well informed of events in Ireland.

A case may also be put on the basis of numismatic evidence, for continuity of rule by Uí Ímair in Northumbria. Two issues of King Eiríkr have been identified. The first imitated the coins of his predecessor Óláfr Sigtryggsson. This could merely be an indication of administrative continuity. However, Eiríkr's second coin-issue imitated that of Óláfr's father Sigtryggr. These coins bore a sword-emblem on the reverse. This has been regarded as a symbol which 'evoked the Hiberno-[Scandinavian] conquest of 919', and it has been identified more specifically as portraying the 'sword of Carlus'.

This is recorded as part of the royal insignia of Uí Ímair in the late tenth century. The association seems plausible. Even if the sword were taken to mean something else, it seems strange that an outsider-king would use images which could provoke memories of a rival dynasty's claim to his position. Indeed, Mark Blackburn has recently emphasised the level of political consciousness and creativity which determined coin-emblems in Viking-Age Northumbria and the degree of royal control exercised over their selection. It may be that this harking back to an earlier coin-design was intended to legitimate Eiríkr's right to rule Northumbria, both as a member of Uí Ímair and possibly as a descendant of Sygtyggr.

Beyond these indications there are personal circumstances in Eiríkr's life which could point to his origins among Uí Ímair. The Life of St Cathroe reports that Eiríkr of York married a kinswoman of the saint, who was therefore related to royal families of Alba and Strathclyde. This assertion contrasts with skaldic poems which describe Gunnhildr as the sole wife of Eiríkr blóðøx. The author of the Life of Cathroe should have been well informed about the events, as the Life is attributed to the 980s, that is a short time after Cathroe's death, and it appears to have been written at Metz where the saint had resided. The marriage alliance which is described between Eiríkr of York and the kinswoman of Cathroe fits with the Irish Sea-Northumbria interests of Uí Ímair.

The record of Eiríkr's death on Stainmore (in that part of modern Cumbria called Westmorland until 1974) also fits with the spheres of influence of Uí Ímair. Stainmore lay on a main route following the old Roman roads from York across to the Irish-Sea coast. In English sources Eiríkr's death is recorded in the same year as his expulsion from Northumbria. The location could suggest that Eiríkr was attempting to reach home-territory. The significance of Stainmore's location *en route* from York to Dublin is not represented in Scandinavian sources. Notwithstanding the assertion in *Ágrip* and *Historia Norwegiae* that Eiríkr died in Spain, *Heimskringla* shows Eiríkr to have been raiding far and wide before falling in his last battle at an unidentified location in England.

Historia regum Anglorum, Part II, and Roger of Wendover also assert that Eiríkr was slain by one Maccus. This name does not appear in the Scandinavian sources. According to David Thornton, Maccus is a name of mixed Gaelic and Scandinavian usage, developed from *macc* (Old and Middle Irish for 'son'). The appearance of this name and the alleged location of Eiríkr's death could suggest a link with the Viking-colonies in Ireland.

This begs a question: if Eiríkr was a member of Uí Ímair, who exactly was he? There are several persons called Haraldr (*Aralt*) recorded in Irish chronicles. Three of these belong to the tenth century, none can be proved to have had a son called Eiríkr. However, it has been noted that Irish chronicles provide little reference to the careers of members of Uí Ímair at York and that, though extensive, they are not comprehensive in their coverage of political events.

Irish chronicles do not yield reliable evidence for someone called Eiríkr in the tenth century. It is possible that the 'Laraic' who raided St Mullins (Co. Carlow) from the sea in 953 has a corrupted form of this name. the only reference given outside the chronicles is to an Eiríkr, king of the Isles (presumably the Hebrides), in the twelfth-century saga *Caithréim Chellacháin Chaisil*. This is an untrustworthy source based on events in the reign of Cellachán, overking of Munster, who reigned from 940 to 952. The author(s) quarried genealogical literature and *Cocad Gaedel re Gallaiba*s a source of names. Limited use may also be made of chronicle-evidence. From Ó Corráin's thorough analysis of this saga, it appears that almost half of the people named in it were contemporary with the events being described. Ó Corráin has demonstrated that the author(s) of that text deliberately sought out and used tenth-century names in the story (apart from names included for political reasons or through artistic licence).

This may have been an attempt to add an air of authenticity. Many other names in the text seem to refer to eponymous ancestors of dynasties who were significant in the twelfth century when the text was written. Their inclusion appears to represent the political agenda of the patron of the text. Other names in the saga may be pure invention. While the content *of Caithréim Chellacháin Chaisil* is unreliable, Alexander Bugge and Alfred Smyth unreservedly identified the Eiríkr of the Isles who is mentioned in it with Eiríkr of York, and consequently with Eiríkr blóðøx. Donnchadh Ó Corráin has more cautiously suggested that 'they may be identical [...] It may equally be a coincidence.'

It would be hasty to jump to conclusions regarding an alternative identity for Eiríkr of York. The evidence is fragmentary. The only possibility which I can tentatively suggest from the available source-material is that he was a son of Haraldr Sigtryggsson. Haraldr ruled Limerick and died in 940. He has been identified as the father of *meicc Arailt*, 'the sons of Haraldr', who were active on the Irish Sea in the late tenth century. Two sons of Haraldr ruled in Mann and the Isles, and Uí Ímair maintained power there (perhaps intermittently) for another century. Smyth and Ó Corráin have argued that the involvements of Uí Ímair in the Hebrides began in the early tenth century. If Eiríkr was a son of Haraldr Sigtryggsson, he would have had a claim to the Northumbrian throne through his uncle Óláfr, and from his grandfather Sigtryggr (it may be worth keeping in mind that Eiríkr's second issue of coins imitated those of Sigtryggr). Eiríkr might also have been a king of the Isles, if *Caithréim Chellacháin Chaisil* can be allowed to carry any weight.

In conclusion the identification of Eiríkr of York with Eiríkr blóðøx can be regarded as late, unreliable and in contradiction of what earlier sources tell us about Eiríkr's life. This identification should be questioned. On the other hand, an origin for Eiríkr among Uí Ímair is plausible and should be considered. It seems that Irish evidence was somewhat overlooked in the nineteenth-century debate concerning the paternal origins of Eiríkr of York. My solution to explain the contradictions both within the Scandinavian evidence and between Scandinavian and Insular sources, is to suggest that there were two persons called Eiríkr. One ruled York, and one ruled Norway. These later became confused in Scandinavian literature. The proposed solution may not be entirely satisfactory. It may be less satisfying to admit uncertainty as to who Eiríkr of York was, but this may do greater justice to the available evidence.

BIBLIOGRAPHY

Primary Sources

Adam of Bremen *Gesta Hammaburgensis Ecclesiae Pontificum* ['Deeds of the Bishops of Hamburg'] (1073–1076).

Anglo-Saxon Chronicle (transl. G. N. Garmonsway, London, J. M. Dent & Sons 1953)

Bede's *Ecclesiastical History of England* (ed. J. A. Giles (London, George Bell & Sons 1880)

Byrhtferth of Ramsey, *The Lives of St. Oswald and St. Ecgwine* in 'Oxford Medieval Texts' (Oxford, Clarendon Press 2009)

Crossley-Holland, K., 'Beowulf' in *The Anglo-Saxon World – An Anthology* (Oxford World's Classics, Oxford University Press 2009)

Egil's Saga transl. Leifur Eiriksson (London, Penguin 2002)

Fagrskinna – a Catalogue of the Kings of Norway (transl.) A. Finlay (Leiden, Brill 2004)

Gododdin by Aneurin, transl. Reverend J. Williams (London, Longmans 1852)

Heaney, S., *Beowulf* (London, Faber & Faber 1999)

Henry of Huntingdon, *Historia Anglorum* (Cambridge, Cambridge University Press 2012)

Historia Norwegie, eds. I. Ekrem & L. B. Mortensen, transl. P. Fisher (Copenhagen, Museum Tusculanum Press University of Copenhagen 2006)

'Jomsviking Saga', transl. N. F. Blake in *Icelandic Texts* editors S. Nordal & G. Turville-Petrie (London, Thomas Nelson & Sons 1962)

Nennius, *Historia Brittonum* (England, independently published 2022)
Njal's Saga translated R. Cook (London, Penguin 1997)
Orkneyinga Saga (transl. Hermann Palsson and Paul Edwards, London, Penguin 1981)
Roger of Wendover *Flowers of History* (New York, AMS Press 1968)
Saxo Grammaticus, *The History of the Danes*, ed. H. E. Davidson, transl. P. Fisher (Cambridge, Cambridge University Press 1996)
Sir Gawain and the Green Knight (transl. S. Armitage, London, Faber & Faber 2009)
Simeon of Durham, *Historical Works* (editor J. Stevenson, Franklin Classics 2018)
Snorri Sturluson, *Heimskringla* (Kent, Dover Publications 2009)
The Poetic Edda by Snorri Sturluson, transl. C. Larrington (Oxford, Oxford University Press 1996)
The Prose Edda by Snorri Sturluson, transl. J. L. Byock (London, Penguin 2003)
The Saga of Grettir the Strong (transl. G. H. Hight, London 1914, Penguin Classics edition 2003)
The Saga of Olaf Tryggvason by Oddr Snorasson (transl. T. M. Andersson (London, Cornell University Press 2003)
William of Malmesbury, *The Deeds of the Bishops of England*, transl. D.G. Preest (London, Boydell Press 2002)

Secondary sources

Aalto, S., 'Categorizing Otherness in the Kings' Sagas' – *Dissertations in Social Sciences and Business Studies* no. 10 (University of Eastern Finland 2010)
Abrams, L, 'The Conversion of the Danelaw' in J. Graham-Campbell et al. (eds) *Vikings and the Danelaw: Select Papers from the Proceedings of the Thirteenth Viking Congress* (Oxford: Oxbow 2001), 31-44
Adams, J., & K. Holman, 'Scandinavia and Europe 800–1350, Contact, Culture and Co-existence' from *Medieval Texts & Cultures of Northern Europe*, Centre for Medieval Studies Hull University (Turnhout Belgium, Brepols Publications 2004)
Adams, M., *King in the North* (London, Head of Zeus 2013)
Bates, C. J., *History of Northumberland* (London, Elliot Stock 1895)
Breeze, D. J. & B. Dobson, *Hadrian's Wall* (4th edition, London, Penguin 2000)
Bunting, B., *Briggflatts* (Northumberland, Bloodaxe Books 2000)

Bibliography

Burne, Colonel A.H., *Battlefields of England* (London, Methuen 1950)

_____ *More Battlefields of England* (London, Methuen 1952)

Calderon M. J. G., *Romancing the Dark Ages – The Viking Hero in Sentimental Narrative* (University of Seville): file:///C:/Users/John/Downloads/Dialnet-RomancingTheDarkAgesTheVikingHeroInSentimentalNarr-2592835%20(3).pdf, accessed 8 January 2024.

Chartrand, R., K. Durham, M. Harrison & I. Heath, *The Vikings* (Oxford, Osprey 2016)

Chesterton G. K., *A Short History of England* (London, BiblioBazaar, 2008)

Christiansen, E., *The Norsemen in the Viking Age* (Hoboken NJ, Wiley Blackwell 2006)

Clarke, G., *Gododdin – Lament for the Fallen* (London, Faber & Faber 2022)

Collins, R., & M. Symonds, *Hadrian's Wall 2009–2019* (Newcastle upon Tyne, Society of Antiquaries 2019)

Collingwood, W.G., 'King Eirik of York' in *Saga Book of the Viking Club*, Vol II Jan 1897–December 1900 (London, privately printed)

Cormack, M., *Egil's Saga, Heimskringla and the Daughter of Eirik Bloodaxe* (Charleston, Department of Philosophy and Religious Studies, College of Charleston 2001)

Cox, D. A., *Exploring Viking Expansion* – MA in Medieval History (West Virginia University 2002)

Crumlin-Pedersen, O., *The Skuldelev Ships I* (Viking Ship Museum and the National Museum of Denmark 2002)

Cunningham, B., *The Annals of the Four Masters as Cultural Icon* (Ireland, School of Celtic Studies, Maynooth University 2019)

Curry, A., 'Slaughter at the bridge: uncovering a colossal Bronze Age battle' in *Science Magazine*, 24 March 2016

Davidson, H. R. E., *Gods and Myths of Northern Europe* (Baltimore, Penguin 1984)

Divine, D., *The North-West Frontier of Rome* (London, Macdonald & Co 1969)

Downham, C., *Viking Kings of Britain and Ireland* (Edinburgh, Dunedin Academic Press 2012)

_____ 'England and the Irish Sea Zone in the Eleventh Century' in *Anglo-Norman Studies* 2003, 26: 55-73

_____ 'Eric Bloodaxe – Axed? The Mystery of the last Scandinavian King of York' in *Mediaeval Scandinavia* 2004, 14: 51-77

_____ '"Hiberno-Norwegians and Anglo-Danes": anachronistic ethnicities and Viking Age England' in *Medieval Scandinavia* 2009, 19: 139–169

_____ 'Vikings in England to AD 1016', https://www.taylorfrancis.com/chapters/edit/10.4324/9780203412770-55/vikings-england-clare-downham, accessed 27.11.2023

_____ *The Chronology of the last Scandinavian Kings of York AD 937–954* (Leeds, University of Leeds 2003)

Duncan, A. A. M., *Scotland, the Making of a Kingdom* (Edinburgh, Oliver & Boyd 1975)

Dunville, D. N., *Wessex and England from Alfred to Edgar: Six Essays on Political, Cultural, and Ecclesiastical Revival* (Woodbridge: Boydell 1992)

_____ 'Old Dubliners and new Dubliners in Ireland and Britain: a Viking-Age story', *Medieval Dublin* 2004, 6: 78-93

Dunville, D. N., 'St. Cathroe of Metz and the hagiography of exoticism' in J. Cassidy, M. Herbert and P. O'Brien (editors) *Studies in Irish Hagiography; Saints and Scholars* (Dublin, Four Winds Press 2001), p.p. 172–178.

Durham, K., *Viking Longship* (Oxford, Osprey 2002)

Edmonds, F., *Gaelic Influence in the Northumbrian Kingdom* (Woodbridge, The Boydell Press 2023)

Ferguson, R., *The Vikings: A History* (New York, Viking 2009)

_____ *The Hammer and the Cross* (London, Penguin 2010)

Finlay, A., C. Lee, J. Mckinnell, C. Phelpstead & E. A. Rowe (editors), *Saga Book Vol. XI* (Viking Society for Northern Research, London UCL 2016)

Graham-Campbell, J., *The Viking World* (New York, Ticknor & Fields 2006)

Griffith, P., *The Viking Art of War* (London, Greenhill 1995)

Hadley, D. M., *The Vikings in England* (Manchester, Manchester University Press 2006)

Hadley, D. M. and J. D. Richards, *The Viking Great Army* (London, Thames & Hudson 2021)

_____ *The Northern Danelaw, its Social Structure, c. 800-1100* (London: Leicester University Press 2000)

_____ (Eds) *Cultures in cContact: Scandinavian Settlement in England in the Ninth and Tenth centuries* (Turnhout: Brepols 2000)

Hall, R., *The World of the Vikings* (London, Thames & Hudson 2007)

Bibliography

Halloran, K., 'The Brunanburh Campaign: A Reappraisal' in *Scottish Historical Review* 84, 2005, 133-48

Harrison, M., *Viking Hersir: 793-1066 AD* (Oxford, Osprey 1993)

Harvey, A., *Forgotten Vikings: New Approaches to the Viking Age* (Stroud: Amberley Books 2024)

Haywood, J., *The Penguin Historical Atlas of the Vikings* (New York, Penguin 1995)

Heath, I., *The Vikings* (Oxford, Osprey 1985)

Higham, N. J., *the Kingdom of Northumbria 350-1100* (Gloucs., Alan Sutton 1993)

Hodges, C. C. & J. Gibson, *Hexham & its Abbey* (Northumberland, Hexham Abbey 1919)

Hollander L. M., *Old Norse Poems* (Sandhurst, Abela Publishing 2010)

Hunter Blair, P., *Roman Britain & Early England* (Edinburgh, Thomas Nelson & Sons 1963)

Jackson, D., *The Northumbrians* (London, Hurst, 2019)

Jakobsson, S., *The early kings of Norway, the issue of agnatic succession, and the settlement of Iceland*, https://www.brepolsonline.net/doi/10.1484/J.VIATOR.5.112357?mobileUi=0, accessed 27.11.2023.

Jarman, C., *River Kings* (London, William Collins 2021)

_____ *The Bone Chests* (London, William Collins 2023)

Johnson, A., 'Battle of Athelstaneford' in *Battlefields Trust Magazine* 24, issue 3, Winter 2020, pp. 10-13

Jones, G., *A History of the Vikings* (London, BCA 1973)

Kapelle, W. E., *The Norman Conquest of the North* (North Carolina, Croom Helm 1979)

Keegan, Sir J., *The Face of Battle* (London, Penguin 1976)

Kjestrud, C. & F. Iverson, 'Introduction: Viking Wars' (Norwegian Archaeological Society *Viking Wars*, 9-12

Lancelyn Green, R., *Myths of the Norsemen* (London, Puffin 1970)

Lappenburg, L. M., (transl. B. Thorpe), *A History of England under the Anglo Saxon Kings* (two vols, Hamburg 1834-1837)

Larrington, C., *The Norse Myths* (London, Thames & Hudson 2023)

Lindow, J., *Norse Mythology* (Oxford, Oxford University Press 2002)

Livingston, M., *Never Greater Slaughter* (Oxford, Bloomsbury 2021)

Loades, M., *Swords & Swordsmen* (Barnsley, Pen & Sword 2017)

Logan Mack, J., *The Border Line* (Edinburgh, Oliver & Boyd 1924)

Lomas, R., *North-East England in the Middle Ages* (Edinburgh, John Donald 1992)

_____ *Northumberland – County of Conflict* (Edinburgh, Tuckwell Press 1996)
Longfellow, H. W., 'The Saga of King Olaf' from *Complete Poetical Works* (Cambridge, Cambridge Editions 1975)
Loyn, L., *The Vikings in Britain* (Hoboken NJ, Wiley-Blackwell 1995)
Low, R., *The Whale Road* (London, Harper Collins 2007)
Lund, N., 'King Edgar and the Danelaw' in *Mediaeval Scandinavia* 1976, 9: 181-95
Lynch, M., *Scotland, a New History* (London, Pimlico 1992)
McTurk, R. W., Alfred P. Smyth, 'Scandinavian York and Dublin', *Saga-Book of the Viking Society* 1974–1977, 19: 471-74
Mackenzie, E., *History of Northumberland* (Newcastle upon Tyne, Mackenzie & Dent 1825)
MacLennan, W. J. & W. I. Sellers, 'Ageing through the Ages' (Edinburgh *Proceedings of the Royal College of Surgeons*, 1999 29:71-75
Magnusson, M., *Hammer of the North: Myths and Heroes of the Viking Age* (New York, Putnam 1986)
Magnusson, M. with H. Palsson, (transl.) *The Vinland Sagas* (New York, New York University Press 1978)
Marsden, J., *Northanhymbre Saga* (London, BCA 1992)
_____ *Fury of the Norsemen* (New York, St. Martin's Press 1995)
Moffat, A., *Arthur & the Lost Kingdoms* (Edinburgh, Birlinn 2012)
_____ *The Borders* (Selkirk 2002)
Morison, S. E., *The European Discovery of America: The Northern Voyages, A.D. 500–1600* (New York, Oxford University Press 1993)
Nighswander, L., 'No Nazis in Valhalla: Understanding the Use (and Misuse) of Nordic Cultural Markers in Third Reich Era Germany' in International ResearchScape Journal Vol. 7, Article 6, 2020
Oliver, N., *Vikings* (London, Weidenfeld & Nicolson 2013)
Oman, Sir Charles, *The Art of War in the Middle Ages* vol. 1 (London, Greenhill 1924)
Page, R. I., *Chronicles of the Vikings* (Toronto, Toronto University Press 1995)
Parker, P., *The Northmen's Fury* (London, Vintage 2015)
Pearson, W., *Erik Bloodaxe – His Life and Times* (Bloomington, Author House 2012)
Pevsner N. & E. Williamson, 'Durham' in *Buildings of England* (London, Penguin 1985)

Poole, R., *Viking Poems on War and Peace* (Toronto, Toronto University Press 1991)
Price, N., *The Children of Ash & Elm* (London, Penguin 2022)
Pulsiano, P., et al (eds.) *Medieval Scandinavia: An Encyclopaedia* (London, Routledge 2019)
Orchard, A., *Dictionary of Norse Myth and Legend* (London, Weidenfeld & Nicolson 2002)
Rene, C. et al., *The Vikings; Voyagers of Discovery and Plunder* (Oxford, Osprey 2006)
Richards, J. D., *Viking Age England* (London, Batsford 1991)
_____ *The Vikings: A Very Short Introduction* (New York, Oxford University Press 2005)
Ridpath, G., *the Border History of England and Scotland* (Edinburgh, Mercat Press 1979)
Roesdahl, E., *The Vikings* (London, Penguin 2016)
Rollason, D. W. et al., *Sources for York History to AD 1100* (York, York Archaeological Trust 1998)
Rixson, D., *The West Highland Galley* (Edinburgh, Birlinn 1998)
Sadler, D. J., *Battle for Northumbria* (Newcastle upon Tyne, Bridge Studios 1988)
_____ *The Hot Trod* (Stroud, Amberley 2022)
Saklatvala, B., *Arthur, Roman Britain's last Champion* (Newton Abbot, David & Charles 1967)
Sawyer, P. H., *The Age of the Vikings* (London, Edward Arnold 1962)
_____ (Ed.), *Vikings* (Oxford, Oxford University Press 1997)
Seward, D., *The Greatest Viking* (Edinburgh, Birlinn 2022)
Schlauch, M. (transl.) *The Saga of the Volsungs, the Saga of Ragnar Lodbrok, together with the Lay of Krak*, (2nd edn., New York, American Scandinavian Foundation 1949)
Sitwell, Brigadier W., *The Border* (Newcastle upon Tyne, Andrew Reid 1927)
Skeie, T., *The Wolf Age* (London, Pushkin Press 2022)
Skene, W. F., *Four Ancient Books of Wales* vol I (Edinburgh, Edmonston and Douglas 1868)
Smout, T. C., *History of the Scottish People* (London, Fontana 1969)
Smurthwaite, D., *The Ordnance Survey Guide to the Battlefields of Britain* (London, Michael Joseph 1984)
Smyth, A. P., *Scandinavian Kings in the British Isles 850-880* (Oxford, Oxford University Press 1977)
Stenton, Sir Frank, 'Anglo Saxon England' in *The Oxford History of England* (Oxford, Clarendon Press 1971)

Terciu, P. C., *Links between Anglo-Saxons and Byzantines until the end of the 11th Century* (Andrei Saguna Orthodox Facility of Theology, University of Sibiu Romania 2016)

Thorsson, O., (ed.), *The Sagas of the Icelanders: A Selection* (New York, Viking, 2000)

Todd J. H., (transl.), *Wars of the Gaedhil with the Gaill* (London, Longmans 1867)

Tolkien, J. R. R., ed. P. Grybauskas, *The Battle of Maldon* (London, Harper Collins 2023)

Trevelyan, G. M., *A History of England* (London, Penguin 1975)

Treece, H., & E. Oakeshott, *Fighting Men* (Leicester, Brockhampton Press 1963

Wainwright, F. T., *Scandinavian England: Collected Papers* (Chichester: Phillimore 1975)

Williams, A., 'Thorkell the Tall and the Bubble Reputation: The Vicissitudes of Fame' in R. Lavelle and S. Roffey (eds) *The Danes in Wessex: The Scandinavian Impact on Southern England, c. 800–c.1000* (Oxford, Oxbow Books, 2016)

Williams, G., *The Viking Longship* (London, British Museum 2014)

Williams, T., *Viking Britain* (London, William Collins 2017)

Wilson, D. M., *The Vikings and Their Origins* (London, Thames and Hudson 2001)

Wise, T., *Saxon, Viking and Norman* (Oxford, Osprey 'Men at Arms' Series, no. 85, 1979)

Wolf, K., *Daily Life of the Vikings* (Westport CT. Greenwood 2004)

Woods M., *In Search of the Dark Ages* (London, BCA 1981)

_____ 'The Battle of Brunanburh: new light on the "Great War" of the tenth century' (Society of Antiquaries lecture 6.10.2020), https://www.sal.org.uk/event/the-battle-of-brunanburh-new-light-on-the-great-war-of-the-tenth-century/, accessed 27.11.2023

Woolf, A., *From Pictland to Alba* (New Edinburgh History of Scotland II, Edinburgh University Press 2007)

_____ *Erik Bloodaxe Revisited* (Edinburgh, University of Edinburgh) https://www.academia.edu/313144/Erik_Bloodaxe_Revisited, accessed 27.11.2023

INDEX

Abbot Cathroe, 201, 204, 205, 210, 222, 258
Ad Gefrin, 102, 107
Aella, 135-136, 188, 198
Aesir, 35, 44, 236
Aedan mac Gabran, 106-107
Aethelflaed Queen of Mercia, 142-144, 146
Aethelfrith, 106-107, 109, 112, 119
Aethelwold of Wessex, 16
Aldfrith, 112, 116, 117, 251
Alfred the Great, 47, 110, 137, 138, 141-143, 148, 158, 196
Amounderness, 205
Arinbjorn, 74, 150-153, 156, 159, 160
Arthuret, 103
Arnvid, 50, 51
Athelstaneford, 119
Atli inn mjóvi ('The Lean'), 46
Aralt mac Sitric, 19
Arnfinn, 134, 265
Ash, 31, 35, 36, 88, 169, 172
Assandun, 77
Astrid, 220

Athelstan, 16, 25, 47, 56, 61, 119, 124, 125, 130-133, 145-147, 150, 161-165, 171, 174-175, 196, 198, 199, 201-209, 223
Audhumla, 44
Aud the Deep-Minded, 40, 214

Bagsecg, 137
Bamburgh, 24, 102, 113, 114, 140, 142, 144, 145, 146, 164, 165, 177, 190, 200
Bang C., 193
Bede, 105-110, 112, 115, 116, 120, 146, 148, 159, 251
Benfleet, 141
Beorhtric of Wessex, 15
Beowulf, 28, 38, 44, 81, 85
Berg-Onund, 129
Brown, Lancelot ('Capability'), 190
Burhred, 138
Berserker, 53, 70, 71, 74, 75, 152, 185, 236, 246

Bernicia, 102, 104, 106, 109, 113, 133, 137, 138, 140, 142, 144, 160, 177, 249
Bestla, 44
Birchlegs, 97-99
Bishop Alcuin, 41, 113
Bjorn Ironside, 63
'Blood Eagle', 132, 136, 230
Bolborn, 44
Bonder, 37-38, 39, 45, 47, 55-56, 66, 67, 131, 139, 236, 237
Boar's Snout, 66, 181, 184
Boniface VIII, 19
Borr, 44
Bowes Moor, 170
Bridei mac Bile, 112
Brunanburh, 16, 26, 64, 77, 80, 123, 147, 161, 165, 174, 190, 196, 199, 204, 205, 206, 223, 226, 263
Bunting B., 168, 190
Burne, Colonel A.H., 147, 202
Byrhtnoth, 22, 23, 29, 67, 182, 184

Cadwallon, 109-110, 249
Calverley, Revd. W.S., 195
Carham, 113, 117
Carlyle T., 26, 40
Castleford, 26, 64, 172, 173, 176, 200
Catterick (Catraeth), 105
Ceowulf, 138
Charlemagne, 47
Chester-le-Street (Conagium), 116, 146
Clifford's Tower, 154
Cnut, 77, 189

Collingwood, W.G., 17, 171, 173, 180, 181, 195, 198-202, 206, 222, 253, 254
Conan the Cimmerian, 189
Constantine of Scotland, 26, 139, 144, 146, 147, 164, 165, 204, 223
Corbridge, 16, 110, 144, 145
Cornwell B., 65, 190
Cuerdale Hoard, 231
Curtis A., 24, 188

Daegsastan, 106
Danish axe, 80
Deira, 104, 106, 109, 113, 137, 140, 154, 161, 249
Denmark, 46, 47, 48, 62, 86, 126, 133, 180, 193, 199, 206, 207, 213-215, 217, 220, 221, 247, 253, 255, 256, 258, 267
Domnall Brecc, 109
Domesday Book, 155, 157, 159
Douglas K., 24, 188, 194
Downham, Professor C., 17, 163, 165, 166, 206-211, 253-272
Dragvandil, 100
Drekkar, 87
Dunnichen (Nechtansmere), 112
Durham, 106, 115, 116, 117, 136, 138, 140, 144, 169, 171, 180, 199, 200, 203, 205, 255

Eadred of Wessex, 16, 26, 64, 144, 145, 146, 163, 171-177, 180, 198, 199, 200, 202, 203
Eadwulf I, 133, 140, 142
Eamont Bridge, 146
Earl Erlend, 96, 133, 179, 180

Index

Earl Hakon, 52, 220
Earl Paul, 94, 95, 96
Eboracum (see York)
Ecgberht II, 140
Ecgfrith of Northumbria, 112, 116, 164, 251
Edington, 15
Edmund Ironside, 77
Edmund King of Wessex, 16, 26, 133, 137, 147, 150, 161, 162, 163, 165, 171, 174, 175, 179, 180, 198, 199, 201, 204, 205, 206
Edward I, 19, 201, 254
Edward the Elder, 16, 143, 146
Edwin of Northumbria, 106, 107, 108, 109, 155, 249
Egbert King of Wessex, 15, 137, 138, 250
Egil, 18, 19, 39, 45, 50, 60, 63, 64, 74, 75, 79, 80, 82, 83, 92, 100, 101, 127-130, 150-156, 159, 160, 180, 188, 189, 194, 198, 201, 202, 204, 209, 214, 216, 217, 222, 242-248, 258, 260, 261
Egil's *Saga*, 9, 18, 54, 92, 100, 127
Egil Vendelkrake, 45
Eikpyrnir, 32
Einar Rognvaldsson, (or Torf/Turf-Einar), 226
Eisenhower General D., 208
Elm, 35, 36, 243
Eoforwic (see York), 114, 154, 155, 238
Erik the Red, 224
Eriksson L., 194
Erling, 94, 126, 215
Ethelred of Wessex, 68, 78, 137, 138, 143, 251, 252

Eugenics, 191
Excalibur, 79

Faroes, 54, 194, 241
Five Boroughs, 161, 162, 165
Fort La Latte, 24
Frakokk, 94, 95
Freydis, 40, 214, 224
Fridgeir, 74, 75

Galton, Sir Francis, 191
Gamle, 126, 215, 219
Gilling Sword, 121
Gjermundbu Helmet, 82
Goddodin, 20, 100, 124, 147
Godrod, 215
Gokstad ship, 24, 87
Gorm the Old, 47, 48, 199, 214
Gothfrith, 144
Great Army, 15, 47, 51, 68, 69, 76, 110, 120, 137, 140, 148, 196
Gryting, 49
Gudrod the Hunter, 45, 132, 213, 226
Guevara C., 118
Gulathing, 58, 59, 129
Gunnhild, 39, 40, 47, 61, 71, 92, 125-131, 133, 150, 152, 153, 156, 160, 178, 180, 181, 188, 190, 201, 202, 204, 207, 210, 212-215, 217-221, 257, 258, 262, 270
Guthorm, 46, 47, 133, 179, 215, 255
Guthrum, 15, 47
Gyda, 47, 48, 74

Hadaland, 46, 47
Hadrian, 102
Hadrian's Wall, 102, 106, 114
Haesten (or Hastein), 141

Hafrsfjord, 15, 45, 52, 60
Hakon the Good, 16, 45, 96, 124, 129, 150, 198, 201, 202, 215
Halfdan, 15, 19, 137, 138, 139, 140, 161, 197, 246, 264
Halfdan Long-Leg, 124, 132, 13
Hálfdan Svarti (the Black), 45, 46, 49
Hallgrimskirkja Cathedral, 194
Halagoland, 214
Harald Bluetooth, 19, 199, 206, 253
Harald Fine/fair/Tangle Hair, 45, 50, 55, 60, 70, 85, 93, 95, 124, 126, 127, 152, 160, 198, 199, 202, 203, 206, 207, 208, 209, 210, 211, 214, 219
Harald Greycloak, 212, 220
Harald Grjotgardsson, 50
Harald Hardradi, 43, 78, 96, 189, 209
Haraldr Gullskegg (Gold-beard), 45
Haraldskaer Woman, 221
Harold II, 68, 77, 80, 96
Havard Gunnason, 96
Heavenfield, 109, 110
Hedemark, 46, 47
Heidrun the Goat, 31, 32
Hersir, 37, 72, 92, 214, 238
Hnefatafl, 38
Hoggspjot spear, 80
Holy Island (see Lindisfarne), 23, 111, 116, 223
Honeycombe, G., 9, 24, 78
Hordaland, 36, 47, 52, 61, 92, 247
Howard R.E., 189

Hring, 19, 56, 65, 80, 199, 206, 253, 255, 2565
Hunthjof of More, 50
Hvitserk, 63

Iceland, 15, 45, 54, 58, 150, 189, 194, 208, 213, 224, 241, 259, 263, 264
Ida, 104, 106, 202, 249, 250
Ivar II, 142
Ivar 'The Boneless', 15, 25, 54, 63, 68, 76, 101, 113, 119, 121, 134, 135, 139, 158, 160, 189, 196, 209

Jaeder, 36
Jarl, 25, 37, 38, 50, 52, 53, 55, 62, 66, 67, 75, 84, 124, 132, 137, 147, 179, 181, 185, 220, 221, 237, 238
Jarrow, 28, 107, 115, 116, 159
Jarrow Vikings (statue), 28
Joan of Arc, 188
Jorvik (see York), 13, 14, 24, 25, 114, 134, 154, 156, 157, 198, 238
Jorvik Helmet, 120, 121
Jorvik Viking Centre, 134, 154

Kalf Arnason, 93
Karve, 87
Ketil the Slayer, 129
Knarr, 87, 239
Knattleikr, 37

Laidlaw, Sergeant-Piper D., VC, 71
Lagertha, 39, 71, 214
Lawrence, Colonel T.E., 211
Leigh J., 24

Lindisfarne, 15, 23, 25, 29, 78, 79, 104, 111, 113, 114, 117, 118, 140, 165, 223
Lindisfarne Gospels, 117
Liofa, 163
Ljot the Pale, 74, 75, 83, 134, 260
Loos, 71

Macchus, 174, 177, 178, 180, 183, 184
Magnus Maximus, 104
Maldon, 23, 30, 67, 77, 105, 182, 183, 185
Mercia, 15, 109, 110, 117, 135, 137, 138, 139, 140, 142, 143, 144, 145, 146, 205
Middleton, Sir Charles Monck, 190
Museum of The Viking Age, 24
Myrddin (Merlin?), 103

Nordicism, 191, 192
Northumbria, 12, 15, 16, 17, 19, 23, 25, 26, 41, 63, 64, 96, 101, 102, 104, 106, 107, 109-122, 126, 131-144, 150, 154, 155, 157-166, 170-180, 184, 195-210, 237, 238, 251, 255, 259-272

Odin, 24, 26, 33, 34, 35, 40, 41, 44, 45, 70, 78, 101, 149, 168, 169, 193, 219, 236, 239, 240, 242-244
Oengus (Angus) II, 119
Oengus Mac Fergus, 112
Olaf Cuaran, 16, 171, 173, 180, 199, 200, 265

Olaf Guthfrithson, 16, 26, 133, 146, 161, 162, 165, 171, 199
Olaf Hrolfsson, 95, 96
Olaf King & Saint, 43, 50, 84, 181, 233
Olvir, 94-96, 127, 128
Onion test, 70
Onund Treefoot, 85
Orkney, 25, 52, 53, 58, 60, 75, 92, 93, 94, 96, 97, 98, 126, 131, 132, 133, 150, 151, 164, 168, 175, 179, 181, 185, 207, 208, 221, 225, 226, 258, 262, 264, 265, 266
Osberg Ship, 15, 87
Osbryht (Osbert), 136
Oslo, 24, 33, 36, 82, 87
Oslo Fjord, 33, 35, 36
Osred I, 117, 251
Oswald, 109-111, 122, 138, 155, 249
Oswulf, 133, 173, 174, 177, 178, 180, 182, 183, 200, 201, 202, 251
Owen I of Strathclyde, 146, 147
Oswy, 109, 110, 111, 112, 113, 122, 155, 249

Pattern welding, 227
Peredur, 103
Penda, 109, 110, 111
Permia, 92
Poe E.A., 189
Polanski R., 111

Raedwald, 107
Ragnall (Ragnald), 16, 142-145, 160, 165, 180, 200, 215

Ragnhild[r] Eiriksdottir, 44, 45, 126, 134, 150, 179, 215, 246, 265
Ragnarök, 26, 31, 41, 166, 168, 189, 239
Ragnar Lodbrok, 39, 56, 62, 119, 124, 135, 158, 197
Raumarike, 46, 47, 56
Repton, 68, 69, 137, 138
Rey Cross, 169, 170, 195
Rheged, 103, 104, 105
Richard III, 167, 187
Ripon, 64, 171, 172, 173, 175, 200
Rognvald Eiriksson, 215
Rognvald of More, 54, 132
Rognvald Brusason, 75
Rolf (Rollo) Duke of Normandy, 266, 267, 268

Saint Aidan, 23, 111, 223
Saint Andrew, 119
Saint Balthere (Baldred), 165
Saint Cuthbert, 23, 42, 110, 111, 112, 116, 138, 143, 144, 223
Saint Olaf (see Olaf), 43, 50, 84, 181, 233
Saint Oswald (see Oswald), 109-111, 122, 138, 155, 249
Saint Wilfrid, 64, 111, 112, 171, 172, 175
Sawyer P., 203, 204, 264, 265, 266
Scott, Sir Walter, 190, 191
Seax, 67, 81, 83, 98, 240
Shetland, 53, 93, 97, 164
Shield *Burg*, 240
Shield Wall, 63, 65, 66, 67, 84, 90, 91, 98, 110, 144, 147, 183, 184, 240

Sigurd Sleva, 215
Sigurd 'Snake in the Eye', 63, 158, 197
Sihtric, 16, 143, 145, 146, 211
Skarsgard A., 193
Skeld, 87
Skorzeny, O., 208
Smyth A.P., 204, 261, 272
Snekke, 87
Snorri Sturluson, 17, 34, 192, 224
Sogn, 36, 45, 46
Stainmore, 16, 19, 26, 30, 64, 78, 101, 133, 136, 166, 168, 169, 171, 179, 180, 185, 188, 189, 195, 196, 198, 200, 202, 207, 210, 211, 222, 226, 257, 258, 270, 271
Stainmore Gap, 170
Stamford Bridge, 66, 68, 77, 96, 189
Svein Asleifsson, 37
Sverre, 97-99
Synod of Whitby, 111

Tankerness, 94, 96
Thing, 36, 37, 56, 58, 236, 240
Theodoric the Monk, 207, 257
Thetford, 173, 176, 200
Thirlings, 159
Thor, 62, 78, 84, 149, 169, 186, 236, 239, 240
Thorfinn, 75, 93, 94, 134, 221
Thorfinn Skull-Splitter, 133
Thorir the *Hersir*, 53, 127, 128, 132
Thorolf, 54, 60, 63, 64, 65, 80, 92, 127, 152, 227
Thorstein, 96
Thrond, 85, 86

Index

Tolkien J.R.R., 30, 123, 190, 214
Torksey, 69, 137
Tortoise F.B., 240
Tostig, 68, 96
Toten, 46
Treece H., 190
Trondelag, 36, 50, 58, 130, 220
Trondheim, 36, 49, 50, 51, 52, 55, 56, 61, 129, 220, 239
Trow Quarry, 28
Trygve, 220

Uhtred of Bamburgh, 29, 190
Uppland, 58
Urien of Rheged, 104

Valhalla, 23, 24, 27, 31, 32, 34, 62, 168, 218, 237, 241, 262
Valkyries, 237, 244
Vermaland, 56
Vestmar, 85, 86
Vestfold, 33, 36, 46, 56, 57
Vigbiod, 85, 86
Vingulmark, 46, 47, 56
Visby, 81
Volkisch, 186, 187, 191, 192

Wessex, 15, 16, 26, 47, 64, 102, 120, 122, 135, 137, 141-145, 154, 158, 160, 162, 163, 165, 172, 174, 175, 198, 201, 202, 203, 223
Westall R., 24, 78, 79
Williams D. T., 20, 28, 29
Woods, Professor M., 180
Woolf A., 164, 166, 170, 180, 181, 199, 201, 203-207, 209, 210, 211
Wulfhere, Archbishop of York, 138
Wulfstan, Archbishop of York, 40, 68, 162, 163, 166, 171-177, 199, 200, 205

Ynglings, 33, 59, 265
Yggdrasill, 31, 32, 169
York, 15, 16, 18, 19, 25, 26, 29, 33, 40, 101, 102, 106, 109, 113, 114, 115, 121, 130, 131, 133-148, 150, 151, 154-166, 168, 169, 170, 172, 175, 177, 178, 180, 182, 183, 185, 188, 195, 196, 198, 199, 201, 203-211, 238, 252, 253